Sarfraz Manzoor

Greetings from Bury Park

Race, Religion, Rock 'n' Roll

Annotations by
Stefan Tränkle

Ernst Klett Sprachen
Stuttgart

1. Auflage 1 6 5 4 3 2 | 2015 14 13 12 11

Internetadresse: www.klett.de / www.lektueren.com

Autor: Sarfraz Manzoor
Annotations: Stefan Tränkle

Redaktion: Jochen Lohmeyer
Layoutkonzeption: Elmar Feuerbach
Gestaltung und Satz: Satzkasten, Stuttgart
Umschlaggestaltung: Elmar Feuerbach
Titelbild: Sarfraz Manzoor
Autorenfoto S. 6: Jochen Lohmeyer
Druck und Bindung: Medienhaus Plump GmbH,
Rolandsecker Weg 33, 53619 Rheinbreitbach
Printed in Germany

ISBN 978-3-12-578046-0

9 783125 780460

Contents

Sarfraz Manzoor

About the Author

Sarfraz Manzoor is a writer and broadcaster. He writes for the *Guardian* and has also written for the *Observer, Prospect, New Statesman, Uncut,* the *Daily Mail, The Independent, The Spectator, The Times* and *Marie Claire.* He has written and presented documentaries for BBC 2, Channel 4, Radio 2 and Radio 4, and he is a regular presenter on BBC Radio 5 Live. Prior to his broadcasting career, Sarfraz Manzoor was a deputy commissioning editor at Channel 4, and before that he spent five years as a journalist for Channel 4 News. He lives in London.

For my mother Rasool Bibi Manzoor and
in memory of my father Mohammed Manzoor
with love and gratitude.

Acknowledgements

For their faith: Alex Linklater, Ian Katz, David Goodhart, Karolina Sutton, Mike Jones, Justine Taylor, Colin Midson, Mary Instone, the teachers at Maidenhall Primary School, Mrs Lovett at Wauluds Junior School, Ms Crowther, Mr Cottier, Dr Dawson and the teachers at Lea Manor High School, John Ramm and the teachers at Luton Sixth Form College, Janey Valentine, Mike Spencer, Adrian Moss, Susan Woodward, Robin Elias, Peter Barron, John Mulholland, Allan Jones, Jim Gray, Narinder Minhas, Charlotte Black, Janey Walker, John Goudie, Matt Morris, Dave Barber, Moz Dee, Mohit Bakaya, Mark Damazer, Lesley Douglas, Bob Shennan, Mark Thompson, Riete Oord, Roger Alton and Alan Rusbridger. In early 2008 my agent and friend Kate Jones died only days after being diagnosed with cancer. Without Kate's faith, encouragement and support I would never have found the confidence to believe I could write this book. But Kate was more than simply an agent; she was also a friend to whom I confided during some of my darkest days. She is sorely missed and will never be forgotten.

For their friendship: Kate Smith, Mary O'Flaherty, Zoe Silver, Kavita Puri, Niamh Sammon, Katia Michael, Emily Tofield, Becky Hodges, Laura Fairrie, Peter Morgan, Craig Lynch, Robert Sebastian, Richard Murphy, Chy Soeng, Grant Ritchie, William Devenny, Simone Pilkington, Michelle Lanaway, Mark Tomlinson, Mark Alderton, Rita Choudhury, Lisa Cook, John Hand, Julia Brown and Scott McKenzie.

Thank you, Amolak.

Thank you, Aysha.

And thank you, Bruce.

My Father's House

I awoke and I imagined the hard things that pulled us apart.
Will never again, sir, tear us from each other's hearts.

'My Father's House', Bruce Springsteen

In the summer of 1995 I was twenty-three years old; an unemployed British Pakistani with shoulder-length dreadlocks, a silver nose ring and a strange fascination with Bruce Springsteen. It had been six years since I had last lived with my family; having left to study in Manchester there had never been a reason to return to my hometown, Luton. After graduating in economics I had assumed I would be deluged with lucrative offers of employment but these had failed to materialise. While my friends were beginning careers in accountancy and medicine I was most successful at being fired from low-paid temporary jobs: I had been sacked from a data-inputting job for only typing with one hand and doodling with the other, and fired from a credit control agency for having stuck an obscene Public Enemy lyric scribbled on a Post-it to my computer screen. The longest job I had was as a directory enquiries operator. Being a slacker had never been a specific career goal but it was a lifestyle to which I seemed suspiciously suited.

My parents had assumed that once I graduated I would return to Luton with a degree and a job, but despite my lack of career and cash I was still not willing to come home. In Manchester I was free; I could stay out late, play music as loud as I wished, wear black leather trousers and red velvet shirts and shake my dreadlocks to Lenny Kravitz. Once a month I

7 **Bruce Springsteen** American singer and songwriter – 11 **to deluge** ['delju:ʤ] to flood (with water or a large number of things) – 16 **to doodle** to draw lines, figures, etc., while thinking about something else – 18 **Public Enemy** American hip hop group – 20 **slacker** lazy person – 21 **to suit** [su:t] to be right or good for sb – 27 **Lenny Kravitz** American singer

would make the three-and-a-half-hour train journey back to Luton to see the family but only out of a sense of obligation. I was barely on speaking terms with my father and most of my conversations with my mother were about how I hardly talked to my father. When I walked through the front door of my parents' home in my blue corduroy jacket with a 'Born to Run' enamel badge pinned on its lapel and my rucksack on my back, my headphones still plugged in my ears, I could sense my father's confusion. I knew he was thinking, 'What are you *doing* with yourself?' and the worst part about it was that I could never explain it to him.

When I rang my father to tell him I had secured my first writing commission he was silent for a few seconds. 'How much will they pay you?' he finally asked in Urdu. I never spoke in English to my parents.

'I don't know,' I replied, 'but it's not about the money. This is my first chance to be published in a newspaper. It's the local paper here in Manchester. The *Evening News*.'

'What are you going to be writing?' he asked.

'It's an interview with an American writer called Elizabeth Wurtzel,' I answered.

Nothing.

'I am coming down to London to talk to her and so I will be in Luton too.'

The interview with Elizabeth Wurtzel would be my first published article. Her book *Prozac Nation* was being published that summer; I had read an advance copy and noticed it contained countless references to Springsteen and his music. Wurtzel was someone who, like me, had found inspiration and sustenance in Springsteen's music. I persuaded her publishers to let me interview her on the promise I would place the interview myself. I then sold the feature to the *Manchester*

2 **sense of obligation** feeling that you should or must do sth *(Pflichtgefühl)* – 6 **Born to Run** album by Bruce Springsteen – 7 **enamel badge** small piece of metal to show support for an organization or (political) belief – 14 **Urdu** language spoken in Pakistan and India – 26 **Prozac** antidepressant drug – 30 **sustenance** ['sʌstənəns] moral support

Evening News. 'If you like the piece you can publish it,' I told the women's editor, 'and if you don't you won't ever have to hear from me again. You have nothing to lose.'

I boarded the Intercity train from Manchester Piccadilly to London Euston on the morning of 16 May 1995. Once in my seat I opened my copy of the *Guardian*, which had a story on the former Pakistani cricketer Imran Khan and his engagement to twenty-one-year-old Jemima Goldsmith. From my jacket pocket I pulled out a CD player and placed the headphones around my head. Bruce Springsteen's *Greatest Hits* had been released only weeks earlier and was in my CD player. As the train rolled slowly out of Piccadilly station I pressed the play button and began planning for the interview.

The interview was scheduled for two o'clock but, having left the directions to the hotel back in Manchester and being unfamiliar with the London underground, it wasn't until almost twenty past two that I was finally introduced, sweating and sticky, to Elizabeth Wurtzel. She was petite; with her enormous eyes and fragile body she looked the dictionary definition of kooky. Elizabeth very graciously accepted my fulsome apologies but each time she looked at me, my dreadlocks tied in a pink bobble and a ring in my nose, I had the feeling she suspected I was not a real journalist. I had scribbled my questions in haste on a sheet of paper and the dictaphone I was using had only been bought that morning. Wurtzel sat cross-legged on the floor opposite me sipping herbal tea while I placed the dictaphone next to her. Once we started talking my nerves disappeared.

Around twenty-five minutes into the interview, Wurtzel suddenly said, 'Hey, are you sure this thing is working?' She was pointing at my dictaphone. 'I'm pretty sure there should be, like, a red light or something?'

18 **petite** small and slim – 20 **kooky** ['kuːkɪ] *inf* strange in appearance or behaviour in an attractive way – 20 **graciously** ['ɡreɪʃəslɪ] in a polite and generous way – 22 **bobble** sth shaped like a small soft ball

Mortified, I picked up the machine and examined the tiny cassette. 'Yeah, you're right,' I said, trying desperately to appear unfazed. It was at times such as this that I felt blessed to be brown-skinned; at least I did not have to be worried about blushing. 'It's not a problem, I'm making notes of what we're saying,' I lied, staring with rising panic at the blank sheet of paper on my lap.

'Are you sure?' asked Wurtzel. 'Hey, let me have a look, see if I can figure it out.'

I handed the offending machine to her and looked on helplessly as she examined it and, with the simple act of changing the direction of one of the batteries, made it work. My shame was now complete: I had been left looking like a fool in front of the woman whom I was interviewing, and whom I secretly fancied and hoped to seduce with my charm. To her eternal credit, Wurtzel remained helpful and charming despite the unpromising start to our interview; she reminded me of the questions I had asked and even extended our conversation to accommodate the earlier difficulties.

This confirmed my long-held theory that anyone who likes Bruce Springsteen is by definition a nice person.

After the interview I took the Thameslink train back to Luton. As the train trundled closer to its destination I began the familiar process of mentally acclimatising to coming back home. Luton gave me a headache.

The following day, before I asked my father to drive me to the train station to take me back to Manchester, I sat on the bottom step of the stairs while he sat at the desk by the front door. It was what passed for his office – a small wooden desk, an office chair, a tray for new mail and a telephone. 'This article I'm writing is going to pay well,' I told him. The easiest way to

1 **mortified** feeling ashamed – 3 **unfazed** not worried or surprised – 15 **to fancy** to be attracted to sb – 15 **to seduce** to persuade to have sex – 16 **eternal** lasting forever – 19 **to accomodate** [əˈkɒmədeɪt] to do what is needed to correct – 23 **to trundle** to move slowly

win approval with my father was to talk about money. 'Might be four hundred pounds.'

He stopped reading the newspaper and looked up at me. 'And what about after that?'

'There's a course I've read about – TV production. It's in Manchester.'

'And this course, how much does it cost?' he asked me, removing his glasses.

'Usually five thousand pounds but there's a chance I can do it for free – they have special bursaries.'

'And this TV business, is it secure?' he asked. 'Is there any future in it?' His voice was not filled with scepticism as I had expected but concern; when I answered that it depended on how good I was he nodded. My father was not a man given to extravagant flourishes of enthusiasm. 'So you might be a journalist?' my father continued. 'That's a good profession. Respectable.'

The next morning I said goodbye to my mother and my father drove me to the train station in our old silver Ford Cortina. I got out of the car, thanked him for the ride and waved him goodbye. As I boarded the train back to Manchester I sighed with relief. I was returning to my life and he was returning to his.

I defined myself in opposition to my father. All that he believed, the values he upheld, the ambitions he cherished I rejected as embarrassing and outdated. When he said he was Pakistani, I declared I was British; he was Muslim, I was confused; he believed in family, I championed the individual; he worshipped money, I claimed it meant nothing. I convinced myself that we were so different, the notion that I might have inherited anything from him appalled me. The sooner I could shed my past the better. When I was younger I didn't want to

10 **bursary** ['bɜ:sərɪ] scholarship – 15 **flourish** ['flʌrɪʃ] a big gesture or movement – 22 **relief** feeling of happiness that sth is over or has not happened – 25 **to cherish** to care for sth that is important to oneself – 31 **to appall** [ə'pɔ:l] to shock – 32 **to shed** to get rid of

know who my father was because I believed my father had nothing to do with me. How wrong can a son be?

My father had an official birthdate but I do not know when he was born. Officially Mohammed Manzoor was born on 1 April 1933. The month of his birth was almost certainly incorrect but the actual year was also possibly wrong. The lives of villagers living in rural India in the thirties were not considered important enough to be recorded with much detail or accuracy.

Mohammed's father was a soldier who would later spend three years fighting for the British in Japan during the Second World War. My great-grandfather had also been in the army and died suddenly in his early sixties from a heart attack.

My mother, Rasool Bibi, was distantly related to my father. She lived in Paharang, a village near what is now Faisalabad, while my father was from the village of Tuttha Musa, near Gujrat. My mother's father owned a store which sold fruit and vegetables. His father and grandfather were both in the army. Her official birthday is 1 August 1933 but again, she does not know the true month or year that she was born. She was the youngest of five sisters and one brother.

When my mother was fourteen her father passed away, a year later her brother's wife and her twenty-two-year-old sister died within months of each other. Without a father, responsible for both her elderly mother and the seven-year-old daughter of her brother, Rasool Bibi would earn money for food by helping her neighbours with their cooking and cleaning.

Mohammed Manzoor and Rasool Bibi married in 1960 – neither could recall the precise date – amidst controversy. My father's family were against the marriage because they thought he could do better. Mohammed's brothers and sisters could

22 **to pass away** to die – 29 **to recall** to remember

not understand why he was willing to marry someone with such poor prospects when there were other more attractive girls available. But Mohammed couldn't care less about such malicious talk and would disarmingly say, Why would I want a more beautiful girl? This one is good enough for me.' If the relatives kept haranguing him he would jokingly accuse them of trying to ruin his life, saying, 'If I married anyone more beautiful she would only leave me.'

On their wedding day my mother wore borrowed jewellery: the gold necklace, the nose ring that was attached to her earrings, the bangles, everything was lent by the women in the village. Years later, whenever my father made any money he would go to Babulal Pattnis, the goldsmith on Dunstable Road in Bury Park, to buy my mother gold bangles and rings. When my mother would protest that she was too old to be wearing such extravagant jewellery, my father replied that he was trying to compensate for the shame of having to accept borrowed gold on their wedding day.

Two days after they were married my father returned to Karachi where he was working and my mother remained in Paharang to look after her elderly mother. She did not join my father for another eighteen months. Mohammed worked as a senior clerk in the Karachi Development Authority and it was his responsibility to allocate plots of land to incoming migrants from India. His brother worked for Pakistan International Airways and through him Mohammed learned about how many Pakistanis were heading for Britain. Britain had been encouraging Commonwealth immigration from India and Pakistan but by the end of 1962 free entry into Britain would be replaced by immigration controls, and employment vouchers would be needed to be allowed to work in Britain. Mohammed was ambitious and did not want his children – as yet unborn

4 **malicious** [mə'lɪʃəs] intended to hurt other people – 6 **harangue** [hə'ræŋ] to speak loudly and in a morally accusing way – 11 **bangle** band worn around the arm or ankle – 20 **Karachi** city in Pakistan – 24 **to allocate** to give – 30 **employment voucher** ['vaʊtʃə] a permit offered to qualified non-Britons to work in the UK

– to have to endure the hardships he had experienced. My father first revealed to my heavily pregnant mother that he was considering leaving for Britain in early 1962; he told her it would be for five years, enough time to earn and save money and return to Pakistan. It would be twelve months before he was finally able to secure the visa which would allow him to leave Pakistan. He left for England in January 1963. My older sister Navela was just one year old and my brother Sohail had been born barely a month before. How could my father have left his young family? He told his wife he must go to England before the children could speak; once they could tell him how much they would miss him, it would be too heartbreaking to leave. My mother claims she did not try to change her husband's mind because for a full year before he left he had kept reminding her that the only way their children were not going to be condemned to poverty was if she allowed him this one chance to carve out a better future elsewhere. And so, keeping any fears and reservations she might have harboured to herself, my mother gave my father her blessing.

Mohammed Manzoor arrived in England in the second week of January 1963. Britain was in the midst of its coldest winter for two hundred and fifty years; whenever he talked about coming to England it was always the bitter cold my father most vividly recalled. It was so cold that in the week my father landed in Britain the Central Electricity Generating Board was urging people to avoid ironing their clothes to reduce the risk of rationing. Britain was still three months from the release of the first Beatles album, Cliff Richard was number one with 'Bachelor Boy', Harold Macmillan was Prime Minister and Laurence Olivier was performing on the London stage. Many years later I would sometimes ask my father for his memories of the swinging sixties; I hoped to hear that he might have

17 **to carve out** to cut into a special shape

seen the Beatles or the Stones or perhaps wandered through Carnaby Street or down the King's Road. But men like my father, the thousands of Asian immigrants who came to Britain during the sixties, were too busy sweating in factories to have time to be swinging in nightclubs.

Mohammed made his way out of Heathrow and hailed a taxi. In his trouser pocket he had a piece of paper with the name and address of his childhood friend Shuja whose brother worked with him in Pakistan. When Shuja had learnt Mohammed was coming to England he had told him he was welcome to live with him. On the piece of paper was an address in Chesham where Shuja lived in a large rented house. Mohammed approached a taxi driver and handed him the piece of paper, pointing at the handwritten address. The taxi driver took the paper and, after reading it, started driving.

The cab arrived at a seven-bedroom house, which already slept thirty-one Pakistanis. Shuja and the others hugged Mohammed and congratulated him for making the journey. It was soon explained to my father that they slept in shifts; some of the men worked nights and others during the day. It was important that the beds were free by the morning as another group of men would be sleeping in them during the daytime.

It was hard for my father to get used to living in England. Everything was different. In Pakistan all meat had been halal but now the nearest halal butcher was twelve miles away. At weekends a man came delivering live chickens; these would be sacrificed and the skin, head and other unused parts would be wrapped in a brown paper bag and thrown into the coal fire.

There was no television where my father lived but there was an old twin-track tape player and in the evenings the men would gather together and listen to old Hindi film songs in the living room. When they were feeling especially homesick they

24 **halal** killed in a manner approved of by Muslim law – 27 **to sacrifice** ['sækrɪfaɪs] to kill an animal and offer it to a god – 31 **Hindi** Indian language

would take a coach to Southall where, on Sunday afternoons, the cinema would play Indian films. The theatre would be full of lonely Asian men who had travelled from across the south-east to see these films.

Meanwhile it was hard for my mother, raising her children without her husband. She was surrounded by relatives who were envious of Rasool Bibi's good fortune in marrying someone who could take her out of Paharang. They would taunt her by saying her husband had already found an English bride. 'Do you really think he is in England and thinking about you? He could have his pick of white girls, why would he want to stick with you?' My mother listened to their insults but told herself they were jealous. Nevertheless, her children were the only ones who did not have a father in their lives. All my mother had to offer her children were letters. Navela and Sohail were confused that their father seemed to be available only in the letters that he sent. 'Mummy, is our daddy made of paper?' Sohail would ask.

No one thought to keep the letters, so the only clues about what my father's life in Britain was like are in the handful of photographs from that period. One was taken in the winter of 1963. My father is wearing a loose slate-grey suit with a black tie and standing next to a vintage automobile. What is so extraordinary about the photograph is seeing my father looking so fabulously cool; the image could have been a scene from a thirties gangster flick. To my eyes he looked the same in the photograph as he did in the flesh; dapper and smart. Even when living in a shared house he still managed to look good. Another photograph shows my father by a cooker stirring a pot. There are four other men in the picture. The men's sideburns suggest it was taken in the early seventies. They are casually dressed in brown sweaters and plain shirts. My father is wearing a tie.

9 **to taunt** to try to upset sb by unkind remarks – 22 **slate** *Schiefer* – 23 **vintage** of high quality and often old – 26 **flick** *old inf* film – 27 **dapper** *adj* describes a man who is small and dressed in good clothes – 31 **sideburns** *Koteletten*

Even in these photographs my father looked out of place; there are few images of him smiling. Perhaps he was tired. No one just worked standard hours; if there was overtime available in the evenings or weekends they would take it. There were occasional excursions; Shuja and Mohammed took a train into London one weekend to visit Buckingham Palace and in the summer of 1972 they went inter-railing across Europe with two other friends. There are photographs of them on a hoverboat and in Hamburg. Mohammed is not smiling. Was it guilt? The knowledge he ought not to be having a pleasant time?

My father lived in Britain for eleven years while his wife and children remained in Pakistan. During this time, he visited only three times: three weeks in 1965, eight months after his father died in 1970 and finally for another three weeks in 1973. I was conceived during the second visit. I was born in the summer of 1971 at my mother's home in Paharang. My father was back in England, working at the Vauxhall car factory. Information took time to travel then and my father only learnt about his new son by letter some weeks later. By then I had already been named Javed by my mother. When my father read the letter he was unhappy with the name. In a hastily written response sent to my mother he told her his boy would be called Sarfraz.

Three months after I was born, we moved back to Karachi. This accounts for the language difference in our family. In Paharang the most common language was Punjabi and in Karachi it was Urdu; I grew up speaking Urdu while the rest of my family mostly spoke Punjabi. Throughout my childhood my parents would speak to everyone else in Punjabi and to me in Urdu. I can understand Punjabi but can only speak Urdu, another difference that marks me and my sister Uzma from the rest of the family.

15 **to be conceived** [kən'si:vd] to be made pregnant

In Karachi, during the first week of December 1971, Indian fighter jets bombed the city. Our home had no windows or doors and we could see the jets flying over our heads as they dropped bombs on oil depots and refineries. The bombing caused a power cut in the area and the lights went out in our house. My mother grabbed me in her arms and, taking Navela and Sohail with her, crouched under the stairs waiting for the raid to be over. I was six months old. After the bombing stopped she took us on to the roof of our house. The burning refineries were pumping black smoke into the sky and buildings were ablaze. When my father heard about what had happened, he became frightened and promised it would not be long before he would be able to bring us to Britain.

On 16 May 1974 Mohammed was joined in Britain by his wife and three children. Eleven years might seem like an unusually long time for a husband and wife to be apart but it was entirely normal at the time. Most of the other Pakistani families whom we knew during the seventies had similar stories. One reason why it took my father so long to bring us over was that not only was he sending money back to my mother, he was also paying for the weddings of his sisters and brothers back in Pakistan. Even as my father's relatives were mistreating my mother by suggesting my father had remarried in England, they were also begging him to send money to fund the building of houses and family marriages. When he sent money meant for my mother, it would be intercepted by the relatives. My mother, vulnerable since her husband was so far away, was powerless.

Then my father arranged for us to come to England. Two months before she was due to fly Rasool Bibi told her mother she was leaving Pakistan. The shock of hearing this threw my grandmother into a fever which killed her just weeks before my mother left the country.

7 **to crouch** [kraʊtʃ] to bend your knees so that you are close to the ground – 8 **raid** attack – 11 **ablaze** in flames – 26 **to intercept** to stop sth or sb from reaching the place of destination – 26 **vulnerable** easily harmed or hurt

My mother arrived at the airport in Lahore with five rupees in her purse, one large suitcase, one bag of luggage and her three children. We flew on the cheapest ticket available, an Afghan Airlines flight from Lahore with a stopover in Kabul. Sohail was given the responsibility of keeping an eye on the passports and the airline tickets. It was he who handed our documents to the airline officials in Lahore, who was first as we boarded the plane. My mother had the seat by the window, I was in her lap with Navela and Sohail in the seats next to her. I wanted to run along the aisles and kept asking my mother to let me go but she did not want to lose sight of me. As soon as the engines started we all fell silent; my mother held my small hands inside hers, she was probably as nervous as I was but she did her best to calm us as the plane began to hurtle across the tarmac. We had not been in the air more than an hour when Sohail began to complain his stomach was feeling strange; my mother had to take him to the toilets where he was sick. By the time the plane landed in Kabul a few hours later we were all feeling queasy, unsettled by unfamiliar travelling and lack of food. Sohail led the way, my mother held me in one arm and grasped my sister's hand. Unfamiliar with the procedures, we blindly followed the other passengers from the plane to the airport to the bus that delivered us to the hotel where we would be spending the night. At the hotel Sohail was separated from my mother and Navela as the males had to be kept apart from the women but because I was so young I was allowed to remain with my mother.

The next morning we changed from the traditional clothes we wore when we had arrived at Lahore airport into what we were going to wear for London. From the suitcase my mother pulled out a pair of powder-blue trousers and matching shirt for me to put on. Sohail and Navela were dressed in bell-bottoms and flowery shirts.

10 **aisle** [aɪl] narrow passage between rows of seats – 14 **to hurtle** to move fast and in a way that does not seem to be totally safe – 15 **tarmac** area where aircrafts start and land – 19 **queasy** sick, dizzy – 32 **bell-bottoms** trousers with legs that become wider at the bottom

We made our way to the hotel restaurant for breakfast. None of us had eaten since the airport and we were starving; I had begun to cry from hunger. Our mother picked up rolls of bread and some fruit from the serving area. As she walked back to the table where we were waiting a woman shouted out that the food was not free and insisted on payment. My mother went through her pockets and picked out the five rupees. 'I'm sorry, auntie, but the food here costs more than that,' the woman explained. I had been crying already that morning and when I heard the woman say we couldn't have food I began to cry again. My mother began to feel agitated. 'Please what can I buy for my children for five rupees? This little one is very hungry; we have not eaten since Lahore.'

The woman from the restaurant was about to reply when she was interrupted. 'Shame on you! Can't you see the little boy is hungry?' It was another passenger, a middle-aged woman who had overheard the conversation. 'Auntie, if you don't have enough money, please let me buy you and your children something,' she said kindly.

My mother smiled weakly and gave her thanks for her good heart. With some money from the woman and our five rupees my mother bought a packet of peanuts and some bread. It was dry and salty but it filled our stomachs.

A coach picked us up from the hotel and took us back to the airport where we boarded the plane that flew us to Paris. During the flight Sohail developed a severe case of diarrhoea and my mother had to look after him because he couldn't stop vomiting. Tending him meant there was no time to think about her own weak condition; she had not eaten since Pakistan.

When the flight arrived into Paris there was another five-hour delay before the next connection. There was no hotel and the time was spent stretched across the seats of the departure lounge. This final stage of the journey was the shortest; we landed in London only an hour or so after taking off in Paris.

26 **diarrhoea** [daɪə'rɪə] *Durchfall*

After we collected our luggage we were directed towards a medical office for a check-up. When they tested my mother, she was so weak they feared she had TB. They had to conduct further tests before they were satisfied she was not in danger. Once she was given the all clear, my mother, Navela, Sohail and me headed towards the exit.

'And who is this little one? Where has he come from?' my father said, picking me up and kissing me on my cheek. I was almost three. Years later my mother would tell me how all through the flight I had kept asking, 'Are we seeing Daddy? Will my daddy be there?' and whenever my father wanted to embarrass me he would repeat how I burst into tears the moment he held me in his arms.

I can only imagine how strange the situation must have been for both my mother and my father. For Mohammed it meant a sudden adjustment in his life from virtual bachelor to married father of three. It can't have been easy. When he had said goodbye to my mother he had been twenty-nine and now he was forty-one.

Recently my mother admitted to me that when she saw my father at the arrivals terminal at Heathrow her first response was not pleasure but cold fear: what if this man lets me down? When she arrived in Britain my mother couldn't speak a word of English, she had Sohail, Navela and me to think of: if my father failed us where could she go? Fortunately my father was an honourable man. Within months of landing in London we were living in our own home, a two-bedroom terraced house on Selbourne Road in Bury Park in Luton.

We did not know that Luton had such a dire reputation. We lived there because my father worked at the Vauxhall car factory which was the largest employer in the town and such a significant presence that it had its own brass band, football team and beauty pageant. The 'Miss Spectacular' contest was

3 **TB** tuberculosis, a lung disease – 21 **Heathrow** main London airport – 29 **dire** ['daɪə] extreme, very bad – 33 **beauty pageant** ['pædʒənt] beauty contest

open to any female employees of Vauxhall; the evening we arrived in Luton the final heat was being held with Valerie Singleton chairing the judging panel.

My father had only managed to buy our home because a group of friends had lent him money for the deposit. Evidently they had not lent him a penny more because when we first moved into the empty house my father couldn't afford to buy beds for us to sleep on. We slept side by side on the living-room floor on bed sheets spread out on the maroon carpet. When we eventually bought furniture it was all from salvage yards and second-hand stores, which my father visited every weekend without fail. The pressure to pay the mortgage and pay off his loans meant he worked all the overtime that was available; white colleagues would joke that Mohammed had moved into Vauxhall and was living in the factory. The more he worked the more frustrated he would be that he was not earning more money. 'I am not a donkey,' he would say to my mother. 'I cannot carry the rest of you on my own. I work like a dog but I am not a donkey.'

My mother, cooking saag aloo on the gas stove and tossing hot chapattis in the air to cool them, must have felt helpless.

My mother had been in Luton less than six months when my father began taking her to textile factories in town. As a young girl when my mother's father suddenly died she had to support her family. To earn money she made clothes for the women in her village, taking the patterned silk and handstitching it into shalwaar kameez. She could use this skill in England as dressmaking was a common means of earning money amongst newly arrived immigrants, and the situations vacant pages of

2 **Valerie Singleton** English television presenter – 5 **deposit** [dɪˈpɒzɪt] money you have to pay as the first part of a total payment for sth – 9 **maroon** dark red-brown – 10 **salvage yard** a place where furniture, machines or cars are broken upso that the material can be used for other purposes – 12 **without fail** without exception – 12 **mortgage** [ˈmɔːɡɪdʒ] the money that you have to pay back over a number of years after you've borrowed it from a bank – 17 **donkey** [ˈdɒŋkɪ] *Esel* – 20 **saag aloo** spinach and potato curry – 21 **chapatti** flatbread – 27 **shalwaar kameez** traditional unisex dress worn in parts of Asia

the local paper often contained offers of work in locally based textile factories. My father would read the advertisements and make notes in his diary. On Saturday afternoons after he had visited the secondhand stores he would take my mother to the factories and tell whoever would listen that his wife had many years of experience making clothes and would be a very good addition to the workforce. No one wanted to give her work because she could not speak English. My father said that this was not a problem. 'It's good she doesn't speak English,' he told them. 'It means she can spend more time working. No chance to chit chat!'

When the managers would say that was all well and good but how were they meant to teach her how to make the dresses, my father had a reply to that too: 'Not a problem. Just tell me what she has to do, I tell her, and she does it. No problem.'

It must have been a strange experience for my mother, mutely listening as my father animatedly discussed and pleaded with a succession of whites for them to give her a chance to work. Everywhere they tried they were knocked back until finally they met one man who said that my mother could work from home.

My father bought a second-hand, black Singer sewing machine and stationed it in the living room. With the sewing machine in position the ritual that would continue throughout my childhood began. Each week a man would come with bundles of material tied up with string; there would sometimes be dozens of such bundles piled high in the living room. With the bundles would come a sample to show what the bundles had to be transformed into. For every finished dress my mother would earn something between forty-five pence and a pound. Those same dresses would then be sold in the nation's high streets.

11 **to chit chat** to talk about unimportant things – 17 **mutely** unable to speak – 17 **animatedly** lively – 18 **to plead** [pli:d] to make an urgent request – 28 **sample** model, example

During the day, my father would be working at the factory, Sohail and Navela were at school and I would be alone with my mother. It was probably boredom which prompted me to start helping but, at four years of age, it became my job to untie the bundles of fabric. When my mother had completed a dress it was my responsibility to lay it flat down on the floor, one on top of another so that they could be tied into bundles of ten ready for collection. When Navela returned home from school she would join my mother at the sewing machine so that when our father came home from work and asked how many, they could give a figure that would satisfy him. After dinner the living room would be transformed into a factory production line with my mother and Navela taking turns on the sewing machine, my father and Sohail hemming and overlooking, while I would count the dresses and arrange them in bundles of ten. As I became older I was given other duties: turning cotton belts inside out with a knitting needle and threading them through the loop holes of the dresses, and changing the thread on the sewing machine when Mum began working on a dress of a different colour.

No matter how hard they worked my mother and Navela never received any praise from my father, only urged to work harder. If they worked into the early hours of the morning they would make mistakes and when the man came to collect the dresses he would sorrowfully tell my father that he was unable to pay for faulty handiwork. This would throw my father into a rage.

When they were not making dresses for Marks & Spencer and British Home Stores, Navela and my mother made their own clothes. My sister would draw out an outline of a dress on tracing paper and design its own unique pattern around the neck. A shalwaar kameez gains its uniqueness from its length and how its neck and sleeves are shaped. When they went

3 **to prompt** to cause – 4 **to untie** to unfasten a knot – 5 **fabric** material clothes are made of – 14 **to hem** *säumen* – 26 **faulty** incorrect – 27 **to throw sb into a rage** to make sb furious

shopping in Bury Park other Pakistani women would approach them and say, 'Sister, can you tell us who made your clothes? They are so beautiful!' and Mum would tell them with pride that she had made them with her daughter.

'Sister, a small request?' they would then say. 'Could you spare some time to make me something as beautiful?'

My mother and sister became Bury Park's leading fashion designers and dressmakers; before they handed the finished garments to their clients Navela would try them on herself and be photographed wearing them.

With the money they earned my father bought my sister a gift: a smaller domestic sewing machine so she could sew at the same time as my mother. The last thing I would hear before I slid into sleep was the groaning of the sewing machines and the dull vibrato of the floorboards.

As a small boy the consequences of poverty were few toys and no holidays; birthdays were family only affairs where each year my mother would prepare the table with samosas, pakoras, spiced chickpeas, plates of crisps and slices of sponge cake and Navela would take the annual photograph of me or my younger sister Uzma blowing out the candles. We never celebrated Navela or Sohail's birthdays and no one outside our family was invited.

I did not appreciate until later how frustrating it must have been for my father to not be able to give more to his children. Whether it was Sohail demanding a cassette radio player or Navela wanting more clothes or all of us hoping for a colour television the demands were continual and the finances limited. When he could he would surprise us. In the winter of 1978 I was seven years old and, thanks to 'Mull of Kintyre', I was obsessed with having an acoustic guitar. My father spent sixteen hard-earned pounds to buy me one. It is my

9 **garments** clothes – 30 **Mull of Kintyre** popular song written by Paul McCartney

happiest childhood memory, the magical sensation of wanting something badly and receiving it.

Unlike some other Pakistani men my father was not frittering his wages. His only vice was smoking. When friends visited our home at weekends they would play cards and talk about the old country while taking turns to suck deeply on the hookah. The gurgling sounded deep and mysterious. During the week he would disappear into the back yard for a cigarette, returning minutes later with the stench of the smoke still clinging to his cream kurta. Eventually, my mother's continual nagging prompted him to give up smoking. I am pleased my father smoked; glad that there were some things he did purely for pleasure and only for himself.

* * *

The doorbell rang. It was September 1979 and we were leaving Bury Park to move into a house in Marsh Farm.

My father opened the door. 'Salaam, Sadiq sahib,' he said, welcoming the visitor into the hall and leading him into the living room.

'Salaam, Manzoor sahib,' whispered Sadiq. Mohammed Sadiq was one of my father's oldest friends. Their friendship went back to the days when they both lived in St Albans. My father worked as a postman while Sadiq earned his living at a local asbestos factory. Sadiq didn't work any more, the accumulation of dust particles in his throat had left him unable to speak in anything louder than a whisper. With his greying hair, pepper moustache, light-brown kurta pyjama and leather *chupulls,* Sadiq looked like a hundred other men you might see walking along Dunstable Road with bags of halal chicken in their arms.

2 **to want sth badly** to want sth very much – 3 **to fritter** to waste – 6 **hookah** waterpipe for smoking tobacco – 9 **stench** unpleasant smell – 10 **kurta** traditional item of clothing worn in Asia – 10 **to nag** to criticize – 16 **salaam** Arabic for *peace,* often used as greeting

'Is a cup of tea possible?' my father asked my mother.

'It's already ready,' replied my mother.

'Where are the little ones?'

I was eight years old and my younger sister Uzma had turned four two weeks earlier.

'Uzma and Javed are in the garden and the other two are upstairs,' my mother replied.

Even though my name was legally Sarfraz, at home my family continued to refer to me as Javed.

'It was the older ones who told you to move, isn't that right?' asked Sadiq.

My mother walked in with a silver tray on which were two cups of steaming hot tea and a plate of egg biscuits. 'Please,' said my father, motioning towards the tray.

'So, why are you turning your back on us, Manzoor sahib? Has the father started obeying the children?'

'The children kept saying they wanted to move from here,' my father explained to Sadiq in between sips. 'The two older ones saw the house and they have been on at me for months saying they want to live there.'

Although we lived in Bury Park my father had insisted that both Navela and Sohail attend a high school that was two bus journeys away. The local schools in Bury Park were overwhelmingly Asian but Lealands was almost entirely white. My father was convinced that this made the school better. It was while walking back from school one afternoon that Navela had seen a house for sale; this was the one that we were set to move into.

Sadiq carefully peeled the skin from the top of the tea and tipped three teaspoons of sugar into the mug. He picked up an egg biscuit and slowly and thoughtfully began nibbling. By this time Uzma and I were also in the living room but

31 **to nibble** to eat with small repeated bites

we knew better than to take a biscuit. We could only help ourselves when it was made clear that guests had eaten what they wanted. Fortunately it was also customary to put out far more than guests could possibly eat; a subtle way of indicating family prosperity.

'That area you are moving to is very white, Manzoor sahib. How are you going to make sure the boys go to the mosque to learn the Koran? Very few Pakistanis in Marsh Farm.'

I looked at my father, hoping for permission to grab a biscuit. But he was looking at Sadiq. 'Their mother taught Sohail and Navela at home, no reason why the little ones can't learn the Koran at home too.'

'Yes, but you know the morals of white people, Manzoor sahib,' Sadiq continued. 'You don't need me to tell you what they get up to. Keep an eye on the little ones. There won't be any Pakistanis in their schools in Marsh Farm. Too many white people around and they will start thinking they are white too. Do what I do: take the children to Pakistan in the summer, let them see their relatives, their country. Otherwise they will become strangers to you.'

My father must have recognised what Sadiq was talking about. It was what every conversation amongst adults seemed to eventually settle on: how to try and protect the children from temptations and reinforce their Pakistani identity. They must have felt they were trying to turn back the tide of progress before it rose to destroy and tear apart their families.

But it was this tide of progress that had carried my father from Pakistan to England. It was this impulse towards improvement that had compelled him to be away from his wife and children. My father was a man perpetually on the move, driven by a relentless desire towards something and somewhere better. His friends frustrated him because they

3 **customary** traditional or usual – 7 **mosque** [mɒsk] building for Islamic religious worship – 24 **temptation** sth very attractive but morally questionable – 24 **to reinforce** [riːɪnˈfɔːs] to make stronger – 29 **to compel** to force – 31 **relentless** continuous

reminded him of who he was, and not what he wanted to be. Most of his friends were men who were not able to talk about the things he was interested in. What they had in common was the old country. When they discussed General Zia or the death of Bhutto they felt connected to each other and their homeland. The only other thing they had in common was children. 'What is Sarfraz going to be when he becomes a man?' one would ask my father.

'What do you mean, he is a man already!' someone else would add.

'My son will be a doctor,' a third would boast. Back then that claim had yet to harden into cliché.

Beyond the realm of children and Pakistan the conversation stumbled; these were not men truly interested in how each other was doing; they only wanted to demonstrate to the rest the extent of their success. My father wanted to discuss politics with politicians, business with industrialists. Instead he was having tea with uneducated factory workers, his awkwardness betraying his frustration at his own unfulfilled existence.

What drives a man to leave his country, to accept demeaning work for more than a decade so that he can bring his family from Pakistan to join him? Why didn't he just find an English girl like many other Pakistani men had? Was it not tempting to forget his Pakistani family and start anew? What was remarkable about my father was how these temptations were unthinkable to him; his moral framework was underpinned by family, responsibility and pride. Those values were who he was, they shaped how he raised his children, they shaped who we became, and yet they were the very values I ridiculed. I condemned him for being tough without appreciating that if he had been softer we would have remained in Pakistan. What

4 **General Zia** General Muhammad Zia-ul-Haq, sixth President of Pakistan from 1977 to his death in 1988 – 5 **Bhutto** Zulfikar Ali Bhutto, Pakistani politician, President (1971-1973) and Prime-Minister (1973-1977) who was hanged in 1979 – 13 **realm** [relm] area of interest – 18 **awkwardness** ['ɔ:kwədnəs] nervous and embarrassed behaviour – 19 **to betray** *here:* to show – 20 **demeaning** degrading and humiliating – 26 **to underpin** to give support – 29 **to ridicule** [rɪdɪkju:l] to make fun of sth

made my father different was that he was consumed with a passion for self-improvement. It is staggering how someone who came to this country in the early sixties, who was never able to fulfill his own potential, and who met with racism on a daily basis, was able to inject into his children – or his sons at least – a sense that the entire world was available to them if we studied hard and worked harder. 'The only way whites will give you a job is if you are twice as good as them and work four times as hard,' he would tell me. Families could progress but only if the children recognised and understood their duties and obligations. This was the most important thing I learned as a small child. My father had brought us to this country and in his eyes it was our duty to work hard, not complain, not expect too much and, most importantly, not let him down.

While, like all parents, my father wanted to be proud of us, it was crucial we did not embarrass him or the family. What 'the community' thought took on an absurdly high significance; we had to act as if our entire lives were being recorded for the critical approval of this community. I found this obsession with keeping up appearances infuriating. 'Who cares what people think?' was a common unanswered question.

But Mohammed Manzoor drew his strength from his community, and also from his pride. In the sixties he worked in a lightbulb factory in Hertfordshire. At lunchtime he would eat his chapattis and the white workers would laugh and point at him, saying, 'That stupid Paid is eating brown paper!' How do you fight the feeling that everyone hates you? That for all your dreams and desires you will never achieve your own potential? By believing completely in your abilities and having pride in what you are. That was my father.

In the early eighties my father was promoted from the production line and became an inspector at the Vauxhall car

1 **consumed** filled – 2 **staggering** shocking and surprising – 11 **obligation** sth you have to do, duty – 16 **to embarrass** [ɪmˈbærəs] to make sb feel ashamed or awkward – 20 **to infuriate** [ɪnˈfjʊərɪeɪt] to make extremely angry

factory. He was required to wear a white overcoat, watch what the factory workers were doing and point out any mistakes that might have been made. It was a job almost tailor-made for his talents because the irony was that while my father preached the sermon of hard work he himself was actually rather workshy.

The ways he got out of work were fairly comical. For all his sternness there was another side to my father; it was a side that my mother and my sisters were best at extracting. When he knew he'd been rumbled, like when he took more chapattis when my mother had already said he'd eaten enough, he would cover his eyes with his hands and peek through the parted fingers like a naughty boy. 'Take it easy with my curry,' my mother would joke, 'we don't want you becoming fat, do we?' Then my father would stand up and start running on the spot, saying, 'See! See how fit I am!'

When it came to work around the house my father always assumed what he called an 'executive supervisor' role. 'Someone needs to be monitoring what you are all doing,' he would say, trying to suppress a grin. 'Supervising is *the* most important job.'

While my mother washed and cut up chicken and I chopped onions' wearing my swimming goggles to stop the tears streaming down my face, my father would be in the living room roaring with laughter at the Laurel and Hardy film on television. (When he was being especially playful he liked to give a little Oliver Hardy wave to my mother.)

'How did you manage to live all these years in England and not cook?' my mother would ask innocently. 'Fish and chips every night was it?'

'Daddy can cook,' I would say, 'I've seen photographs of him in the kitchen.'

8 **sternness** seriousness – 9 **to extract** to take out sth – 10 **to rumble** *inf* to find out the true facts

'If your daddy ever sets foot in this kitchen then I swear to Allah that I too will take a photograph,' Mum would retort.

'So, don't you have anything to say for yourself?' Navela would ask him playfully.

'What are you talking about? The most important part of cooking is not the chopping and the slicing. Anyone can do that! The most important part of cooking is the recipe. Ask your mother where the recipe came from. Go on, ask her.'

It was true – the roast chicken that we cooked was based on a recipe that my father had passed to my mother. It was how he had cooked chicken in the sixties.

My father loved gardening. For us the garden was not only a place of beauty but a source of food. At Bury Farm our garden was a slab of concrete, but when we moved to Marsh Farm my mother was able to grow potatoes, onions and mint leaves, which she ground into chutney. There were also flowers; my parents would choose which colour flowers they wanted to plant and my father would buy the seeds. It was very important to my father that we maintain a neat and tidy garden, which was why mowing the lawn was a significant responsibility. Long grass – like long hair – suggested a certain moral laxity which invited the ridicule of others. When my father pointed out that the neighbours had recently cut their grass while ours was looking unkempt he was not merely making an observation. All his obsessions with pride and keeping up appearances were apparent in his compulsive desire to ensure that our garden lawns were kept neat. On Saturdays my job was to mow the grass in the front and back gardens. While I was busy operating the lawnmower, my mother would sit at the edge of the lawn trimming with a pair of scissors the wisps of grass that the lawnmower could not reach. When that had been done it was then Uzma's role to collect the cut grass and dump it in the dustbin. After that finally my father would emerge, take out

2 **to retort** to answer quickly – 14 **slab of concrete** big cemented area – 16 **chutney** ['tʃʌtnɪ] cold sauce made of fruit, sugar, spices and vinegar – 21 **laxity** carelessness – 24 **unkempt** untidy (esp. hair) – 30 **wisp** a thin untidy piece (hair/grass)

a plastic rake and gently rake over the freshly mowed grass, making sure that none remained. This usually took no time at all but once he had finished he would make a great play of what he had done. 'See how neat it now looks?' he would say to us.

'Listen to him!' my mother would say, laughing. 'Spends two minutes going over the garden and tries to pretend it's all his work! No shame! No shame at all!'

Dad would be trying to suppress his own laughter. 'Why are you saying such a thing? You know that in any job there have to be workers and there has to be management. My role is to be a supervisor.'

'Dad?'

'Yes, son.'

'Does supervise mean getting everybody else to do the work and then claiming credit for it afterwards?'

By now we would all be laughing as we bundled back into the living room to settle in front of the television for the weekly ritual of watching Dickie Davies and the Saturday afternoon wrestling.

The wrestling was an obsession for my father. All activity in the household on Saturdays was planned around it; if the family were out shopping they knew to be home by four thirty. Why wrestling was so important was never explained. My father was also a huge boxing fan and I had grown up watching Muhammad Ali fight; I can understand his love of Ali but why Giant Haystacks and Big Daddy exerted such influence I do not know. And yet, the communal ritual of watching the wrestling featured regularly throughout my childhood.

When we watched television we could push the pause button on our lives while other lives played out before us. During the IRA hunger strikes I rushed into my parents' room each morning to ask my father if Bobby Sands was still alive; I

1 **rake** gardening tool to gather up dead leaves – 19 **Dickie Davis** TV presenter, best known for presenting "World of Sport" – 26 **Muhammad Ali** American heavyweight boxer originally known as Cassius Clay who converted to Islam – 33 **Bobby Sands** member of the IRA who died on hunger strike in 1981

followed the trial of the Gang of Four in China and the Yorkshire Ripper in Britain and I looked forward to *Question Time* just as much as *Knight Rider.* In the evenings, after my parents had gone to bed and Navela and I had watched the late movie together, my father would call me up to his room to discuss politics and listen as if he really cared what I made of Labour's chances in the general election. Years later my mother told me that my father really enjoyed those conversations, that talking to me about politics made him feel that we had something in common.

My father was obsessed with tidiness. Apparently he had even been like that many years earlier when he had lived with a dozen other men in a shared house. His friends from that time would speak of how, even if the entire house was a chaos of mess, Mohammed Manzoor's area would be spotless and he'd complain to the others about the state of the house. This obsession meant that he asked us to go to extreme lengths in order to have a tidy house. For example, where the sewing machines were used by my mother and sister the carpet would be messy with rags of excess fabric and tiny pieces of cotton thread. My father would ask my sister and me to clean the carpets by hand. The vacuum cleaner could not, he told us, be expected to clean the carpet thoroughly. Far better for us to get on our hands and knees and pick up each thread and rag individually. We didn't find this peculiar, for us it was just another game to play. We would choose opposing sides of the room and compete over who could collect the most strands; Uzma used an old hairbrush to exfoliate the room. When we had finished we would each offer up our piles of threads, fluff, pins and buttons to our father for inspection. But there was

1 **Gang of Four** leading group of four Communist Party Officials in the Chinese Cultural Revolution (1966-1976) who were convicted in a show trial in 1981 – 17 **to go to lengths** to make big efforts – 20 **rag** small piece of cloth – 20 **excess** not needed and left over – 21 **thread** very thin cord made of cotton, wool or silk – 27 **strand** single thin thread – 28 **exfoliate** to remove dead skin cells from the skin, *here:* to clean – 29 **fluff** thin soft hair

never a sense of accomplishment from this task, we always felt like we had let him down again; by failing to pick up every single strand from the carpet we had merely confirmed how we could not be trusted to do even the simplest task.

If it wasn't hand cleaning the carpet there were countless other ways to try and keep me occupied. The answer you could never give to the question 'what are you doing?' was 'nothing'; saying that I was reading a book was almost as bad. When I remember my teenage years the one thing I wanted to do most was just that: nothing.

For a man so outwardly proud my father seemed remarkably relaxed about allowing his wife to work and his children to wear second-hand clothes. The jumble sales were held in the assembly halls of the Maidenhall school and my junior school in Marsh Farm. I would look forward to these with the same passion that later would be reserved for Bruce Springsteen concerts. Jumble sales and libraries were where I satisfied my desire for stories and stimulation; there were no new books in our home but dozens of secondhand issues of *Reader's Digest* which I would devour in the evenings before I went to sleep. My mother and I would stand at the school gates thirty minutes before they opened and as soon as the teacher admitted us through I would dash into the central hall where there would be tables filled with piles of clothes, books and toys. My mother would rifle through the clothes picking out trousers, shirts and jumpers; she could make clothes for Navela and Uzma but I had to manage with my brother's hand-me-downs and whatever she found in the piles.

My mother only bought me shoes that were much too big for me, which meant that throughout my years in junior and high school I had to wear two pairs of socks to ensure my feet did

13 **jumble sale** flea market – 20 **to devour** [dɪˈvaʊə] to eat (or read) quickly and eagerly – 23 **to dash** to run quickly – 25 **to rifle through** to search quickly through sth – 27 **hand-me-downs** clothes that his elder brother used to wear

not helplessly slide around inside my shoes. Once she bought me a pair that was so big I had to fill the toes with screwed-up newspaper; at school I was briefly called 'Ronald McDonald'.

As embarrassing as wearing outsized shoes and secondhand clothes was for a young boy, I was not especially upset about it; my father had done an excellent job of hammering down his children's expectations of him while at the same time maintaining very high expectations of us. Many years later when I was living away from home, friends told me that their parents had given them something they called 'unconditional love'. But Asian parents of my father's generation knew nothing of unconditional love, a sitar came with fewer strings attached.

* * *

My best friend at school was Scott McKenzie, a freckle-faced, chestnut-haired lad who lived only minutes from my home. Ours was a somewhat unlikely friendship. I liked reading books and Scott was a star in the school football team; I was painfully shy around girls while Scott was the boy all the girls fancied; and while I was still sharing a bedroom with my brother, Scott's bedroom was an Aladdin's cave of treasures filled with posters of Bryan Robson and Steve Coppell, a dartboard and record player. Since he lived so close I was allowed to visit Scott's home in the evening. His mother would ask about his homework and Scott would be jealous when I told him that my father never asked such questions. 'You're so lucky,' he would say. 'My dad won't let me out of the house unless I've finished it.' My father cared nothing for homework, what mattered was that I passed my exams.

3 **Ronald McDonald** clown character used as mascot by the McDonald's fast-food restaurant chain – 12 **sitar** instrument with 21 to 23 strings used throughout the Indian subcontinent – 12 **strings attached** with special conditions or restrictions – 13 **freckle-faced** freckles are small brown spots on the skin – 14 **lad** boy – 20 **Bryan Robson and Steve Copell** football players who both played for Manchester United in the early 80s – 23 **jealous** ['dʒeləs] unhappy because sb has sth you want

In the evenings as I massaged his feet, my father would be reading the newspaper while my mother would be in bed beside him. Their bedroom smelled of incense. I would sit at the bottom of the bed, slowly and firmly squeezing his feet and calves, and then he'd begin. 'So, how old are you now?'

It seemed to be a rhetorical question but once I found a small notebook into which he had written the names and birthdays of all his children. 'Twelve,' I'd reply.

'Twelve? Practically a man then. Do you know what I was doing when I was twelve? I was looking after my sick father and my sisters. I would go to school and then work in the evenings so that my family had food to eat.'

I would listen while pressing the soles of his feet, rubbing my fingers over the rough corns that scarred his toes. His feet were caked with so much thick dead skin that I would sometimes need to shave it off with a razor blade. It was a curiously satisfying experience watching the shavings peel off his feet.

'So, do you know what you want to do when you leave school?'

'No, not really, haven't thought about it.'

'Haven't thought about it! What sort of answer is that? Look at your mother. Even before you can remember she has been looking after you. You have no idea what she has been through, the sacrifices that she has made. Now it is your time to make sacrifices. Parents do their job so that the children will do their job in later life.'

Every meaningful conversation during my childhood was a variant on that theme and they could all be summarised into one statement: do not let me down. Do not forget the sacrifices I made to come to this country, to bring you here. Do not forget where you come from and who you are. Do not forget us. It was a huge burden to place on a young boy's shoulders. But I

3 **incense** ['ɪnsens] substance that is burned and produces a sweet smell – 14 **corn** *here:* a small and painful area of hard skin that forms on the toes – 24 **sacrifice** ['sækrɪfaɪs] the act of giving sth up that is valuable in order to help sb or get sth that is more important

now understand him better. He was, I think, embarrassed by working at Vauxhall. He wanted me to say to him that I would do him proud and not give him cause to be ashamed. When I heard him speak like that I felt afraid of growing up, scared of the consequences of letting him down.

I was fifteen years old when, in the autumn of 1986, my father was made redundant from the Vauxhall car factory. When I learnt that my father would imminently be unemployed I, as a typical self-absorbed teenager, only viewed it from my perspective. With my father out of work it meant money would be even tighter and I would be under greater pressure to find holiday work. I assumed this meant he would be at home all day. There would be no escape.

I failed to see that, for my father, the concept of being unemployed was deeply shameful. He was someone who believed with almost messianic passion in the very idea of work; it was not something he was willing to sacrifice merely because he did not have a job. Which was why, even after he was made redundant and even when he had nowhere specific to go, my father would wake at seven and immediately get dressed. He would then read the newspaper at his desk, a square table we had bought from a second-hand furniture store.

To judge from the mail, my father had no friends. The only letters were the very occasional aerogramme from Pakistan, but mostly it was bills and bank statements and annual reports from companies that my father had bought shares in. Years before the privatisation of the nationalised industries created millions of shareholders my father was buying and selling on the stock market. Despite his constant protestations that our family had no money, he seemed to find the cash to trade in stocks and shares. My father did not make any money from

7 **redundant** unemployed – 8 **imminently** soon – 9 **self-absorbed** caring only for oneself – 16 **messianic** like a messiah; with religious zeal – 27 **shares** *(Aktien)* – 30 **protestations** claims

his trading but that might have been because he had very little money to invest. Every few days reports would arrive from oil-drilling companies based in Australia, chemical conglomerates and pharmaceutical businesses. They did not make for fascinating reading, filled as they were with daunting graphs and indecipherable pie charts and statements about 'extraordinary general meetings'. There would also be guides to buying and selling penny shares and updates on the companies to watch.

Once he had absorbed the daily information my father would call Arthur. Arthur Bryant was my father's stockbroker, someone he had known since we lived in Bury Park. I imagined him as Charlie in *Charlie's Angels* since he only ever appeared to exist on the other end of the telephone. After my father was made redundant he became convinced that there were great fortunes to be made in the stock market, if you had the initial outlay. 'Money makes money,' he would tell us. 'If someone were to give me one hundred thousand pounds I could turn it into a million, with the knowledge I have. But you need to have the money to invest.' That was where my mother and Navela came in, working on the sewing machines while my father chatted to Arthur. Every conversation started with the same words: 'Good morning, Arthur, how's the market today?'

I never heard Arthur's assessment but I would see my father making notes in his diary before issuing instructions about buying five hundred of one company and selling three hundred of another.

With the paper read and the shares traded, my father would say goodbye to my mother, appearing for all the world as if he was leaving for work. In fact the entire day would be spent with his friends. These visits were not entirely social. My father was the first port of call for any Pakistani who was

4 **conglomerate** business organisation consisting of different companies – 5 **daunting** impressive to a frightening degree – 6 **indecipherable** [ɪndɪ'saɪfrəbl] – 13 **Charlie's Angels** US-produced TV series in the late 70s – 17 **outlay** money spent as a first investment in sth – 32 **port of call** first peron to speak to *(Anlaufstelle)*

interested in buying a house but was ignorant of how to secure a mortgage; he spoke English well and knew how to deal with bank managers. He didn't charge a fee for his time. Later, when men would call on him to help with their passport and visa problems, he would spend afternoons filling in forms so that they could bring their wives to England. He did not charge for that either. At the time I did not know what he was doing in those afternoons that he disappeared; I was simply grateful he was not at home.

After his redundancy my father could not claim that he was the main breadwinner for the family; my mother and Navela were earning the family income with their dressmaking. No one dared to make the obvious observation to him that he did not have the authority to lay down the law if he was not bringing in the money. We continued to behave as if nothing had changed.

While I lived at home it did not occur to me that my father might have felt embarrassed and emasculated after losing his job. Maybe he felt disappointed in himself, which was why it became so imperative that we should not disappoint him. But the only thing I felt at the time was frustration. Too absorbed in myself, I did not notice that when the local paper arrived every Thursday my father would scan the situations vacant for work; sometimes he would ring to enquire farther but not once did he get an interview. When my father would speak to his bank manager or the local estate agents he would joke with them, 'I know as much as you do, you should give me a job. Consultant. I could do that for you.' He was not actually joking, of course, but I would hear laughter coming from the other end of the telephone. The very idea.

My father represented the past; that was what he talked about, what he celebrated and what he wanted to preserve.

2 **mortgage** ['mɔːɡɪdʒ] agreement to borrow money esp so as to buy a house – 18 **to emasculate** to make a man feel less male by taking power and confidence away from him

My eyes were fixed firmly on the future, a life far from Luton and all its limitations. We were so different and yet anyone who saw us together could see which side of the family my features were from: the high forehead, the full lips, the fleshy earlobes and, most telling, the coarse curls of my hair. My hair was the most visible reminder of my father; I hated my hair.

My brother and sisters all had straight hair inherited from my mother; hair that could be grown long, combed easily, hair that could fall in front of their eyes or be tossed around by the wind. My mother used to tease me and say I had steel wool on my head; Navela would try to persuade me that I was an eight-year-old spitting image of Paul Michael Glaser in *Starsky and Hutch. As* a teenage boy the limitations of what could be done with my hair were a source of constant irritation. I wanted hair that would grow long, hair that I could whip in the air as I sang along to 'Living on a Prayer' or 'The Final Countdown', hair that would keep falling in front of my eyes so that I'd need to flick it back in a sexy, possibly seductive, way.

My older sister cut our hair at home. The hallway was the temporary barbershop. We would sit facing the mirror that hung from the wall, an old bed sheet draped over us and tucked into our collar. She used the same scissors that my mother would use for cutting fabric before stitching dresses together. I was a recalcitrant client; I resented not being able to go to an actual barber. 'Don't you realise white people pay to have hair like yours?' my father would ask me. 'Those mad fools spend money to have hair that you have for free!'

Navela also was responsible for cutting and dyeing my father's hair. Once my father's hair had been shorn Navela would pour the hair dye into an old saucer and stir the tarlike goop before dabbing it onto a small square of sponge. She

12 **to be spitting image of sb** to look exactly like sb – 12 **Starsky and Hutch** US-produced TV series in the late 70s about two policemen – 16 **'Living on a Prayer', 'The Final Countdown'** hard rock songs released in 1986 – 18 **seductive** [sɪˈdʌktɪv] sexually attractive – 21 **to drape** to cover or decorate with folds of cloth – 24 **recalcitrant** [rɪˈkælsɪtrənt] refusing to obey or be controlled – 28 **to dye** to give a different colour to sth – 30 **tarlike goop** *teerartige Pampe*

would then brush my father's temples with the dyed sponge until his hair shone like a vinyl record.

By seventeen my desperation to leave Luton for somewhere else was only marginally more intense than my resentment at my father for having held me back. My teenage life had been nothing more than a failed checklist. Mostly disappointment remained safely buried, only expressed through listening to songs like Janis Ian's 'At Seventeen'. I was too scared to get angry in front of my father and I was riddled with guilt at the prospect of blaming him for anything. Who was I to complain? When he and my mother had suffered and endured so much. That guilt, the feeling that I ought not to feel like I deserved any better, meant that I never went through that teenage time of rebellion when you think that your parents know nothing and when you tell them that. I was too aware of the price that had been paid to give me the luxury of being able to complain. My frustrations remained suppressed.

At college I discovered Bruce Springsteen. In his music I found a new way to understand my relationship with my father. In 'Independence Day' Springsteen sings in the character of a son speaking to his father. Springsteen's father had been a bus driver and he had never approved of his son's rock and roll. Springsteen described his father as taciturn and unemotional. I identified. 'Independence Day' is the story of a son trying to tell his father that he is now his own man and that the old rules don't apply any more. When Springsteen sings it he doesn't sing with anger, he is not taking any pleasure when he tells his dad that 'they ain't gonna do to me what I watched them do to you'. What most impressed me about 'Independence Day' was the empathy that Springsteen had for his father. It isn't that he is

1 **temples** *Schläfen* – 4 **resentment** feeling of anger because one has been forced to accept sth one does not like – 8 **'at Seventeen'** released in 1975 – 9 **to be riddled with** to be full of – 20 **'Independence Day'** released in 1980 – 23 **taciturn** ['tæsɪtɜːn] tending to speak very little – 30 **empathy** ['empəθɪ] ability to imagine oneself in the position of another person

angry with his father for having different values and believing in different things. 'There's nothing we can say can change anything now,' he sings, 'because there's just different people coming down here now, and they see things in different ways and soon everything we've known will just be swept away.' Those lines made me understand the fear that drove my father and men like him: that all the things they had experienced, the values they had tried to pass on to their children were all for nothing. Until I heard 'Independence Day' I'm not sure this fear was something I had even bothered to consider. That was what made the song so important; it opened my mind to the pain that my father was feeling and it made me think of what he might have been feeling.

At the end of the song Springsteen tries to explain that in wanting his freedom he is only trying to secure what is rightfully his, not deliberately trying to hurt his father. 'Papa, now I know the things you wanted that you could not say,' he sings, 'but won't you just say goodbye, it's independence day, I swear I never meant to take those things away.' That last line always blew me away. Bruce was saying that it was not selfishness or malice that was driving him; it was just the order of things, this was what happened with the passing of generations.

The realisation that the tension between my father and me was not unique, that it was something as old as time, something that Springsteen also experienced, was a huge comfort. I was not alone. When my father was driving me insane, I would sing 'Independence Day' to myself and imagine I had the courage to say those words to him. I never did.

In the autumn of 1989 I left Luton to start university in Manchester. My brother had graduated from Nottingham the previous year and it was always assumed and expected that

21 **malice** ['mælɪs] wish or intention to harm or hurt sb – 25 **comfort** ['kʌmfət] sth that makes you feel better after feeling worried or sad

I would follow him to university. For my parents attending university was a sign of success and status; for me it was a means of getting the hell away from them. When I finished university I remained in Manchester for another three years, returning to Luton only because of guilt, duty and Bruce Springsteen. On the day that I graduated from university Springsteen was playing Wembley Arena; I skipped my graduation day and went to the concert. When my father later asked when my graduation day was I told him that it had been and gone.

I did not know it at the time but while I was growing up away from home my father was changing. When I had lived with him, he had mouthed the right words about religion but had never shown much interest in exploring it. After the Eid visit to the mosque my father would mock the imams, saying, 'They are all thieves. They collect cash and say it's on behalf of the mosque but a few months later the imam gets an extension on his house!'

But while I had been going to see Oasis at the Hacienda my father had developed a more profound understanding of his faith. He dressed less in his beloved shirts and ties and move in the traditional kurta pyjama. When I rang home from my Manchester home to speak to the family my mother would tell me that he was at the mosque. When I asked why, she would explain that he had said that he found it soothing and inspiring to discuss religion with the imams. He even had begun to set aside an hour a day to read the Koran.

In his later years Mohammed softened. Living away from home I did not notice the way that the others did. He discussed making a pilgrimage to Mecca with my mother. Seventeen-year-old Uzma was astonished when he had taken her to PJ Shoes and bought her a pair of knee-length boots. I had been

14 **Eid** [i:d] Muslim holiday that marks the end of Ramadan – 19 **Oasis** English rock band – 25 **soothing** ['su:ðɪŋ] making one feel calm – 30 **pilgrimage** journey made to a holy place

shocked when he had not raised any objections to my going to see Bruce Springsteen six nights running at Wembley Arena. At the time I assumed that we had worn him down. Now I think that he was genuinely becoming more at ease with his children. When we spoke he was less argumentative and more interested in hearing what I thought. He seemed less angry, less bitter at my life choices. Perhaps he had given up on me or perhaps his faith was encouraging him to try fresh ways of reaching out to me. Perhaps he had even started to believe in me. I didn't think that at the time, only later.

Knowing now that my father was not the authoritarian dictator I had constructed in my imagination, I understand better his reaction when, in early 1993, he did not explode with anger when I came home with a new hairstyle. I did not see my dreadlocks as blatant rebellion; it was not done to deliberately outrage my father but I was still wary of his reaction. When I returned home with my new dreadlocks I kept a large woollen hat on my head. 'Your son has had a haircut,' my mother said as I edged past them.

I rested my acoustic guitar by the side of the wall and faced my father. 'So, take your hat off, let me see this new hairstyle.'

I smiled, pulled off my hat and shook my head until the dreadlocks were freed and flailing.

'Is that another hat?' he asked, not yet betraying any reaction.

'No, this is my hair.'

'This is your hair?'

'Yes.'

'All this is *your* hair?'

'No, some is extensions that have been weaved in.'

'Don't you understand? Your son wants to be Jamaican,' my mother said in a tone of mock patience. 'He doesn't want

15 **blatant** ['bleɪtnt] done openly without caring whether other people are shocked – 16 **wary** ['weərɪ] not completely certain about sth or sb – 23 **to flail** to wave about

to be Pakistani, he is not a Muslim. He wants to be black. Congratulations: two Pakistanis have given birth to a Jamaican son. Have you brought some ludoos to celebrate this special day?'

My father did not fly into a rage. Not then and not later. He was only disappointed and embarrassed. When Sadiq came to visit us I would be banished upstairs and Uzma would deliver my curry and chapattis to my bedroom. While I understood that it must have been strange to see their son looking so alien I couldn't see at the time why it should be the cause of such disappointment. But I think I understand now. For my father my hairstyle was emblematic of something far deeper; in rejecting my coarse curls I was rejecting him and everything that he stood for.

Two weeks after the Elizabeth Wurtzel interview I received a phone call from my brother telling me my father had been taken to hospital. It was the last Sunday of May and I was watching *New York, New York* on television at my flat in Manchester. 'You need to come to Luton,' he said.

I did not have a car and there were no trains travelling south at that hour. It was past midnight but in desperation I called my friend Paul. He had friends round, but once I told him the reason I was calling he immediately offered to drive me to Luton. Thirty minutes later Paul was outside my home in West Didsbury with two of his friends. In the small hours of the morning we set off for Luton and Dunstable Hospital.

I was told later what had happened. My father had been in his bedroom reading the paper. Harold Wilson had died the week before and his death had put my father into a reflective mood. He had been reading about him when from nowhere he had found himself burping uncontrollably. The burps had become

3 **ludoo** Pakistani dish – 7 **to banish** to send away as a punishment – 12 **emblematic** being a sign of sth – 13 **coarse** [kɔːs] not smooth but rough – 28 **Harold Wilson** (1916-1995) British Prime Minister (1964-1970, 1974-1976) – 31 **to burp** [bɜːp] to get rid of air from the stomach through the mouth in a noisy way

more frequent and more painful. My mother had suggested a glass of warm milk but it had not improved the situation. An ambulance was called. He had struggled downstairs. Uzma and Sohail were telling him not to worry but they could see he was fading. He was glistening with sweat. The ambulance had not yet arrived. My mother was saying, don't worry, the ambulance is coming. My father had tears in his eyes. My mother would later say she knew why he was crying. He was crying because he knew he was leaving his wife to fend for herself, just like she had done for so long while he had been in England and she had been in Pakistan. My mother always said that my father was not crying because he feared death but because he feared for the lives of those he left behind. His family.

I was not there to see my father collapsing or crying. By the time I reached Luton and Dunstable Hospital he was already in intensive care. In the room were my mother, Uzma and Sohail. My older sister Navela, who was married and had a small baby boy, was also there. It must have been serious for her to make the visit as we hardly ever saw her since she moved out of home. The little boy was crying in his mother's arms. The television flickered silently in the corner of the room. I looked at the wan faces of my family. No one said anything to me. My brother's eyes were bloodshot. Uzma looked defeated. My mother looked as if she had reached the far shores of disbelief. Each of them looked up at me with an expression that implied that my hell was only just beginning.

It was hard to tell if he was in pain. Lying on a hospital bed with tubes invading his nose and mouth, he did not look peaceful. His breathing was loud and mechanical. Blinking machines surrounded him. He was hooked up to a drip. Were there any flickers of life? None that I could discern. Nurses

5 **to glisten** ['glɪsn] to shine – 9 **to fend for oneself** to look after oneself – 22 **wan** [wɒn] pale and tired – 23 **bloodshot** having the white part coloured red – 30 **hooked up to a drip** connected to a machine putting liquid into a vein – 31 **to discern** [dɪ'sɜːn] to recognize

drifted past. I tried to engage one in conversation. Her manner was bright but the words were bleak.

My mother joined me at the bedside. 'Take a good look at your father. Look at what he has become.'

I looked at my father but I was not seeing him. The man I knew was proud, strong, intelligent, ambitious; he could tell you the price of oil and gold when the stock market closed, he was someone whose life was a relentless quest to achieve and know and gain and become. My father was all about becoming. And he was always smart and cared obsessively about the image that was projected of himself and his family to the outside world. So who was this man lying in a forced sleep on this hospital bed? It was my father, but stripped of all the qualities and characteristics that made him the man I loved and feared. When his brain was deprived of oxygen, everything that made my father what he was slipped away. Everything that he knew, believed in, cared about, fought for and against was erased. The spirit of my father had vacated the hospital ward. We just had the sleeping flesh.

For seven days we took turns to sleep in the relatives' room of the hospital. Friends came and offered their prayers. Sadiq came with water from Mecca that he poured into a silver bowl that had verses from the Koran engraved on it. My mother dipped her fingers in the water and rubbed it on my father's lips as she recited some lines from the Koran. In the villages where our families came from entire families were reading the Koran day and night, hoping that Allah would reward them by giving my father his life back. Men my father had helped came and offered their prayers and best wishes. These were the men whom my father had helped with mortgages, passport applications or forms to try and bring their wives into the country. They all said the same thing: that my mother

8 **relentless quest** continuous search – 15 **to deprive sb of sth** to take sth that is necessary away from sb – 18 **to vacate** to stop being at a place

would get her husband back. Allah was merciful and kind and generous and he would listen. 'I swear on my children's lives,' said my mother one night, 'that I will go to Mecca and lie down in front of the Kaaba and give my own thanks to Allah if He will just give me my children's father back.'

'Sister, don't worry. Allah listens to everything. He is listening now.'

When we went home we watched the news. At the same time that my father was fighting for his life so was Christopher Reeve. He had fallen off a horse the day before my father's heart attack. The news networks were running footage of Reeve when he was Superman.

The last day of May was a Wednesday. My father had been in a coma since Sunday night. That day the *Manchester Evening News* published my interview with Elizabeth Wurtzel. They sent me a copy of the paper that same day. I opened it and saw the full-page feature with my name in print for the first time. It was the first thing I had done in my career that my father might have been proud of if he had seen it; but he was sleeping. Unaware.

The doctors warned us the chances of him waking from the coma were negligible, it was only the machines that were helping him breathe but the risks of infection that came with weakness meant his time was limited. Each morning my mother would use swabs of wet cotton buds to moisten his lips, she would rub Nivea intensive lotion on to his face and brush his teeth. But with his condition deteriorating we had been advised to say our goodbyes. My mother instructed each of her children to separately say our farewells. 'Go to your father and ask for his forgiveness,' she said. 'Ask him to forgive you for all your mistakes.'

9 **Christopher Reeve** American actor who played Superman – 11 **footage** [ˈfʊtɪdʒ] the length in feet of cinema film used for a scene *(Filmmaterial)* – 25 **swab** cleaning cloth – 27 **to deteriorate** [dɪtˈɪərɪəreɪt] to become worse

I did not know what to say. It felt embarrassing speaking to someone who probably could not hear what I was saying. 'Daddy, I don't know if you can hear me,' I whispered, 'but I want to say I am sorry if I ever let you down.' My father remained silent and still. I reached out and gently held his hand. 'I know that I haven't done everything you wanted me to do and that I have sometimes embarrassed and ashamed you but I want you to know that I really… I really…' Even alone in a room with my father slipping from life, I found it hard to say the word, it was not a word we ever used in our family. 'I really *care* about you and I promise I will try my best to make you proud of me.' I was still holding his hand when the rest of the family joined me. It was then that the tears started falling.

'Let them out, son,' said my mother, 'let the tears out.' I squeezed hard on my father's soft, still hand, looked into his face and saw my own. The next day I had my dreadlocks cut off.

My father never awoke from his coma. On 6 June 1995 Mohammed Manzoor died. The next day I helped carry the open coffin out of the hearse, along the path of our back garden and into our house. We laid it gently on the carpet of the living room. According to Muslim tradition the women of the family were not allowed to attend the funeral. This would be the last glimpse that my mother would have of my father. 'Why have you left me? Why have you left me alone?' wailed my mother while her friends held her close and quietly said prayers to Allah. 'You should have taken me with you! Why have you left me alone?'

Navela and Uzma sat with my mother, tears streaming down their faces. I gazed into my father's face, his skin a sick yellow. Later that afternoon Sohail and I lowered his coffin into the ground and covered it with soil. Two days later I turned twenty-four.

20 **hearse** [hɜːs] vehicle which is used to carry a body in its coffin to the funeral – 25 **to wail** to cry out in grief or pain

His clothes were still hanging in the wardrobe in his bedroom. The blue shirts with their white collars, the charcoal-grey trousers and the ties from British Home Stores. Old issues of the *Financial Times*. His spectacles case. The gold-plated tie pin and tie that Uzma had bought him for his birthday eight weeks earlier, the first birthday present she had ever bought for him. Everything in its place as if my father was coming home any moment. As if the last few days had been just a cruel nightmare from which I would soon awake. I slept on the floor in the living room with my mother who was too traumatised to sleep in her bedroom. During the night I found myself waking with a jolt and I'd walk softly to where my mother was sleeping. She would be lying on a duvet spread on the living room carpet. I would lean close towards her and ensure I could hear her breathing. Each night I watched her and waited in fear that her breathing might stop in the middle of the night.

Three months after my father died I returned to Manchester. On the walls of my bedroom were the same posters of Woody Allen and Winona Ryder, the same Fender Stratocaster I had been trying to master, the same piles of cassettes and compact discs that I had left behind. The months immediately after my father's death were filled with confusion and pain. It hurt leaving Luton after only three months since I knew how painful my departure would be for my mother and the rest of the family. But I was leaving to start a master's course in documentary making, which might, I hoped, lead to a job in the media. I had to try and see if it led somewhere, I reasoned, otherwise the only other option was a job in Luton. My mother and brother had been supportive of my decision to start the course. 'Go, try to succeed. I will keep things going here,' Sohail had said to me. 'We will all work harder to give you the chance to make it.'

1 **wardrobe** large cupboard – 4 **spectacle case** little box to put one's glasses in – 12 **jolt** sudden forceful shake – 13 **duvet** ['du:veɪ] large bag filled with feathers used on a bed – 19 **Fender Stratocaster** famous electric guitar model built from 1954 to the present day

I was pleased to be given that opportunity but I couldn't escape the guilt I felt at leaving the others to their pain.

On the train going back to Manchester an old couple sat opposite me. They were both in their late seventies, I guessed, and they took great care with their appearance. The man wore a tweed fedora and had a neat moustache, the woman had straight white hair, a powdered face and wore pink lipstick. Thoughts kept spinning around my head like: why are these two allowed to grow old together while my parents were not? Why was it that just at the moment that life was meant to be getting easier for Mum and Dad, just when they were planning on going to Hajj together and starting to take some time for themselves, that should be the moment when death claimed my father?

In Bruce Springsteen's album *Darkness on the Edge of Town* there is a song called 'Candy's Room'. Springsteen sings: 'In the darkness there'll be hidden worlds that shine.' I don't recall ever being particularly moved by that line before but after my father died that one line felt like a lifeline thrown to a drowning man. The first time those words came to me was in the early hours of the morning. I was in my room in Manchester and I got out of bed and wrote it out in block letters on a piece of blank paper. I fixed it to my bedroom wall so that it was in my direct line of sight when I was in bed. I stared at those words as if they might hold the secret to the universe.

'In the darkness there'll be hidden worlds that shine.' I cannot be certain what Bruce Springsteen meant with those words but what they mean to me is this: there is pain right now but it will lead to rewards that can only be found by going through the pain. It was not the promise of better days which made those words so powerful; it was the suggestion that there was a purpose to it, that the only way to know the better days ahead

6 **fedora** a man's hat with a wide brim – 12 **Hajj** [hædʒ] the annual pilgrimage to Mecca

was to endure the present anguish. Since my father had died, anguish was all I and my family had known and it seemed a meaningless torment. But it was those words from Springsteen that I had scrawled in black felt-tip pen and pinned to my wall that comforted me by implying that the pain was not in vain.

One afternoon twenty years ago while I was rifling through my father's suits looking for loose change that I could borrow I found a diary. Flicking through the pages, I came across the usual scribbled notes referring to stocks and shares. On one page my father had written two dates. Below them he had written 'death of beloved mother and father'. He never spoke about his parents but reading that offered a tiny insight into my father as a man and a sentimental one at that. In his bedside drawer he kept a tattered black fan with a painted red dragon. This fan had been bought by my father's father when he had served in the army, fighting for the British against the Japanese in the Second World War. Sons never get over losing their fathers.

In a corner of Stockwood cemetery reserved for Luton's deceased Muslims a simple black marble gravestone marks where Mohammed Manzoor lies buried. The block beside him is reserved for my mother. It's more than ten years now since Mohammed Manzoor died and I feel that I know him better now than I did when he was alive. The hidden world which his departure illuminated was the realisation that I was more like him than I had ever conceded. My anger mutated my father into a heartless brute who was incapable of love. Any memories that contradicted this were buried or obliterated; resenting my father was the fuel that drove my ambition, but it also drove me away from him. I was not interested in seeing things from his point of view, I hadn't reflected on why he felt the things he did. I did not want to know. When I had the chance to ask my

1 **to endure** [ɪn'djʊə] to suffer sth that is painful – 1 **anguish** very great pain – 3 **torment** very great pain – 14 **tattered** old and torn – 14 **fan** an object made from folded paper or other material used to move the air around – 26 **to concede** to admit that sth is true – 26 **to mutate** to change – 28 **to obliterate** to destroy, to remove all signs

father questions, I chose not to. But by not being able to direct those questions to him I was forced to confront them on my own. As my own adult life has progressed, my admiration for my father has grown. I wish I had asked more questions when he was alive, I wish I had tried to humanise him when I had the chance. I wish in vain; it was only when he died that the desire for answers arose.

My greatest regret is that he did not live to see how his gamble to come to this country played out. He died in the same week that my very first article was published; any success I have had came when he was not around to savour it. The one person whose approval means most to me is unable to grant it. Where once it was resentment which inspired me, now it is the hope that in my own life I can do his memory proud. These days I am a willing prisoner of my father's house.

11 **to savour** [ˈseɪvə] to enjoy intensively

The Ties That Bind

Everybody's got a hunger, a hunger they can't resist.
There's so much that you want, you deserve much more than this.
But if dreams came true, oh, wouldn't that be nice.

'Prove it all Night', Bruce Springsteen

I owe my life to two strokes of incredible luck: I was not born female and I was not the oldest son. I was almost three years old when I arrived in Britain. My brother Sohail and my sister Navela were old enough to remember life in Pakistan. My younger sister Uzma was born in Luton and I remembered nothing else.

When my family arrived in Britain to join our father, he was a stranger to his children. He worked shifts, sometimes leaving in the early evening to go to work and returning early the next day. While he worked I stayed at home with my mother, and Sohail and Navela were enrolled at the local junior school. They lasted only a few days because neither my brother nor my sister could speak much English – they only words they knew were: 'I'm sorry, I don't speak English.' My brother and sister were transferred to a special school for three months where they were taught English before rejoining Maidenhall Junior School.

There were other adjustments to be made. We had not known who our neighbours were until my brother was caught urinating out of his bedroom window in the middle of the night. When my brother had lived in Pakistan there had not been an indoor lavatory, if he needed to urinate he just had to wander out into the sugar cane fields, so now, when the call

14 **shift** *Schicht* – 17 **to enrol** to register – 24 **adjustment** slight change

of nature came, he preferred to answer it by sliding open the bedroom window and pissing on to the street. It was only the persistent complaints from the neighbour which persuaded him from continuing to drench the pavement.

Those early years in Bury Park were hard times. The National Front were winning local elections; the three-day week was keeping my father at home. My mother kept candles under the sink in case of power cuts. Everything we bought was from second-hand stores or jumble sales and they were bought with Green Shield stamps. I would sleep in my parents' bed, Navela slept on the second-hand sofa in the living room. Sohail slept on two dining-table chairs that were placed opposite each other and tied together with two of my mother's old dupattas. Later, my father was given an old hospital trolley bed by his friend Sadiq; it had wheels and was so narrow that at night my mother had to tuck Sohail's blankets in tight under the thin mattress so he would not fall out during the night.

On the evening of 12 September 1975 my mother was sewing until the small hours of the morning. The next day she gave birth to my sister Uzma. When we brought Uzma back to the house there was no crib so she would lie on clothes that were laid out on the floor of the living room. 'It will flatten the back of her head,' my mother would tell Navela, 'like we did with your brother.' For the first six months of my life I had slept with my head resting on rice bags as it was believed a flat head was more attractive than a curve. Navela liked to put make-up on baby Uzma and draw eyebrows on her face as if she were a little doll.

The television carried news about IRA bombs in Guildford and Birmingham; the men at Vauxhall joked with my father that these days being Irish was even worse than being a Paki. My mother cleaned the house, made dresses in the living room and chapattis in the kitchen. We had no central heating; when

4 **to drench** to make wet – 5 **National Front** far right British political party – 10 **Green Shield stamps** stamps that were give as bonuses with every purchase – 29 **IRA** Irish Republican Army; Irish terror group

it was cold we would turn on the three-bar electric heaters. In the evenings we would sit by them and watch *The Life and Times of Grizzly Adams* and *The Rockford Files* while trying to stay warm from the orange glow of the bars. But this was an expensive way to stay warm so my father encouraged us to find other ways to heat the home. There was a fireplace in the dining room and during the winter when the house would become particularly cold my mother would ask Sohail to break up some of the cheap, secondhand furniture and throw it into the fire.

There was little money but my brother and I still found ways to entertain ourselves. We played marbles in the hallway and in the evenings we'd test each other on the capital cities of different countries, using an old atlas that was covered in bottle-green cloth. In the summer of 1976 Sohail made a cricket bat from a plank of wood. Using an old hacksaw, he had sawn along two L-shaped lines to make a handle, which he wrapped with one of my mother's old dupattas. We'd spend the summer afternoons playing cricket in our concrete back garden while our mother would put out a plate of melon seeds to dry in the sun. When it was too hot to play Sohail would take one of our bed sheets and hang it over the clothes line in the garden. The two of us would crouch under the makeshift tent drinking water filled with ice cubes.

The nearest high school to our home in Bury Park was called Beech Hill; it was where Navela and Sohail would have gone after leaving Maidenhall but my father was adamant that he did not want his children attending an all-Asian school. 'I don't want my children to grow up uneducated,' he'd say. 'I don't want them turning into criminals.' He was convinced the best way to ensure this was for us to be educated with white children. This was not the same as being friends with whites, which he believed to be both unlikely and possibly dangerous.

12 **marbles** small hard glass balls – 23 **makeshift** sth that is used because there is nothing better – 27 **adamant** [ˈædəmənt] determined not to change a decision

Navela suggested Lealands High School in Sundon Park which was three miles and two bus rides away but new and overwhelmingly white. Sohail was allowed to attend but my father refused to let Navela go. 'It's different for girls,' he would say. 'I don't want you mixing with boys.' For three months my father and sister argued, and during that time, Navela did not attend high school because the school insisted she comply with a uniform that required her to wear a skirt. My father was adamant that no daughter of his would be seen wearing such revealing clothes. Eventually the school allowed my sister to wear trousers. She was the first girl at Lealands to be given permission to not wear a skirt.

Sohail was working during the weekends at a grocery store on Dunstable Road which was minutes from our home. The money went to my father, but he bought Sohail a Meccano set and a pair of Dr Martens boots. For the first week he had them my brother would go to sleep with his boots by his bedside, unable to believe they were really his. At school my brother was captain of the rugby, athletics and cricket teams. His sporting prowess was his ticket towards approval and acceptance from the whites; the trophies he was winning the school made him a popular pupil and anyone knew that if they dared call him a paki they would be given a thorough beating. Meanwhile Navela was being picked on at school. The other girls taunted her, made fun of her hairy legs and told her that she smelled. And the truth was that to them she did smell; we only bathed once a week. Navela wanted to tell our parents about being bullied, but there was enough tension at home already. What good would it do to give them more to worry about?

At home the pressure from my father on my mother to be more productive at dressmaking was relentless. Sohail and I helped where we could but it was Navela who would come home, help with the cooking and cleaning and then work until

15 **Meccano set** model toys construction set – 20 **prowess** great skill or ability – 24 **to taunt** to upset sb by making unkind remarks

one in the morning on the sewing machine. When my father worked the evening shift, the tension would ease; we had bought a record player and Navela would play 'You're the One That I Want' and 'Hopelessly Devoted to You'. She wished she could have gone to the cinema to see *Grease.* My sister adored pop music; it was because of Navela that I had seen Queen singing 'We Are the Champions' on *Top of the Pops,* because of her that the Eurovision Song Contest was essential viewing in our home.

Sohail would spend his evenings playing sport for the school teams, but Navela had too much to do at home. My sister had little time for her studies and her schoolwork suffered, which mattered only to her: my father had already forbidden her from going to college. 'I need you to work at home; how can this house manage without all of us working together?' Navela left school on 17 May 1980; two weeks later she was working at a textile factory just across the road from the college of higher education.

Navela loved fairy tales. After work she would go to the library and borrow collections of fairy tales which she would pass on to me when she had read them. On Saturdays Navela would try to teach me calligraphy. Beauty mattered to my sister.

When we moved to Marsh Farm, my father, mother and older sister were all working but we still never seemed to have any money. Where is the money going?' Navela would ask my father. 'I work at Eastex and you get the money, I work at home and you get the money. Mum works and you get the money but there never seems to be any money! Where does it go?'

The rest of us would never have dared to speak like this to my father but Navela felt she had earned the right to be disrespectful. She was the oldest child, she brought in money but it was also her temperament; Navela was as fiery as a green

22 **calligraphy** art of writing beautifully by hand

chilli. I was at once appalled and filled with admiration by Navela's utter fearlessness. Even today, it is still more difficult to be a strong-willed independent Asian girl than boy; harder still for Navela in 1980. 'Listen to your daughter talk!' my father would respond, his words dripping scorn. 'She thinks she knows all the answers! Look at my clothes, are they new? The money you are making puts food on our table, it is making sure this house you wanted is warm at night. You won't understand these things until you have your own family and your home. Running a house costs money!'

'But we never *do* anything to our house, Daddy,' Navela would fire back. 'We've never redecorated; the wallpaper is the same as when we moved in and the carpet is worn out. We can't be spending *all* our money on food. And your clothes *are* brand new: new cufflinks, new ties, new suits. The only time I ever buy clothes is for Eid – the rest of the time I make them myself and so does Mum and Uzma.'

'You want to talk about clothes? Don't you know how shameful it is for your mother and me seeing you dressed in your jeans going to work? Have you any idea what our friends are saying about you, about us?' There was nothing wrong with jeans on boys but my parents believed that girls shouldn't wear such things. Particularly not tight jeans, and especially not on their daughter. What made it worse was that Navela favoured wearing jeans that were crimson and skintight. 'Your daughter, she has no shame,' my father would say to my mother. 'Look at the way she walks when she is wearing those clothes, as if she wants people to look at her. What am I expected to say if anyone sees her?'

'What's wrong with what I am wearing?' Navela would respond. 'I am not showing any flesh and I paid for these with my own money.'

'This isn't about money, it's about honour!'

1 **to appal** [ə'pɔːl] to shock deeply – 2 **utter** ['ʌtə] complete – 5 **scorn** anger – 25 **crimson** deep red colour

'But what's wrong with jeans?'

If the argument persisted I would go to my bedroom and listen to Radio Luxembourg or try and read but I would be unable to drown out the sound of my father and sister arguing. Navela wasn't allowed to leave the house in the evenings so instead would keep Uzma awake for hours by trying on clothes and asking her to take her photograph in different outfits. Uzma could not understand why Navela would spend so much time dressing up in clothes, applying lipstick and eyeliner and foundation when she was not going anywhere.

While Navela was working at the textile factory Sohail was at sixth-form college. An old friend of my father called Sufi had been giving my brother driving lessons. Sufi worked with my father at Vauxhall but his family lived up north, so he was free at the weekends to teach Sohail how to drive his Datsun Sunny. My brother passed his driving test on the third attempt and was soon scouring the pages of the *Luton Herald* for a cheap second-hand car. He eventually found a gold Vauxhall Viva which my father bought for seventy pounds. Dressed in his stonewashed denim jacket and jeans, his face bristling with stubble and wearing mirrored sunglasses, Sohail would take the Viva for aimless drives into town with the windows down and bhangra bursting from the speakers. At the weekends he would lovingly repair the bodywork, filling dents with gauze and letting me help with vacuuming. When he replaced the old car stereo he gave the old one to me. My friend Ben explained how I could wire speakers up to it and have my own music system in the bedroom I shared with my brother.

Sohail no longer played sports for the college but he went weight training three times a week; he also bought bodybuilding magazines and the walls of our bedroom were plastered with images of past Mr Universes. The men all had

10 **foundation (cream)** substance rubbed into the face before face powder is put on – 20 **to bristle** ['brɪsl] to stand up (of hair) – 21 **stubble** short stiff hair – 23 **bhangra** form of music originated in the Punjab region (Pakistan/India) – 24 **bodywork** main outside stucture of a car – 24 **filling dents with gauze** [gɔːz] *Dellen mit Gewebe ausspachteln*

the same expression of concentrated serenity, the arms would be either outstretched like a Greek god or posed to display the bulging biceps. Sohail read books on body building; we knew Arnold Schwarzenegger when he was a body builder. When he caught me looking at the magazines Sohail would insist that I felt his biceps. 'Can you feel that? Does it feel hard?' he would ask proudly. 'Don't you wish you had muscles like that?'

I loathed being thin. At junior school I was convinced a tapeworm was getting to my food before me; it was the only explanation for why I remained rake thin no matter how much I ate. The photographs of body builders on the bedroom wall did nothing for my self-esteem. My father believed the best cure for low self-esteem was public ridicule. This meant that whenever anyone came to visit there was an inevitable moment when they would ask how the children were. It was particularly pointed when Shuja came to visit because my father had known him since childhood and the longer my father had known someone the freer he felt to humiliate his children in their presence. Although he was the same age as my father, Shuja seemed older; his eyes were deep set and he looked like he was wearing eyeliner, but in fact it was charcoal. The henna in his hair had turned it orange. 'Manzoor sahib, is your son eating correctly? He looks painfully thin. Not like his brother at all.'

'Yes, he is very thin. We tell him to eat more but nothing seems to work. Son, pull your shirtsleeves up. Let him see your arms. Do you see how thin they are? Practically sticks.'

'You are so right! He is all bone!' Shuja exclaimed. 'Son, you should eat more meat. You want to grow up to be a strong lion of a man, don't you?'

I would not answer, I would just run back to my room. I wished I could have been more like my brother who could walk around with only a shirt. I would secretly do press-ups and sit-ups in my bedroom, borrow my brother's Bullworker, load my

1 **serenity** calmness – 8 **to loathe** [ləʊð] to dislike very much – 9 **tapeworm** *Bandwurm* – 34 **Bullworker** exercise device to build up muscles

bag with more books than I needed to make it heavier on the walk to school. It made no difference.

My father believed that all my physical deficiencies could be cured by drinking a glass of milk a day. The two fixed rituals of my teenage years were reading the Koran and drinking a glass of milk; one for spiritual nourishment and the other for physical well being. I always drank the milk slightly warm at the end of the day. After seeing *Rocky* I became convinced that I needed to drink milk mixed with raw eggs but the first and only time I tried it I retched and hurled into the kitchen sink.

The bedroom I shared with my brother became mine in the autumn of 1984 when Sohail left to study in Nottingham. The photographs of the body builders were replaced by film posters from the local video store and a map of the world. I missed my brother when he was away; when he came home it was always in brand-new cars that he had hired for the weekend. In the glove compartment there would be albums on cassette: *Can't Slow Down, Thriller and Lost in Music.*

To be popular at my high school it was essential to wear the right clothes. The cool students wore Diadora trainers, Farah trousers, Pringle sweaters and sportswear emblazoned with Lacoste. I would doodle the logos of Sergio Tacchini and Fila in the back of my exercise books, but most of my clothes came from the discount stores in Bury Park. When Sohail came back to Luton he would secretly take me shopping in the Arndale Centre and, with his own money, buy me clothes that my father never would. He bought me a pair of dazzling white Hi-Tec Capitol trainers and a navy-blue Lyle & Scott sweater. During holidays we would visit Sohail in Nottingham; with his redundancy money my father had bought the house where he lived and the whole family would travel to see him and spend the weekend painting and cleaning the house to prepare it for the new set of students. Sometimes I went to see my brother

3 **deficiency** [dɪˈfɪʃnsɪ] state of not having sth that is essential – 6 **nourishment** [ˈnʌrɪʃmənt] food – 10 **to retch** to feel like vomiting – 10 **to hurl** to throw with force – 20 **trainers** shoes used for sports – 30 **redundancy money** money you receive when you are unemployed

on my own; on those visits he would take me to see *Robocop* and *Fatal Attraction*.

While Sohail was enjoying university life, Navela was still living at home. She could not forgive my father for not letting her pursue her education. While my father insisted it was because of finances, Navela was convinced it was simply because she was female. If a daughter went to university she was out of sight, out of her parents' control and liable to descend into a moral cesspit of depravity. It was bad enough that a son could venture there but for a daughter to be lost in sin was unimaginable. What angered my sister most was that the opportunities being given to my brother and later to me were made possible because of her efforts.

Navela was a huge influence on my life. It was because of her that I started listening to the radio. She turned me on to Steve Wright, a DJ whose afternoon show provided the soundtrack to my eighties childhood. I became such a fan that when I was at school I would ask Navela to record the entire three-hour programme on to three blank cassette tapes. In the evenings when the rest of the family were sleeping I would turn on my cassette player and hide it under my blankets. I would then switch off the lights, tuck myself under the covers and go to sleep with *Steve Wright in the Afternoon* in my headphones.

When Uzma and I returned from school we were expected to help Navela and our mother with their sewing. We would help with the collars and the belts; the collars were inside out so Uzma would poke them out with a knitting needle, being careful not to pierce the fabric. The belts had to be pulled inside out. Uzma and I would have races to see who could do twenty belts the quickest. When a dress was finished, a tag with the number 67 – our house number – would be attached so that the man who came to collect it would know it was made by our family.

8 **liable** likely – 9 **cesspit of depravity** *,Kloake der Verdorbenheit'* – 10 **to venture** to risk going somewhere dangerous

When Navela was not working on dresses with my mother she would design them for other people. She had a book of sketches she would show to prospective clients; once she had made a dress she would make sure to be photographed in it herself before handing it over. One of my mother's friends had a daughter who went to the London School of Fashion; despite being a fashion student this girl would ask Navela to design her own clothes.

My father knew something about what it was like to not see one's potential fulfilled, and yet while he encouraged me to study hard I never heard him say anything similar to my older sister. The idea that Navela could have utilised her love of fashion in ways other than making dresses for pennies at home never occurred to him. His biggest priority was trying to find a husband for her; when they argued and he was feeling particularly bitter, my father would complain that my sister had given him a huge headache. 'Who is going to want to marry you? Do you realise what a burden you are on me, having to find someone willing to accept a girl who talks back?'

Three times during the eighties my father took my sister to Pakistan to find her a husband. Navela insisted that any husband of hers had to be older and taller than she was. On the third visit she met someone who fulfilled her requirements and in early 1991 the family, except me and Sohail, travelled to Pakistan for my sister's wedding.

When Navela returned, she and her new husband moved into our home. I met him for the first time when I returned from Manchester one weekend. It was strange to think that this fair-skinned man with a thin moustache and his shirt tucked inside his chinos was now part of our family, and had replaced my father as the most important man in my sister's life. When we talked our conversation was stilted and punctuated with uncomfortable pauses. I asked him what he did and he told

3 **prospective clients** possible future clients – 12 **to utilise** to use sth in an effective way – 32 **stilted** very formal and unnatural – 32 **to punctuate** to interrupt

me it was something to do with biochemistry. He asked me about Manchester and I told him it was better than Luton. I asked him what he made of life in Britain. He pulled a face as if chewing a piece of mango pickle. 'Life is very hard,' he complained. 'People here work like dogs for their money.'

Bloody cheek, I thought to myself. There are millions desperate to come to England and now you're here, you're complaining. 'Life is hard here but you do have the chance to have a better life than in Pakistan,' I reminded him.

He shook his head. 'There is poverty in Pakistan, of course there is, but the rich live very well there. Servants, imported goods. A lifestyle you cannot imagine.'

I had thought my brother-in-law would thank the stars we had taken him away from Pakistan, but instead he appeared to be in shock at the realisation that in Britain the good life required hard work. That was one of the problems with arranged marriages and importing husbands and wives from Pakistan: they thought marriage was a free ticket to an easy life.

My sister had always been the most outspoken of all of us and now, emboldened by her husband, she began to refuse to pass her earnings on to our father. 'I have spent my life working for you,' she said. 'Now I want you to pay me back all the money I have given to the family.' All our lives my father had been the undisputed authority figure in our family; nothing happened without his consent and his was the final word. Suddenly it no longer mattered how loudly my father shouted, his daughter no longer felt compelled to obey. 'I want what is mine, what is rightfully mine and what I have earned,' my sister demanded.

'What rubbish are you talking?' my father would retort. 'Where have you learnt this talk of your money and my money?

4 **pickle** vegetable that has been preserved in vinegar – 6 **cheek** *inf* disrespectful person – 17 **arranged marriage** marriage arranged by someone other than the couple – 20 **outspoken** expressing openly what is thought or felt – 21 **to embolden** to encourage – 30 **to retort** to answer quickly

The money I was making at Vauxhall – did I ever say that was just for my needs?'

But this was no longer enough for my sister. 'Who made the greatest sacrifices, Daddy? Who? It wasn't your son, was it – he got to go to university. It was me, Daddy. I was the one who didn't get the chances. Now it's my turn – now I want my share.'

My father would listen with anger and bewilderment: where did his daughter learn such impudence? 'The greatest mistake I ever made was bringing you people to this country,' he would shout so loud the whole house would hear. 'I thought I knew what I was doing, but may Allah forgive me for what I have done. If someone had told me that after all my efforts my children would speak like this to me I swear I would have left you back in Pakistan.'

After five months of fierce arguments Navela and her husband moved out of our home.

Afterwards we would see Navela at the Purley Centre market or walk past her in the street. She would say hello but make little effort to visit our home. Having spent so much of her life living in accordance with our father's wishes and desires Navela seemed now to be deliberately maintaining a distance. My parents were too stubborn to visit her. 'If your daughter wants to see us she knows where we are,' my father would say, but I was not so proud. During weekends and afternoons I would stop by at her place, play with her young son and drink tea in her living room.

* * *

In 1988 Sohail returned from Nottingham. When his friends asked my father what Sohail was doing he would tell them he was looking for work and that times were hard. He did not want to reveal that Sohail had graduated with a poor degree and was

8 **bewilderment** [bɪˈwɪldəmənt] confusion – 9 **impudence** lack of respect

working at a pizza restaurant. Back in Luton, my brother drifted from job to job. He worked as a waiter, in a factory that made hospital beds, and on the construction of the British Library, where many years later I would write this book. My father and brother barely spoke; Sohail would return home late after work smelling of cigarettes and eat the chapattis my mother left for him in the kitchen. He would be out of the house before my parents were downstairs in the morning.

After Sohail's poor results at university, my father would throw my brother's situation at me. 'Is that what will happen to you if you go to university?' he would ask. 'Will you shame the family like he has?'

My mother would ask me to talk to Sohail. 'Ask him what he is doing with his life. Is it any sort of life? Dressing like a tramp and not speaking to his own parents?'

What my parents did not know was that Sohail was planning to leave Britain. His friend Zahid had spent the summer in the United States and had returned full of stories about how amazing it was and how the two of them should try and get work. Frustrated by the lack of decent work in Luton and with tension running high in the family, my brother agreed, and in the summer of 1989 he told my father he was leaving for the United States and he did not know when he would be back. The plan was to travel to New York and take a hired car down to Florida where Sohail and Zahid had a friend who would help them find work. My brother had bought a one-way plane ticket; bored at home, he wanted excitement and there was nothing keeping him in Luton.

The only time I ever saw my father cry was on the day Sohail left home to take the coach to Heathrow. Even after he had shouted at him and told him he had ruined his life my father still reached over to hug Sohail. His eyes were shiny with tears. Sohail was leaving and we did not know when we would hear from him again.

It was in the early hours of the morning, four days after Sohail had left. The telephone would not stop ringing. Shaking the sleep out of my head, I picked up the phone. It was Sohail and he wanted to speak to my father. I went upstairs but by now the whole family were awake. My mother and Uzma joined me on the sofa in the living room as my father talked to my brother. Sohail and Zahid had arrived in New York and were driving from Myrtle Beach to Charleston, North Carolina, in two hired cars when Zahid was involved in a car crash. My brother's closest friend had died in his arms on a highway four thousand miles from home. I knew Zahid; he was always smiling, positive and full of life. I broke down in tears. My father rang Zahid's family to make preparations to bring the body home for a Muslim burial. Sohail returned home.

While I was away at university Sohail finally agreed to visit Pakistan and find a bride. In 1993, the whole family – except Navela – went to Pakistan for his wedding.

I had to be persuaded to attend. It was not that I didn't want to go to the wedding itself but rather that I didn't want to go to Pakistan. I eventually agreed on the condition that I only spent a week there.

I have very few recollections from the trip. Each day was a flurry of meeting cousins and aunts and uncles. What I remember most clearly was a conversation where I was talking to some of my cousins and they were telling me how appalling England was. I sat sipping tea as they denounced England as being the home of sin and decadence and amorality. I could not be bothered to disagree or argue with them and so sat in silence. Finally they stopped talking. The room was quiet. 'So tell me,' piped up one of the cousins, a portly man with a large belly and full moustache, 'could you help me get to England?'

Sohail was to marry Nazia, a girl who grew up in the same village as us and who was distantly related. I remembered

22 **recollection** memory – 23 **flurry** a sudden short period of activity – 26 **to denounce** to criticize – 30 **to pipe up** to suddenly start to speak – 30 **portly** *hum* fat

seeing her the last time I was in Pakistan; it was hard to forget her as she was the only Pakistani girl I had met with green eyes. She was only twelve back then but now she was eighteen.

The night before the wedding we slept in our uncle's house. There were two rope beds in the room, Sohail lay in one and I in the other. Neither of us could sleep. I don't remember much of what I said to my brother that night but I do remember the sense of feeling deeply connected to him. It was his last night as a single man, tomorrow his life would be changed for ever. We both knew Sohail's relationship with the rest of the family would never be the same. If our family had been one where brothers spoke openly and honestly about their feelings, I might have enquired whether he was excited or scared about getting married, I might have told him I was pleased that I was there to see his marriage. As it was I asked him if he was all right and he told me he was.

On his wedding day my brother was clean-shaven and dressed in a charcoal suit with a rose in his lapel. Nazia wore a blood-red wedding dress and was almost invisible under a mountain of gold jewellery. I was the official photographer and was busy snapping the bride and groom from every angle. The ceremony was in the main room of the Intercontinental Hotel in Lahore, Sohail and Nazia were seated at the front, facing scores of relatives. My father and mother were standing, watching the proceedings. My father had a grave expression on his face, he looked stressed. My mother wore gold earrings, a necklace, bangles and lipstick, and was smiling. I looked across at the relatives who were all chatting and laughing and listening to the wedding songs being played on the public address system. I thought these are my relatives, I am part of them and they are part of me. Some even looked like me. I could lie and say I was different, that I had nothing in common with these people

21 **bride and groom** woman and man who have just got married

except the colour of our skin, and yet the truth was there in the shape of our noses and the fleshiness of our earlobes. In that instant I felt a sense of connection, a sense of being part of something bigger than my direct family that I had not felt before.

* * *

Uzma and I returned to England shortly after the wedding but the rest of the family remained for another week. When they returned, Sohail and Nazia moved into my parents' home. By then, I had graduated from university but was still living in Manchester. I had assumed that since my brother had relented and agreed to an arranged marriage my parents would be pleased with him. When I rang home however, Uzma would report about the tensions back in Luton and how my parents were barely on speaking terms with Sohail. I did not understand what the cause of the trouble was, Sohail had not disgraced the family, his wife was from the same village as my mother. Despite that, my father was not happy. His daughter had let him down and somehow so had his eldest son. When my brother dressed in tracksuit bottoms and went unshaven and dishevelled, my father believed he was insulting his good name. My father's life had been driven by self-improvement and he had assumed that his children would continue that journey. His anger towards Sohail was born of the frustration that his eldest son was not only failing to make progress but also actively undermining all his hard work. 'The worst mistake I ever made was to come to Britain,' my father would claim. 'I came to this country thinking I was doing the right thing. I did not know I would end up losing my own children. Too much freedom in this society. The parents do their best for their children but at the end the children turn round and say, "Who are you?" '

11 **to relent** to finally give in – 20 **dishevelled** very untidy (esp. the hair) – 25 **to undermine** to weaken or destroy gradually

Sohail was planning on leaving my parents' home and buying his own house but the death of my father thrust him unexpectedly into the unwanted position as head of our family. My mother, who with my father had attacked and criticised him, was now reliant on him. I could only be thankful that it was him and not me.

Three months after my father's death I was back in Manchester and the responsibility of maintaining the household fell entirely on my brother's shoulders. He was working in a factory but he knew he needed to find a way to make more money. While I had always protested that money meant little to me, my brother did not have a choice. Through fearlessness and hard work he established his own property business and he used the money to take the family out of Marsh Farm. He bought two houses on a nice street in a smart part of Luton; he lived in one with his wife, and my mother and sister lived in the other.

He made sure that I was aware of his contribution. 'The only reason you can do what you do is because I do what I do,' he would tell me. 'You don't have to worry about Mum and see that the bills are paid. I'm the one who does that, you're the one travelling the world to see Bruce Springsteen.' Like my father Sohail saw success only in financial terms. 'The money you're making is peanuts, how are you going to plan for your future on that? You know that Mum complains you don't ever talk to her – she says you come home, eat her food and then as soon as your Sikh friend calls you, you're out of the door until God knows when. Is that a way to treat your own mother?'

'But what am I meant to say to her?' I would protest.

'She's our mother, and it's my job to tell you what she says to me. She thinks you're too proud to talk to her. That's what she

5 **reliant** [rɪˈlaɪənt] depending – 27 **Sikh** follower of Sikhism, a religion founded in the fifteenth century

says. She says that you have forgotten how to talk to your own family. You don't have anything left to say to us.'

I listened and said nothing.

* * *

It was the first week of 2004 and I was in Luton spending New Year with my family. I had been living in London for some time by now. I was stretched out on the sofa watching a Pakistani drama serial with my mother who was sitting in an armchair. 'Do you want a mug of tea, son?' she asked me.

I nodded. As she rose from her seat my mother suddenly fell back into the chair. 'What happened?' I asked.

'I don't know, I just felt a stab of pain. It's gone now,' she replied.

Once she had returned from the kitchen my mother began to complain of pins and needles in her feet. She complained that she was feeling feverish, and when she tried to stand up her body failed to hold her weight. It was Sunday evening. Uzma suggested taking her upstairs to her bedroom. We both helped her upstairs.

I rang my brother to tell him what was going on. Sohail didn't think it was anything serious and said to keep an eye on her. He would take her to see the doctor in the morning. Meanwhile, my mother was now saying she had lost some feeling on one side of her body. This seemed worrying so I went on the internet and began searching for what the problem might be; I had a suspicion it was a stroke, and once I began reading about the telltale signs I became convinced of it. I rang the night doctor who arrived in the early hours of the morning, took her temperature and her pulse and said that she was suffering from complications relating to high blood pressure. I didn't

25 **stroke** when a blood tube in the brain suddenly bursts or is blocked – 26 **telltale** showing that sth exists

believe him and told him I was concerned she might have had a stroke. He told me I was mistaken. Without expert knowledge I was unable to argue on the specifics and reluctantly allowed him to leave.

The next morning I awoke and found my mother weeping with pain; I rang my brother who drove us to the emergency ward at Luton and Dunstable Hospital. An Indian doctor examined her and confirmed she had suffered a stroke. He took us into another room and told Sohail and me that it was too early to know how serious the stroke had been. This would require a CAT scan, which was not possible until the following day. In the meantime there was no way of knowing her chances of survival. I asked the doctor what the worst case scenario was.

'It's possible that bleeding is occurring in the brain,' he told me, 'so it is possible she might not survive the day. In the case of a brain haemorrhage there is really very little we can do.'

The doctor departed and Sohail and I were left trying to absorb what he had told us. We both returned to our mother who was lying on a hospital bed in the emergency ward with pale-green curtains dividing us from the other patients. 'The doctor has said they're going to do some more tests to find out what's going on,' my brother said quietly, 'and until then they can't tell us what's happening.'

I didn't say anything. I just kept looking hard into my mother's face, studying the lined forehead and worried eyes, and wondering whether she would be alive by the end of the day.

The CAT scan revealed that there was not a clot on the brain but the impact of the stroke had left my mother unable to move one side of her body. She could not walk or eat solid food, and when she spoke she slurred her words distressingly. The hospital kept her in the ward for two weeks and during

11 **CAT scan** x-ray computed tomography – 17 **haemorrhage** [ˈhemərɪdʒ] flow of blood, esp. a long and unexpected one – 29 **clot** half-solid lump of blood *(Blutgerinsel)* – 32 **to slur** to pronounce unclearly – 32 **distressing** upsetting

that time there was hardly a minute that she was not with one of her family. I took leave from work and shared the time at her side with Uzma and my brother. The ward she was in was for the elderly; the woman in the bed opposite was in her nineties and spent the two weeks unconscious, another woman was suffering from pneumonia and kept pleading with the nurses to call her daughter to ask her to visit. My mother was the only woman in the ward whose children spent all day with her.

When I had called Navela to tell her that our mother was ill she had driven to the hospital and brought her children. By now, she had four of them. I hadn't asked Sohail or my mother whether I should call Navela, it just seemed the right thing to do. When she turned up unannounced with her children in tow, my mother burst into tears. Uzma and I left them together, both crying uncontrollably as Navela's children looked on in bafflement. Navela sat with our mother for two hours talking about the children and Shaukat. She said that she was happy and she missed her, and that she often thought of calling but each time she backed off, worried at the reception she would receive. When it was time to leave, Navela gave our mother a hug and promised she would be back. She did not return.

* * *

Gradually over the two weeks my mother was in hospital, she was able to start walking very slowly as long as she had someone to hold on to. Her walk was unsteady and when we watched her it was as if she might falter and fall at any stage. But she was making improvements and, with the threat of further strokes receding, the hospital told us she could go back home.

When she returned home initially my mother was unable to walk; the prospect that she would need full-time care was

6 **pneumonia** [njuːˈməʊnɪɑ] serious disease of the lungs *(Lungenentzündung)* – 16 **bafflement** confusion – 25 **to falter** to walk unsteadily – 27 **to recede** to move away into the distance

looming. Feeling that she might now be a burden, my mother became very depressed. She was a woman who prided herself on not being reliant on others; if anything, the rest of us still relied on her.

But now my mother needed help with everything: Uzma had to feed her with a small spoon; if she wanted to walk anywhere someone had to be there for her to hold on to; a lady from the council had to come each morning to help her dress and wash herself. For my mother this was an unbearable loss of pride; to have a stranger, and a white woman at that, helping her into a bath was an indignity too far. 'Would it not have been better if I had joined your father when he left rather than have to become a burden on you?' she would say. 'All you children are busy with your own lives. I spent my life looking after you and now that I am in this state who is going to have time to take care of me?'

It was not going to be me. Having taken two weeks off work I returned back to London, leaving Sohail, Nazia and Uzma to care for our mother. Since everyone worked there was no one to keep her company during the day. Having read about aftercare for stroke victims I made enquiries about community groups for elderly Asians. What most depressed my mother was feeling alone during the day; if there was somewhere she could go where she could spend time with other older Pakistani women it might, I hoped, improve her mood and perhaps her health. When we suggested this to my mother she became even more miserable. 'So this is what I have been reduced to then, is it?' she said. 'A problem for the rest of you. Someone to throw out of the house like a dog?'

'I'm trying to find a place where you can go to meet other people like you,' I would reply. 'We're not trying to throw you out, it might be nice to go somewhere different, that's all.'

'That's the problem, son. Your daddy has gone somewhere and you know my only wish is that he could have taken me

1 **to loom** to appear as sth dangerous that is likely to happen

with him. Then I would not have to endure this living hell of being a burden to my own children.'

We did not take my mother to a community day centre, not because of her reluctance but because no such place existed. Since Asians are known for their extended families and how they respect their elders, there were no groups in Luton of the type I was seeking for my mother. It was assumed there wouldn't be a demand.

And so my mother spent the days alone watching Pakistani soaps on satellite television until the others returned from work in the evenings. 'It's easy for you, isn't it, coming home and saying the right words and then leaving,' Sohail would say to me when I came back to Luton. 'It's me who has to be here all the time. What would happen if I suddenly said I didn't want to do it any more? What would happen if I said now it's your turn to look after Mum. Why don't you invite her to spend a week at your place in London? Give the rest of us a break? You don't think like that, do you, because you're selfish. You just say what you need to to get everyone off your back and then off you go back to London to live your life.'

It was hard listening to Sohail because he was telling the truth: the rest of my family had paid the price for my freedom. I had the luxury of being the younger son.

My mother's health improved and the scare about long-term care lifted; gradually she began to regain the ability to walk and talk. However, one of the most painful consequences of the stroke was that she never regained her sense of taste. My mother, the woman responsible for the most amazing food I had ever eaten, could not taste her own cooking.

I returned to life in London but I knew what was in store for me each time I came home. The usual lectures about responsibility from my brother. As a consequence, my visits to Luton became less frequent and my relationship with Sohail practically non-existent. Sohail and I seemed to have nothing

4 **reluctance** [rɪ'lʌktəns] unwillingness

to say to each other; he did not respect what I had achieved in my life and he felt that everything that had been achieved was due to his efforts.

Although I was not speaking to my brother I continued talking to Uzma. My younger sister was working for a brewery company and living with my mother. That had not been the plan; she too had wanted to go to university after college and had been arguing with my father about being allowed to go. Many Asian girls whose parents did allow them to continue their studies did so on the condition that they studied nearby and so could remain at home. But Uzma did not want to study in Luton and had been fighting to be allowed to leave home like both her brothers. She had been having one such argument on the day that my father suffered his heart attack. It was now inconceivable that Uzma would be able to leave home. At the time she was working in the same textile factory that Navela had worked in fifteen years earlier; it was soul-crushing work for someone as intelligent as my sister, but with our father gone financial demands meant she was unable to leave.

Music and fashion were her only escape from the tedium of the real world. Uzma loved Bruce Springsteen almost as much as I did. I had indoctrinated her when I was sixteen and she was twelve, and on each tour I would make sure to take her to a Springsteen concert. Her other great passion was clothes. Uzma would rifle through vintage clothes shops for interesting clothes that she would wear in imaginative ways. While other Asian girls would parade through the Arndale Centre in their identikit uniforms of shalwaar kameez or hijabs, Uzma would be in a fake-fur coat, knee-length boots and nose ring. She would wear green eyeliner and maroon lipstick, she was obsessed with maintaining her inch-long fingernails. During

5 **brewery** [ˈbrʊərɪ] place were beer is made – 20 **tedium** boredom – 22 **to indoctrinate** to train someone to accept a set of ideas without questioning them – 28 **identikit** very similar in appearance – 28 **hijab** head covering traditionally worn by muslim women

the winter she wore a bright-pink coat and black velvet gloves. It was her way to demonstrate that she too had dreams that stretched beyond Luton. It must have been hard for Uzma when I called to tell her about my holidays and concerts and parties and friends; it was a world that she ached for herself but which she had been denied. Eventually Uzma did manage to leave the textile factory. She became an accounts clerk; new work friends would ask her out for evening meals and she was able to accept. Sohail appeared indifferent to Uzma's aspirations; she remained an embarrassment because she was unmarried and wore clothes that hinted at a personality.

I had always been close to Uzma; my relationship with my brother was much less secure. The scare of our mother's stroke had made me think about Sohail and me, and how sad it was that even in such a small family tension and jealousies kept us apart. When I was a young boy I would hear my parents' friends advise them not to educate their children because once they had an education they would no longer have anything to say. That, I knew, was how my brother and mother felt about me. It was particularly ironic that I was working in a career where the ability to communicate effectively was critical and yet I was failing completely to communicate with my own family; I was writing articles about the impact of my father's life on my identity as a British Muslim and my own mother was hardly speaking to me. To the outside world I might have been a success but as a son and a brother I was an abject failure: selfish, uncommunicative and a disappointment.

In the autumn of 2004 I was contacted by a BBC documentary director who wanted me to present a television programme about my hometown. The director, who was called Riete, wanted to include my family in the programme but when I

7 **accounts clerk** [klaːk] person responsible for the bookkeeping of a company – 26 **abject** [ˈæbdʒekt] pitiful and showing no pride

discussed this with Sohail he was very resistant. My mother was in Pakistan at the time, we had sent her to Lahore for the winter to escape the cold. Riete was adamant that the programme needed the participation of my brother and sister but Sohail wouldn't hear of it. 'Why do you want to make a programme about the family?' he asked me. 'Who is going to be interested?'

I told him that the BBC was interested.

'Well, if you want to be making this kind of thing that's fine for you, but I am a very private man. I don't like other people knowing my business.'

Although he kept insisting there was no possibility he would be involved with the documentary, Sohail did agree to meet Riete to discuss the programme. She drove from London and visited our home where she had dinner with my brother and the rest of the family. Being incredibly persuasive and charming, Riete managed to change Sohail's mind and he agreed he would take part in the programme.

Luton Actually was broadcast in the spring of 2005; amongst other things it transformed my relationship with my family. The day after it was broadcast Sohail was in a grocery store in Bury Park when a man approached him to ask if he was the person he had seen on television the previous evening. My brother smiled and confirmed that he was. Later that afternoon his bank manager called, and then his carpenter. When he took the children to Wardown Park he noticed how the parents of other children would be pointing at him and turning to explain to the others who he was. This continued for weeks, strangers approaching my brother to tell him how much they loved the programme and what a decent and honourable older brother he was.

My brother would call me in London to tell me the latest story of who had contacted him following the broadcast of the documentary. Usually the only time my brother contacted me was to admonish me or lecture me, now he would call to ask about what else I had coming up and even to suggest future programmes. It was something of a shock to have my brother sounding enthusiastic about my work. 'You know, at the estate agent's two people came up to me to say they'd seen the programme,' he would say. 'The whole town saw it, I think. Hey, maybe we should set up business together and make documentaries!'

One evening a few months after the documentary aired I was sitting in Sohail's living room. 'You know it's taken me a while,' my brother said, 'but I now see that I have been slagging you off, saying you were lazy and good for nothing and that I was the one who had all the right answers. It's only now, after all this time, that I realise that it was you that had got it sussed and I was the fool. All my life I have been working like a dog and what do I have to show for it? High blood pressure, diabetes, panic attacks. Meanwhile you've been out having fun, enjoying life and seeing the world and there isn't a thing wrong with you!'

I listened as I played with his daughter Romessa. 'But you always said that you didn't like travelling,' I said.

'I said that but I think the truth is that how can you know you don't like something if you have not tried it? I think I was just afraid of doing anything different. And you know what happened the one time I went to America. That was hard, to have your friend die in your arms like that. It put me off travelling or going anywhere, but how do I know that if I go to Italy or Spain or China I won't like it? I have spent almost my whole life in this town and I have just realised that if I don't get my life in order I am going to die in Luton and not have seen or done anything!'

2 **to admonish** to speak with disapproval or tell sb to do sth – 12 **to slag off** to criticize – 15 **to suss** *inf* to understand

In all the years that I had known him I had never heard my brother speak like this. 'I mean, you go to Glastonbury every year. Maybe I should go to Glastonbury and listen to Coldplay and all this music that you like. Maybe I should be listening to Bruce Springsteen. Maybe Bruce could teach me a thing or two!'

The next time I was in my brother's home I noticed that next to his CD player in the living room was a brand-new copy of *Born in the USA*.

What I had always found so infuriating about Sohail was, despite having spent thirty years in Britain, how Pakistani he was; his friends were all Pakistani and he remained resolutely unintegrated. Despite having been educated here his values were thoroughly traditional. My brother did not have any crisis of identity, he was not torn between two cultures. He was a Pakistani: that was why he had bought two houses next to each other so that he could live next door to our mother; it was why he liked to visit Pakistan once a year and catch up with the relatives. In the past I had been guilty of judging my brother's lifestyle as unadventurous when in fact the truth was that the only reason I could be the archetypal younger son because he was the archetypal older brother: I owed him my life. When I was young I felt guilty about feeling resentful of my father since I knew the struggles he had endured. These days I appreciate how much I owe not only to my father but to the rest of my family. Navela, Sohail, Uzma and I have all followed the lives determined by gender and our place in the family, each of us living our own separate lives, but drawn together by the ties that bind.

21 **archetypal** [ɑːkɪˈtaɪpl] being the typical example of sth

Blood Brothers

Now we went walking in the rain talking about the pain from the world we hid.
Now there ain't nobody nowhere no how gonna ever understand me the way you did.

'Bobby Jean', Bruce Springsteen

I did not know it then, in that first week at sixth-form college during the autumn of 1987, that my life would be changed for ever by the boy sitting on his own in the upper common room with his eyes closed and his head rocking to the music he was hearing on headphones stretched over his maroon turban. He wore a faded denim jacket with its collar up and his clenched fists were beating out a silent rhythm on an invisible drum kit. He had the hairiest face of any sixteen-year-old I had ever seen.

The first time I saw him it was lunchtime. The college radio station was blasting out 'Pump Up the Volume' and I was in the common room with Kate, whom I had met whilst working during the summer at a sandwich-making factory. The boy was tugging at his headphones, trying to free them from the bandages of his turban, when he spotted my friend. 'Hey, Kate, how's it going?' he said before offering me his hand and saying simply, 'Hey, mate, how's it going? I'm Amolak – my mates call me Roops.'

My new college was predominantly Asian, but before then I had virtually no Asian friends. I saw the sons of my father's friends occasionally but Lea Manor High School was almost entirely white and when I was around Asians I tended to feel

20 **to tug** to pull

a bit of a fraud. I had always felt grateful I was not Sikh; being Asian was hard enough without a religion that insisted believers wear enormous bandages on their head and forsake cutting facial hair. Within seconds of meeting Amolak it was obvious that while he might have looked like Chewbacca in jeans, he had the confident air of someone completely oblivious to how ridiculous he looked.

'Hey, I'm Sarfraz. So what you listening to then?' I asked him, noticing the dog tag around his neck and the metal stars and stripes badge on his jacket.

Amolak stopped fiddling with his headphones. 'What am I listening to?' he said slowly, as if it was the most inane enquiry ever made. 'I'm listening to the truth, my friend. I am listening to wisdom. I am listening to philosophy. I am listening to The Man, The Boss.'

By the time I was sixteen I considered myself to be reasonably knowledgeable about pop music; about Bruce Springsteen I knew this much: he had sung 'Born in the USA' and Asian boys from Luton had no business listening to his music. These two pieces of information provided me with all the ammunition I needed. 'What the hell are you doing listening to Bruce Springsteen for?' I asked. 'Isn't he just a millionaire who goes around dressed in lumberjack shirts pretending to care about the working class?'

'Don't start arguing with Roops,' said Kate, laughing. 'You're not going to win.'

As someone who loved arguments so much that I looked forward to when Jehovah's Witnesses came knocking, no further encouragement was needed. 'But seriously though,' I continued, 'doesn't Bruce Springsteen make, like, *rock* music?'

Amolak bristled.

1 **fraud** [frɔːd] someone who is not what he claims to be – 3 **to forsake** [fɔː'seik] to give up completely – 5 **Chewbacca** very hairy Wookiee character in the Star Wars films – 6 **oblivious** not noticing – 9 **dog tag** identification tag worn by military personnel – 12 **inane** [ɪ'neɪn] extremely stupid – 31 **to bristle** ['brɪsl] to react angrily

'And anyway,' I carried on, enjoying his reaction, 'he's really old, isn't he? In his thirties! What you listening to middle-aged music for?'

Amolak stood up. 'Listen, my friend,' he said deliberately as if he was repeating a speech he had made many times before, 'Bruce Springsteen is a direct connection to everything that is meaningful and significant in life. And anyway what the fuck do you listen to then? That fool Rick Astley? Bros? Let me tell you something right now: Bruce pisses on all them twats.'

I was passionate about music but Amolak was evangelical; he seemed so secure in his conviction that I began to regret having ridiculed Bruce Springsteen whose music I hardly knew.

'Hey, we're just chatting,' I told him. 'To be honest, I don't really know much about Springsteen, I've heard "Born in the USA" and that's about it.'

'You know what you need to do? You need to stop chatting your rubbish and open those big ears of yours,' said Amolak.

'OK, you got a tape I can hear?' I asked him.

'I'll make you one,' said Amolak as he fished out his headphones and began slipping them under his turban once more. The conversation was evidently over.

'How do you know him?' I asked Kate as we left Amolak to his music.

'Oh, we've been friends for ages. We went to Maidenhall together and then we were at Challney as well. He's definitely a bit of a character,' she giggled.

'You're telling me! I thought he was going to punch me when I said that thing about Bruce.'

'Yeah, he's a bit mad when it comes to Springsteen, practically worships the man. It's like religion to him and when he starts he just doesn't shut up!'

8 **bros** short for brother – 9 **twat** [twæt] *inf* unpleasant or foolish person

'It'll be cool if he does give me a tape, be good to see what he's on about.'

A few days later during morning assembly I felt a tap on my back. 'Here you go, geezer, here are the tapes you wanted.'

'Cheers – by the way I saw the video for his new song.'

'What? "Brilliant Disguise"? You dog!'

I had seen the video on breakfast television that morning and it felt good to have the better of my new friend. 'It was all right,' I said airily.

'So what's it like?' asked Amolak. 'Raas man, I can't believe you've heard it before me!'

I smiled and asked him what was on the cassette tapes.

'Only the greatest music ever recorded, my friend,' Amolak replied. 'You woke up a boy and tonight you will go to sleep a man.'

* * *

The evening after college followed the usual sequence: I came home and ate in silence in the living room while my father read the newspaper. When my parents went upstairs to bed I watched television with Uzma before the regular call came to go upstairs and massage my father's feet. It was not until after eleven that I was finally able to fall into bed, slip one of Amolak's cassettes into my Sharp twin-tape machine and slide the headphone jack into the socket. The bedroom was dark as I placed the headphones on my ears and reached for the play button.

The first thing that struck me was his voice; I had been expecting music and singing but Bruce Springsteen was not singing, he was just talking with an acoustic guitar playing in the background. 'When I was growing up,' he was saying, 'me and my dad would go at it all the time, over almost anything.' I was confused. This was not a song, it was a spoken word

4 **geezer** ['gi:zə] *inf* strange often elderly person – 10 **Raas!** *sl* Wow! – 23 **socket** part of electrical equipment into which another part fits

introduction to a song; it was a man recalling his childhood and his relationship with his father. As I listened to Bruce Springsteen I realised this was like nothing I had heard before. I had taken to having a white sheet of paper on the wall next to my bed where I could write the details of any song that I liked while listening to the radio. There were hundreds of songs on that list, but in all my years of listening to music there was nothing to compare to this. The pop singers I knew sang about dancing on the ceiling and total eclipses of the heart, not their troubled relationships with their fathers.

A piercing harmonica announced the start of the first song. 'I come from down in the valley,' it began, 'where, mister, when you're young, they bring you up to do just like your daddy done.' From those opening words I wanted to know what happened next. I lay on my bed in the darkness and listened to the story unfold, it was a motion picture told in words and music. As each song unfurled I kept asking myself how I had lived for sixteen years without this music, without even the knowledge that it existed. Listening to the cassette made me realise that everything that I had fed my ears before then was nothing more than the plastic posing of irrelevant fools. Having stumbled in the dark for so long, on that September night I was blinded by the light. Everything significant that I did or achieved in my life in the years that followed had its roots in the emotions I experienced that evening. That night Bruce Springsteen changed my life.

The following afternoon after college I was walking towards the bus stop on my way home when I spotted Amolak.

'Hey, Amolak, I listened to the tapes you gave me.'

Even though all his other friends called him Roops I insisted on calling my new friend by his actual name; I found nicknames irritating.

9 **eclipse (of the sun)** disappearance of the sun's light when the moon passes between it and the Earth – 17 **to unfurl** to unroll and open – 21 **to pose** *here* pretend to be more than one really is

'Yeah? So what do you think?'

'I don't know what to say. It's like nothing I have ever heard before.'

'See, I told you! The Boss rules!'

We were walking towards the main road, just two of hundreds of students finished for the day but I didn't want to go home. There was so much more to know. 'So listen, is there any chance you could get me some more stuff?' When I asked him my voice was low and conspiratorial and layered in shame; I did not like to admit that I had been so completely wrong when I had been cheerfully knocking Springsteen earlier in the week, and I felt like an addict trying to score some stuff from a dealer.

'Yeah, I can record some copies of the albums for you, no worries. But you got to read the lyrics. It's the words that make him The Boss.'

During the next few weeks I had a crash course in Bruce Springsteen. Amolak taped some of his albums for me and I borrowed others from the college library. In between classes I would sit and read the photocopied lyrics from the album before I spoke to Amolak. For my friend, so long a lone disciple, I was a project, someone with whom he could share his passion. We spent our lunchtimes discussing Springsteen.

'So what did you think of that tape I made you the other night? *Darkness on the Edge of Town.*'

'Only heard it about five or six times so still trying to get it into my head. That first song I don't really get.'

'What? "Badlands"? You're joking, right? That's one of his classics!'

'I don't know. It's hard to make out the words and I don't have the lyrics for it yet but I tell you what, I love "The Promised Land", that's fucking amazing. That bit where he sings, "I've done my best to live the right way…" '

9 **layered** covered – 22 **disciple** [dɪ'saɪpl] follower of a great teacher

'"I get up every morning,"' continued Amolak, '"and go to work each day, but your eyes go blind and your blood runs cold..."'

Neither of us were singing the words but there was a rhythmic punch to our delivery, each word sliding into the other. Around us Asian girls glided past, some in traditional shalwaar kameez but most in western dress, their eyes meeting ours briefly before continuing their conversation. Amolak nodded at them in acknowledgement without missing the beat of the verse. By now we were both walking faster, oblivious to the students and the posters on the walls advertising the coming student elections, immersed in the lyrics of the song: 'take a knife and cut this pain from my heart...' And now 'The dogs on Main Street howl 'cause they understand, If I could take one moment into my hands, Mister I ain't a boy, no I'm a man, And I believe in a promised land.'

Every Sunday evening my father would drive me to Amolak's house in Bury Park. When Amolak spoke to my parents he would speak to them in Punjabi, which immediately endeared him to them as it meant he was respectful enough of his elders not to speak to them in English.

Amolak lived in a large terraced house near my very first school. His mother, a large woman with a friendly face and bad back, would come in to say hello and bring us tea and biscuits. I always made sure to say hello to his father who would be sleeping on the sofa in the adjoining room. Amolak's father was a huge man with a white turban and a flowing white beard that he kept in a hairnet. I had always assumed that Sikh men had very long hair under their turbans but one afternoon I found this to be not always the case. I came to say hello to his father only to find him sprawled on the sofa with his turban on the

12 **to immerse** to enter deeply into an activity – 19 **Punjabi** language spoken by the inhabitants of the historical Punjab region (north western India and Pakistan) – 31 **sprawled** arms and legs spread out carelessly

coffee table and his head revealed to be almost entirely bald save for a few strands knotted with a small handkerchief.

Amolak and I would spend the evening in the living room where there was an old record player. On the wall hung a portrait of Guru Nanak. In one corner of the room was a display cabinet in which there was a brass wheelbarrow, a gondola made of gold-coloured plastic and a selection of plates and glasses. Like the special plates and glasses in my home they were never used. For three or four hours we would talk – ostensibly about Bruce Springsteen but actually about our lives. I had had friends before but there was no one with whom I could speak with such honesty as I could with Amolak; with white friends I always had to explain things – why I didn't drink, why I didn't have girlfriends, why I wasn't allowed out at night – but with Amolak no explanations were necessary. He understood. We were sixteen-year-old boys so we did not speak about our feelings; we talked about song lyrics instead.

'The thing about Bruce,' Amolak said, 'is that it's like he knows everything you've ever felt, everything you've ever wanted and he can describe it better than you. That's what I love about him so much; there isn't a situation you will ever go through that Bruce will not have a song for. I'm serious, you hate school: "No Surrender"; you hate where you live: "Thunder Road"; you hate your dad: "Independence Day"; you hate your girlfriend: "Brilliant Disguise"; you hate your life: "Badlands". He's there for you no matter what you're going through.'

'What I don't understand,' I said, peeling the skin off my mug of tea, 'is how come no one else at college likes Springsteen. I mean, if you listen to the words you would think everyone would be really into it but let's be honest, everyone thinks we're nutters.'

1 **bald** [bɔːld] without hair – 5 **Guru Nanak** the founder of Sikhism and the first of the ten Gurus of the Sikhs – 6 **brass wheelbarrow** *Schubkarre aus Messing* – 10 **ostensibly** seemingly one thing, when it really is sth else – 31 **nutter** mad or strange person

'Hey, you thought I was a nutter, remember!' retorted my friend. 'You know the story. I was watching *Top of the Pops* and saw the video for "Dancing in the Dark". Must have been the summer of 1984, I reckon. I was doing my English homework in front of the telly and this song comes on. I remember looking up and thinking, this is good, I wonder who this guy is. The next day I bought *Born in the USA* and you know the rest. My mates thought I was a fucking clown! "Hey, Roops, you think you were 'Born in the USA'? Got some news for you, mate. You were born in Dunstable Hospital, right here in Luton!" I didn't listen to their chat and do you know why? It was because I felt sorry for them. I forgave them because they knew not what the hell they were saying. Bit of *Jesus of Nazareth* for you there. See, the thing is, mate, I had all this extra wisdom, this special knowledge and those muppets were still listening to bloody bhangra! And I tried to educate them. I'd bring in *Nebraska* and *The River,* say to them, "Listen up, you fools, you might learn something," but they didn't want to know. So in the end I thought fuck you all. You try, but if they don't want to know something that might change their lives, what can you do, hey?'

When I listened to Amolak preaching the gospel of Bruce while Springsteen played on the record player, it was hard not to believe that the two of us were more enlightened than the rest of our college. *Thunder Road* and *Born to Run* gave me new dreams to aspire to; a world that could yet be mine.

Amolak's mother would offer us another mug of tea or urge me to eat the egg biscuits that remained on the table. 'So he's brainwashed you too?' she would joke. 'I can't talk to my son for two minutes without him talking about this Bruce.' His parents, like mine, did not appreciate that this was about more than music. 'To my mum, I might as well be listening to Engelbert Humperdinck,' claimed Amolak. 'She doesn't understand the whole Bruce thing at all. Dad just thinks all white singers are

15 **muppets** group of TV puppet characters created by Jim Henson – 31 **Engelbert Humperdinck** popular singer of love songs who adopted the name of the famous German composer

taking drugs. When I tell him I'm listening to Bruce he just says "druggie". I used to try and argue with him and say no, Bruce is very anti-drugs and he is a really great role model but have you seen my dad? Six foot five and built like a brick shithouse. No point arguing.'

I had thought that by telling my father how successful Bruce Springsteen was it would validate my enthusiasm for him but he had responded by saying that if I enjoyed music so much why didn't I try to make money out of it myself rather than making someone else richer. 'You can't really expect them to understand, can you?' I said. 'I mean, if people our age think we're weird, what's the chance that our parents are gonna get it?'

'The thing about our parents' generation,' Amolak responded, 'is that they didn't have the time to have hobbies. Take my old man. He came over from India, got treated like a fucking leper and ended up working on a building site. Before he knew it he was working like a donkey carrying bricks up a ladder and breaking his back so that the rest of us had dahl with our chapattis. I mean, it's not like he had time to start stamp collecting or bird watching, is it? So they look at you and me and can't understand the idea of doing something just because we fucking like it.'

In my new friend I had found someone else who loved America and hated Luton with the same passion as I did. On his bedroom wall Amolak had hung a confederacy flag and he would come to college wearing a stars and stripes bandanna around his neck. Were it not for his turban, he would most likely have strutted around Bury Park in a ten-gallon stetson. Meanwhile I was reading *On the Road* and Studs Terkel. The best part about my friendship with Amolak was the knowledge that I had made a friend for life. We could not choose our

7 **to validate** to make sth officially acceptable – 17 **leper** ['lepə] person who suffers from the infectious disease leprosy – 27 **bandanna** large handkerchief – 29 **stetson** tall hat, worn esp. in the American West by cowboys

families, we might not even be able to choose our spouses but at least we had the freedom to choose our friends.

When I first became introduced to Bruce Springsteen, I sleep-walked through my classes in economics and mathematics and spent my evenings in my bedroom wearing my headphones whilst listening to Bruce albums as I mouthed the words from the photocopied lyric sheets. When the student council gave me my own lunchtime show on the college radio station I used it as an opportunity to evangelise for Bruce; for one show I played the entire third side of the live box set. When Amolak and I were not listening to Springsteen, we were trying to emulate his look. I restricted myself to wearing black waistcoats similar to the one he had worn on the video for 'Tougher than the Rest' and a large buckled belt like on the cover of *Tunnel of Love*. Amolak, as well as the waistcoat and belt, had cultivated long sideburns, and wore a variety of chains and a silver dog tag engraved with 'Born to Run' and a pair of black cowboy boots. (When, during the early nineties, Springsteen began favouring a goatee with ponytail Amolak followed suit; a decision he claimed later explained his complete absence of success with women during this time.)

In many ways Amolak was different from me. I was Muslim and he was a Sikh. He was brash and cocky and never happier than when boasting about how drunk he got the night before, while I never drank. He watched *Dallas* and I loved *Cheers;* he thought that listening to anyone other than The Boss was treachery whereas thanks to Springsteen, I had discovered Bob Dylan and John Mellencamp. Amolak walked around our college like he was a king, wise-cracking with the boys and flirting with the girls, while I was tongue-tied and shy.

1 **spouse** husband or wife – 12 **to emulate** to try to copy sth – 12 **waistcoat** *Weste* – 16 **sideburns** *Koteletten* – 19 **goatee** little pointed beard on the bottom of the chin, like the hair on a male goat´s chin – 23 **brash** too confident – 23 **cocky** self-confident in an unpleasant way – 29 **to wise-crack** to try and make clever jokes

I envied how much at ease he seemed around girls but I also knew that it was only around me that he was truly himself; the rest was a performance. When it was just the two of us he would confide how frustrated he was by his turban. 'Fact is there's no way I'm getting any pussy with this on my head,' he would tell me. He would point out how blistered the tops of his ears were from being bandaged. 'Girls ain't going to see past this, are they?' he would complain. What girl is gonna want to kiss me with me looking like this? Plus I get mash-up headaches cos of the weight on me head.'

It had not occurred to me that wearing a turban would cause headaches but it made sense now that he mentioned it.

'So why don't you get your hair cut?' I asked him.

'You've seen my dad, right? He would kick the living shit out of me. And then throw me out on the street. He's a bloody priest at the temple, no fucking way I can do it while I'm living at home.'

It was only when he referred to his appearance that Amolak's supernatural confidence disappeared; the turban, beard and moustache were a constant reminder of the chasm between how he saw himself and how others saw him. It also made his love of Bruce Springsteen's music seem hollow; Springsteen's songs were about being true to yourself and being the best you could be and yet it was only fear that was forcing my friend to retain his turban.

When I saw Amolak clean-shaven and without his turban, at first I did not even recognise him. He had not discussed it with me, and he hadn't warned me. I walked towards him to shake his hand but he ignored it and gave me a bear hug instead, smiling broadly like a lifer handed a surprise parole. 'I fucking did it, mate,' he said.

'You look really cool,' I replied honestly. 'I thought you said you couldn't do it because of your dad? What happened?'

6 **blistered** sore from rubbing – 20 **chasm** a very deep crack in the surface of sth, a large difference between people – 30 **lifer** person who has been sent to prison for life – 30 **parole** the letting out of a person from prison before the official period has ended

'Truth is I've been thinking about it for a few months but I didn't want to say anything to you in case I bottled it.'

'But you kept saying that you couldn't let your dad down.'

'I know, mate, I know, but something just changed, you know, something just clicked inside. I thought, what is the fucking point of banging on about Bruce if I can't live what he's singing about? You get me? It's like his whole message is about being true to yourself and being the best you can be and…' His voice trailed off.

'How's your dad taking it?'

'Not good,' he replied. 'Didn't talk to me when I got back from the barber, Mum didn't make me dinner… they probably think I'm going to be bringing a white girl home next.'

'You're not that lucky,' I joked.

'Yeah, they'll get used to it. It's only hair for fuck's sake.'

But it wasn't only about hair, it was about freedom and it was about a question we constantly asked ourselves when we were teenagers: whether it was possible to say you were a Springsteen fan if you couldn't live your life by the values of his music.

In the spring of 1988 rumours began emerging that Bruce Springsteen might tour later that summer. The speculation, contained in articles that I cut out from *NME, Sounds* and *Melody Maker,* was both exhilarating and terrifying. To see Springsteen in concert would be unimaginably thrilling but the prospect of persuading my father to allow me to attend was deeply depressing. For Amolak, who had been a fan since the age of fourteen, it was unthinkable that he would not be going to see him in concert. 'I don't give a fuck what Dad says, I'm going,' he told me bluntly.

'Yeah, but what if your dad says you can't go?' I asked.

'There is no way, mate. No way.'

2 **to bottle it** *sl* to back out the last minute before you do sth dangerous

I could tell that he was secretly terrified that he would not be allowed to attend. 'I reckon if we both tell our parents that the other one is going they won't mind so much,' I suggested. 'I think my dad would feel better if he knew that I was going with you, he might go for it then.'

This was probably nonsense as I guessed that my father would most likely say that Amolak was leading me down the wrong path, that I needed to ditch him and start remembering what college was really for.

'You think? It's worth a shot, I guess.' He was looking rather forlorn.

'I mean, the papers are saying Wembley Stadium in June, I could ask them if I could go as my birthday present, lay on the guilt trip about how I never get any birthday presents and all that. That could work.'

Whilst we waited for the rumours to harden into facts I began buying bootleg tapes from mail order suppliers I found advertised in the back of music magazines. Each cassette was listed on badly typed catalogues that would arrive in the mail from addresses in Manchester and North Wales and cost around five pounds each. Reading the catalogues was like studying a map of exotic foreign lands, each title promising so much: *Born to Run* outtakes, *The River* home demos, live concerts from 1975 onwards. It seemed extraordinary to me that I could, when I had the money, listen to songs by Bruce that weren't on any album, hear concerts I hadn't attended. The legendary Bottom Line concerts in New York from 1975, the epic Winterland show from 1978, the three nights at Wembley Stadium from 1985 were all concerts I had salivated over and now they were arriving through my letterbox in small packages wrapped up in plain brown paper. Receiving the tapes was about more than just hearing new Bruce music; each time I got a new package in the mail it felt like I was part of a secret community defined not by geography, race or religion, but

8 **to ditch** to get rid of – 11 **forlorn** alone and unhappy – 17 **bootleg** made illegally

by passion. I had no idea who the people sending me those bootleg tapes were but I believed that they, like me, were citizens of an imagined community of like-minded people.

I knew I had to attend the Springsteen concert. It wasn't just about seeing Bruce: I knew that if I was able to go, my life would change for ever. For weeks I plotted how to raise the concert with my parents. I had told my mother about how Amolak was going and how much I wanted to go but her approval was worthless unless I could persuade my father. To increase the chances of my father agreeing I adopted a strategy of trying to please him in other aspects of my life. I began buying cartons of weight-gain powder and drinking them with warm milk each night in an effort to bulk up. Three times a week I went weight training at a local gym. I knew that would please my father who continued to complain at how painfully skinny I was. When I was not lifting weights I would volunteer to wash and vacuum the car, do the dishes, massage his feet.

What has happened to your son?' my father said to my mother one day when I had been particularly ingratiating. 'He must want something.'

'It's that Bruce,' my mother explained.

'He's coming to play a concert in London,' I added, 'at Wembley Stadium in June. He doesn't play very often. Amolak's parents say he can go...'

'Who goes to these concerts?' my father asked.

'Just people who like Bruce,' I explained, 'intelligent people... He writes about politics so lots of people who are there will be interested in that.'

'Politics? What does he write about politics?' asked my father, suddenly more interested.

'Well, he's written songs about being unemployed and the economic recession and people who work in factories being laid off work... His songs aren't about normal boring subjects, it's about the real world, it's like watching *Panorama*.'

6 **to plot** to make a secret plan – 13 **to bulk up** to make bigger or heavier – 19 **ingratiating** [ɪn'greɪʃieɪtɪŋ] trying too hard to please sb

I do not know if my father was persuaded by my arguments or whether he simply took pity on me, but he agreed that I could go to the concert. He even offered to buy me a ticket.

The *Tunnel of Love* tour started in the United States at the end of February 1988. I kept up to date with the latest news by calling an information line organised by a British Springsteen fan club called Badlands. Anyone who rang the number could find out the latest Springsteen news, including what songs he had played on each show. I would call the phone line every evening, making a note of set changes. The closer we got to the concert date, the more excited Amolak and I became: Amolak had been a fan for three years but it was going to be the first time he had seen him live. 'Thing is, when the show starts I'm going to be somewhere else in my head,' he told me. 'I'm going to be tapped. We might as well not be standing next to each other, in my head it's just going to be me and the man. No one else. So don't be trying to chat to me.'

My friend never let me forget that he had been a fan longer than I had. I could not turn back time but I still believed I was the bigger fan. I had read every biography I could find about Springsteen, I had bought unreleased live concert tapes and when the tour started I wrote to a venue in Detroit enclosing a twenty-dollar bill and requesting an American tour shirt so that I could wear it around the Arndale Centre months before the tour reached Britain.

It was not yet eight o'clock on a summer Saturday morning in the last week of June. Amolak and I sat opposite each other in the near-empty carriage, plastic bags containing food from our mums on the seats next to us. My mum had prepared chapattis which she had filled with vegetable curry and rolled up and wrapped in silver foil. Along with the chapattis were a couple of vegetable samosas that had been made the previous night.

22 **venue** place where sth is arranged to happen – 32 **samosa** stuffed pastry and popular snack in parts of Asia

'Don't you think it's weird?' I said to Amolak. 'That Bruce is staying in London and that's where we are going.' It wasn't really a question, more a statement filled with a sense of awe.

'I know, I wonder what hotel they are staying at? If we knew, we could call and see if we get through!'

'Yeah, I *bet* Bruce answers his own phone!'

'It would be fucking cool though, wouldn't it, to meet him?'

'I reckon we will, you know,' I replied.

When we arrived at Wembley, the grounds of the stadium were practically deserted. As we tried to find where the entrance point was we walked past burger vans and merchandise stalls. Nothing was open. We seemed to be the first people there. 'You don't think we're too early, do you?' I asked Amolak. 'There isn't anyone else here.'

'Yeah, there is,' he responded.

We had reached the edge of the stadium. In front of us was a steep flight of steps and at the very end of the steps were the turnstiles which allowed entry into the stadium itself. Sitting and standing around the turnstile entrance was a small crowd of around twenty or thirty men. Amolak and I walked along the circumference of the stadium looking up at those who were already there. From their vantage point the men looked down at us. They seemed to be in their twenties and thirties. Some were dressed in shorts. A few were wearing *Born in the USA* T-shirts. Proper adults. Proper fans. What must they have thought when they saw us? Two teenage Asian boys overdressed for the hot sun, carrying plastic bags stuffed with food, stumbling around looking lost and overwhelmed.

When Bruce Springsteen appeared on stage all I could think was: that is really him. There I was and there he was. Wearing a dark suit, holding what looked like a bunch of red roses just like in the poster for the tour. My eyes flashed across the

18 **turnstile** small gate with four arms spinning around on a central post – 21 **circumference** length round the outside of a circle – 22 **vantage point** good position to see sth

hundreds of fans wearing T-shirts with his image on them and settled back almost instantly on the man on the stage. 'Hello, London,' he said. 'Are you ready for a ride?'

My memories of the actual concert are snatches of sound and images. I was near the front of the stage and by the time he came on, I hadn't been to the toilet for most of the day and hadn't eaten for hours. Having been up for twelve hours was taking its toll. Even before the concert started I was thirsty, starving and shattered. Once the gig started I was hardly able to concentrate on the music for the first half-hour or so; it took all my energy to not be swept away by the crowd surges that rippled through the front of the stadium. Each surge swept me off my feet and hurtled me every which way; each time I was thrust further forward my chest felt like it would implode under the pressure of thousands of bodies pressing behind me. To try and create some space I held my arms up and rested the back of my forearms on the back of the person in front of me. Within a few minutes my shirt was drenched in sweat and I was feeling weak from hunger. Somewhere in the crowd was Amolak but I had no clue where he was. Instead, it was just Bruce and me on our own with seventy-two thousand others crashing the party.

I didn't see Amolak during the concert, we had lost each other in the race to reach the floor of the stadium. I took the train back to Luton alone, my T-shirt damp with sweat, my throat ravaged and my stomach crying for food. I woke the next morning with every muscle in my body aching. My back was still sore and my feet felt as if they had run a dozen marathons. My voice was reduced to a hoarse croak from singing so heartily. Everything hurt.

After my first Springsteen concert I should have felt exhilarated and yet I felt desolate. I had not imagined I would feel so low. There seemed little point in speaking to Amolak,

4 **snatch** a small and incomplete piece – 11 **surge** a sudden powerful forward movement – 26 **to ravage** [ˈrævɪdʒ] to damage badly – 32 **exhilarated** [ɪɡˈzɪləreɪtɪd] excited and happy

perhaps he had not come down from the thrill of the concert and I did not want to admit how depressed I was feeling if he wasn't. It was not until the next day that I saw him in college. He was dressed in the same tour shirt that I had bought. We walked silently into the common room and sat opposite each other, saying nothing. It was as if one was waiting for the other to reveal their hand. 'So, what the fuck do you say to that?' I finally said to him.

Amolak shook his head. Seconds passed in silence as we both sat staring into the middle distance. It was a sign of how close I was to my friend that we could be together and not say anything. 'You want the truth?' Amolak said at last. 'I still can't fucking believe I was there.'

I nodded my head sympathetically. It was hard to get my head around the reality that I had been in the presence of the man whom I had obsessed about for the past nine months. 'I'm feeling so shit right now,' I said sadly.

'Me too!' Amolak cried. 'It's like I am totally filled with this really deep sadness or something, and I can't get rid of it.'

I told Amolak that I had started getting sad before the end of the concert, the knowledge that it would soon be over almost ruining my enjoyment. We had spent so long dreaming of this one evening that now it was over there seemed nothing left to look forward to; the real world was encroaching again; exams, parents and everything else that we had relegated to the back of our mind came racing to the front.

'Do you think we'd be happier if we saw him again?' I wondered glumly.

'He's a fucking drug, ain't he,' declared Amolak, 'and you know what the cure is, don't ya?'

'What's that?' I asked him.

'We gotta see him again!'

24 **to encroach** to take over – 25 **to relegate** to put into a lower place – 28 **glum** [glʌm] sad, in low spirits

However, it was another four years before we next saw Springsteen in concert. It was the summer of 1992. Springsteen had split up the E Street Band and released two albums on the same day; I was in my last few months of studying in Manchester. When the tour was announced I was so determined to get the best seats I travelled down from Manchester to London and was outside Wembley Arena by lunchtime on Tuesday afternoon; the box office was not due to open until Thursday morning. I was one of the first in line but by the end of the first night there were hundreds of us waiting, trying to keep warm. Even though I did not actually know anyone there was a wonderful sense of camaraderie. Shared passion for Springsteen transcended other boundaries; there were fans who had, like me, travelled across the country just to wait in line. For someone who was only twenty-one it was a wonderful thing to be surrounded by other fans who could regale me with tales of having seen *The River* tour back in the early eighties. When the box office finally opened I was able to buy front-row tickets for all six concerts; row A smack in front of the centre of the stage.

Amolak had decided he did not fancy spending two days sleeping on concrete for tickets and was instead relying on me to secure him tickets. Since each person was only allowed to buy six tickets, all my allocation went on my seats. So a system was arranged which meant those who didn't want as many seats would still buy their allocated four tickets and sell the extras at face value to those who needed them. These would not be as good as those we bought for ourselves but it would at least mean your friends would be able to get in.

On the first night of the Wembley residency I woke early and ironed my clothes. Being so near the front it was possible that Springsteen would actually see me and I wanted him to notice the Pakistani lad in the front row. I decided that rather than

13 **to transcend** to go above and beyond the limits of – 16 **to regale** [rəˈgeɪl] to entertain with – 27 **face value** official value or cost of sth

dress in regulation T-shirt and jeans I would dress up: black trousers, white shirt, paisley tie and blood-red bandanna. Just before rushing out of the house towards the train station I grabbed my vinyl copy of *Born to Run,* just in case I ran into Springsteen himself. It could happen.

Amolak was attending the concert with his brother and nephew. They had seats up in the gods, so far from the front he took binoculars. We met outside the Wembley Arena. It was late afternoon and the touts were busy trying to buy and sell tickets; there were a few hundred fans milling outside the arena when I met Amolak. 'This is it, dude,' said my friend simply.

'Cool to not have to queue up all day like last time,' I replied. 'I can just walk past everyone and take my seat. Right. At. The. Front.'

'Yeah, all right, don't rub it in for fuck's sake,' said Amolak hurriedly. His brother and nephew were trying to find parking and my friend told me he would catch up with me later.

I wandered over to the side entrance of the arena where some other fans were floating around. Some had carrier bags with CDs and vinyl records. I didn't feel quite so stupid having my copy of *Born to Run* with me.

I had always known I would meet Bruce Springsteen. I didn't know how or when it would happen; I assumed it would be when he was old and largely forgotten, when he could no longer sell out stadia and arenas, when most of his fans had lost the faith. But I met him earlier than I had hoped. The first glimpse I had of him was through the window of a people carrier, a smudge of face and a wave of a hand as the vehicle passed through the gates that led to the artists' entrance. 'That was him!' someone shrieked. Within seconds fans rushed towards the entrance shouting, 'Bruce! Over here, Bruce!'

The people carrier came to a halt, a thick-necked bodyguard emerged, opened the passenger door and out stepped Bruce

2 **paisley tie** classical tie pattern of Indian or Persian origin – 7 **gods** seats high up at the back of a theatre – 9 **tout** *derog* person who offers tickets that are in short supply at a price higher than usual – 11 **dude** [du:d] man – 28 **smudge** *here* unclear image

Springsteen. I could see him through the bars of the gates as he walked slowly towards us. I was at the front of the crowd that was waiting for him, our hands outstretched holding objects for him to sign. The closer he came the faster my heart raced. By the time he was amongst us, a strange calm descended on the fans. Everyone politely waited their turn to give him a book, a poster, an album to sign. With an almost embarrassing shyness I handed him my copy of *Born to Run,* saying, 'Hi, Bruce, any chance you could sign this?'

'Sure, no problem,' he answered but his eyes never met mine; he was too busy scanning the other outstretched hands and trying to ensure everyone got their own personalised scribble. It was over in seconds, the evidence of our meeting a smeared signature in spidery writing scrawled across the cover of my beloved vinyl record.

'You're lying! Tell me you're fucking lying!' Amolak was, understandably, less than thrilled when I told him who I had met.

'Mate, I'm serious, he was out here just half an hour ago,' I told him as I took out *Born to Run* from my carrier bag.

Amolak grabbed it from me and began to examine it as if it was something holy, akin to the Turin Shroud. His brother and nephew were falling about laughing at his bad luck to have missed out on meeting Springsteen but Amolak was failing to see the joke. To add insult to injury his seat was nowhere near as good as mine. After the concert he told me that he could, thanks to his binoculars, see someone wearing a red bandanna waving his right arm in the air.

I had never been as happy in my life as when I stood at the front of the stage waiting for Bruce Springsteen to appear. Unlike Wembley Stadium there was no crush, no waiting for ten hours in the heat, starving. Here, my seat was reserved and there wasn't a better one in the house. The highlight of the

22 **akin to** similar – 22 **Turin Shroud** a linen cloth bearing the image of a man who is believed to be Jesus Christ

concert for me was some way into the show when Springsteen had just finished one song and was about to introduce another. His shirt was drenched in sweat. I was standing by the front of the stage, right by the microphone as Springsteen strode towards the front of the stage, unstrapped his Fender Telecaster guitar and said to me, 'Could you hold this? I just wanna take my shirt off.' I automatically stretched out both hands and found myself grasping the neck of Bruce Springsteen's fabled Telecaster guitar, the one he had played for twenty years, the one that featured on the cover of his live box set. I held on to the Telecaster while those around me looked on in envy and disbelief. Springsteen slipped off his dripping shirt to reveal a T-shirt. He walked back towards me, took the guitar from me and said, 'Thanks.' Why had he chosen me? Did he have a sixth sense in identifying his most devoted fans? Did he see in my eyes how much his music meant to me? He chose me, more probably, because there wasn't anyone else with brown skin in the front row, there wasn't anyone my age and nor was there anyone dressed in a tie and wearing a bandanna.

The following year Bruce Springsteen returned to Britain for a full national tour. I managed to secure seats by sleeping outside Sheffield Arena. I had heard he was going to be staying at the Midland Hotel in Manchester; as I was living in the city it seemed too good an opportunity to miss. Ringing the Midland, I booked myself in for one night under the name 'Bill Horton'; the girl on the reservations desk had obviously never heard 'Cautious Man' or she would know where I had borrowed the name from. Mr Horton was due to arrive late that evening, I told her, and could she reserve the room in that name. He would pay on his credit card on arrival. That afternoon I took the 42 bus from West Didsbury into town, walked into the Midland and told the receptionist I was due to meet Bill Horton. 'Ah yes, Mr Horton isn't due to arrive until a little later.'

'Oh, that's a shame,' I said. 'Is it all right if I wait in the bar for him?'

'Certainly, sir, that's not a problem,' she replied.

I headed towards the bar and sat down. About twenty minutes later Roy Bittan – pianist for the E Street Band – and Jon Landau, Springsteen's manager, walked into the bar together and sat down. I tried to look as if I didn't know who they were whilst at the same time listening in on their conversation. A waiter came and asked if I wanted a drink. I asked for a coffee. Meanwhile Zack Alford, the drummer with Springsteen's band, walked in and sat opposite me. Any moment now, I told myself, Bruce Springsteen himself will come walking in. Any moment now.

While I waited I managed to muster up the courage to introduce myself to Bittan. As I shook his hand I told myself, 'These are the hands that played the introduction to "Backstreets"!' As soon as I left the bar I called Amolak. 'Shit! Why do I keep missing all this?' he said.

Uzma had missed out on seeing the Wembley concerts and had cried each of the six nights I had seen Springsteen. I told her that if she could persuade our father to let her go I would take her to see him. To my surprise, permission was granted and Uzma took the train up to Manchester on the day of the Sheffield concert. I told her about my experience in the Midland and suggested we spend the afternoon outside the hotel before taking the train to Sheffield. We were not the only ones who had this idea, there were around thirty other fans all wanting their albums signed. I had brought my red bandanna and my copy of Dave Marsh's *Glory Days*. We were unsure whether we would meet him or not but excited by the possibility. As I was chatting with Uzma, a white-haired bodyguard walked out and told us that Bruce was about to leave the hotel. He would sign autographs and pose for photographs. All he expected from us was that we line up in an orderly queue. I could see Uzma smiling with nervousness and disbelief.

Suddenly the man himself was standing before us. 'Hi, Bruce,' said Uzma.

'Hello,' Bruce replied.

'Would it be possible to have a photo taken?' she asked.

'Sure, we can do that!' he replied, smiling broadly.

I took the photograph. Then it was my turn. He signed my book and bandanna and posed for another photograph. Just as I was about to let the next fan have their moment in the sun I turned to Springsteen and said, 'Bruce. Three words: "Point Blank", acoustic.'

The following night I was sitting in the Sheffield Arena with Amolak and my sister. It was 16 April 1993 and we were in the front block ten or fifteen rows from the stage. Uzma was having the time of her life. It was her first Springsteen concert and it was so wonderful to see her having so much fun. Springsteen had just finished singing 'Badlands' when he requested an acoustic guitar and told the audience: 'A fella came up to me and asked for this song. I don't know if he's out there tonight, but if he is, this is for you.' He began slowly strumming the acoustic guitar before singing, 'Do you still say your prayers darling, before you go to bed at night? Praying that tomorrow everything will be all right?' He was singing 'Point Blank'. I doubled up, buried my face in my hands and wept. Amolak hugged me. 'Point Blank' was one of my favourite songs. I never imagined I would hear it sung acoustically. The fact that Springsteen had remembered my request and then decided to actually listen to my suggestion was overwhelming. As I continued to cry uncontrollably and as Bruce Springsteen continued to sing 'Point Blank', Amolak said to me: 'You see, buddy, dreams do come true.'

* * *

In the winter of 1998 Bruce Springsteen made an appearance inside the Royal Courts of Justice for a lawsuit he was bringing

23 **to double up** to bend at the waist, usually with pain or laughter

against a company which had released illegal recordings of his early work. At this point I was a journalist working on Channel 4 News and my editors, knowing my Springsteen obsession, kindly agreed to let me be their offical court correspondent. What this involved, incredibly, was having to sit inside the court and spend the day listening to Bruce Springsteen give evidence.

On the second day of the case I found myself sitting on a wooden bench only two feet from Springsteen himself; it was a surreal experience which became even more extraordinary when the judge ordered a twenty-minute recess, meaning the lawyers all retired outside and I was left sitting with Springsteen in a near-empty courtroom. 'So, what you reading?' Bruce asked me.

I showed him my copy of *The Grapes of Wrath.*

'That's a great choice. You'll learn more from that than any newspaper,' he told me.

I told him that I was rereading the book as I wanted to appreciate the *Tom Joad* album more; he smiled and told me about how his parents used to live in California. We talked for about twenty minutes. It was strange and yet it didn't feel strange. I had always believed that if I actually managed to talk to Springsteen it would not be a daunting experience; he wasn't a freak like Michael Jackson, he wasn't as opaque as Dylan. I imagined him as simply a regular guy with an extraordinary talent. That was what I most liked about him; even when I was listening to him in my Luton bedroom I could imagine talking to him and having a normal conversation.

When I rang Amolak he went ballistic. 'You complete bastard! I don't fucking believe this!' he yelled. 'What is fucking going on that you keep meeting him and I keep missing out? Right. I'm coming down to the High Court tomorrow.'

11 **recess** [rɪ'ses] pause – 15 **The Grapes of Wrath** novel by John Steinbeck – 23 **daunting** causing you to lose courage – 24 **opaque** [əʊ'peɪk] not able to be seen through, hard to understand – 29 **to go ballistic** *hum* to go crazy, to freak out

The next day I sat with the other reporters at the front and Amolak sat towards the back in the public gallery. During an interval I strolled over to Springsteen – who was almost a friend by now – and made some small talk about how well I thought the case was going. Meanwhile Amolak was charging towards us. This was his first time meeting Springsteen. Bruce and I were laughing about something when Amolak walked over and offered his hand. 'Bruce, I just want to thank you. I want to thank you for your music and everything it's given me over the years. It's meant a lot, it really has.'

I looked at Amolak; his voice was breaking with emotion. He had probably spent the past thirteen years rehearsing this moment.

'Hey, thanks,' said Bruce in his familiar Jersey drawl. 'That was always the plan, y' know. To make music that meant something to people. That's why I do what I do, you are the reason.'

We walked with Springsteen and his lawyers as they headed out of the building where he was mobbed by other fans who had been unable to get into court. I shook Amolak's hand and said: 'So you finally met him, man.'

Amolak's hand was shaking.

* * *

There were many more concerts during the following years. As we became successful in our careers Amolak and I ploughed more money and time into seeing Bruce Springsteen concerts. We were there in Spain for the first night of the reunion tour in 1999; we saw him in Paris, Bologna and Barcelona two years later; we travelled to New Jersey to see him on home ground. It was during one of those New Jersey shows at the Giants Stadium that I had my most uncomfortable experience at a

Springsteen concert. I was standing on my own, having lost Amolak in the rush to reach the front, and next to me was a man wearing a baseball cap and drinking beer from a plastic cup. He was in his thirties with a sunburnt face and dull brown eyes. The show was yet to start when the man nudged me and said, 'So you're a Bruce fan, huh?'

'I sure am,' I replied, smiling.

'So how do we know you're not a terrorist here to blow this whole stadium up? Hey?'

The question floored me. I felt myself tensing inside.

'So, go on, if you're a Bruce fan what's your favourite Bruce song, huh?'

I was back on firm ground. 'Not sure to be honest,' I said slowly. 'I like "Backstreets" and "Incident on 57th Street"... I know it's a bit obscure but "Two for the Road" is also really great and "The Promise" has got to be up there...'

The red-faced man looked startled. 'Dude, you're a fan, no doubt about it,' he said, taking a gulp of beer.

When *The Rising* tour reached Wembley Arena in the winter of 2002, Amolak and I were at the very front. When work prevented my friend from going I went alone; I thought nothing of flying to the United States to see him play two charity concerts in Asbury Park. The week before I flew to the United States to see the opening night of the *Rising* tour a friend invited me to a Bollywood themed party in central London. Most of those attending the party were young, hip Asians and a scattering of whites. I walked through the room watching the trendy Asians with their impeccably styled beards and hyper-gelled haircuts and the girls with their immaculately applied make-up and plucked eyebrows. I share a skin tone with these people, I remember thinking, but that is all. This is not my world, these are not my people, this is not how I like to have my fun. I left early.

5 **to nudge** to push gently, usually with one's ellbow – 28 **impeccable** free from fault, flawless – 28 **hyper-gelled** ['haɪpəˌdʒeld]

One week later I was standing outside the Meadowlands Arena. The only people lining up were local New Jersey folk: lawyers and waitresses, nurses and military men. I was the only non-white person, the only non-American and one of the youngest in line. When they first saw me join the queue I could tell that some were slightly puzzled. I stood out. But it only took two sentences of conversation, me explaining I had come from England and revealing how much of a fan I was, for the faces to break out into smiles and for me to be invited into conversations. I might not look like these people, I might speak in a different accent and follow another religion but in my heart I felt more connected to the fans I found waiting for Springsteen in the New Jersey night than I did with the Asians at the Bollywood party a week earlier.

The last time Amolak and I went to a Bruce Springsteen concert together was the second week of November 2006.

We walked out of Wembley Central underground station and made our way towards Wembley Arena. Eighteen years earlier we had seen him at Wembley Stadium; that building had been torn down and the new stadium was still under construction. The arena, where we had seen Springsteen fourteen years earlier, had also been renovated. Our tickets allowed us into the pit right by the front of the stage and it was from there that my friend and I watched Springsteen and the Seeger Sessions band. It was, of course, an awesome concert and the most moving moment came when Springsteen struck up the opening chords of 'Bobby Jean'. The song, from *Born in the* USA, is about the enduring power of friendship, and when we had been at college Amolak and I had considered it our song. Neither of us ever referred to it in such terms but some things do not need to be said. When Springsteen sang, 'Down we went walking in the rain, talking about the pain that from the world we hid, and there ain't nobody nowhere no how who's ever gonna understand me the way you did,' Amolak had his arms round my shoulder and he was singing those words to me.

After the concert was over the pair of us repaired to an Indian restaurant that was only minutes from the arena where we ordered samosas and keema naans.

'Fuck me, that was good,' cried Amolak as we sat down to catch our breath and have a drink.

I reached for my wallet to pay. 'Hey, this is gonna be on me,' he said, 'American Express black card – time for some black power tonight.'

It had been many months since I had seen my friend; he had been working in the United States and my career had kept me busy. And yet the curse and blessing of such close friendships is that they are never truly lost or forgotten. We had not fallen out, but we needed Bruce Springsteen to remind us why we had been friends in the first place. That evening after the concert we talked and I could feel the years fall away; we talked about the early days at sixth-form college and our messianic passion for Springsteen, about the years spent trying to live up to the values we heard in his music. We were no longer boys, we were now men and the conversation inevitably turned to how much life had changed for both of us during the years.

As we talked I remembered how ever since college Amolak and I had been outsiders; we were not like the other Asians because we had 'white' tastes and we were not like the whites because of our families and traditions. When we had nothing to hold on to except our dreams of escaping, we had Bruce and we had our friendship. Now all those years later, with our different lives, the music of Springsteen and our friendship still endured. Amolak and Sarfraz. Roops and Saf. The Luton boys. Blood brothers.

The Promised Land

Mister I ain't a boy, no I'm a man and I believe in a promised land.

'The Promised Land', Bruce Springsteen

In the summer of 1981 I was ten years old, wearing pyjamas under my trousers to make my legs seem less skinny and still being bathed by my mother who insisted I wear my Y-fronts in the bathtub to protect my modesty. The summer holidays always began with grand plans; I would resolve to build my own telescope, learn how to write backwards like Da Vinci or teach myself Morse code. These aspirations usually evaporated in the summer heat and the summer of '81 was spent looking forward to the Royal Wedding, watching the Ashes and playing cricket with my friends. Each school holiday my father made his customary promise to take us to London Zoo but each holiday those hopes were dashed. Once or twice during the summer holidays my father would ask his old friend Sufi – he of the snowy beard, furry hat and unreliable Datsun – to drive us to St Albans to see their friend Adalat. Uzma and my mother both suffered from car sickness; before setting off my sister would take a tablet to prevent her being sick. The pill would be crushed and sprinkled on to half a boiled egg which she would eat with her mug of tea. The tablets didn't seem to work for my mother and the journey would invariably be punctuated with Sufi pulling the car on to the hard shoulder to allow my mother to vomit heartily before wiping her face with a tissue and wordlessly motioning to Sufi to start the car again. Travelling

7 **Y-fronts** men's underwear that have a fly as part of an inverted Y formed by the seams – 13 **Ashes** test cricket series played between England and Australia twice a year

with my mother meant always having a plastic carrier bag to hand.

St Albans was as far as our family managed during the summer holidays. It wasn't just money – although we didn't have much of that – it was just that my father didn't see the point of holidays: why spend money going somewhere when you could stay where you were and save it? There was nothing unusual about his attitude – he was typical of an entire generation of Asian fathers. I grudgingly accepted this but returning to school from summer holidays was always rather embarrassing since we were expected to write essays on what we had been up to. Trying to fill a few pages of an exercise book with an uneventful trip to St Albans proved beyond my literary talents; meanwhile Scott would be busy detailing his family holiday to Tenerife and Richard would be describing how his mother had taken him to the Canaries. But it was Mary, a pretty blue-eyed blonde, who trumped us all the day she brought her holiday slides into junior school. Mary had been across the Atlantic: she was the first person I had ever known who had actually been to the United States of America.

I had been fascinated with the United States for as long as I could remember; for me it was a magical crucible from which spewed fantastic films and marvellous music. It was where *The Streets of San Francisco* was based and where Kojak worked; it was certainly not somewhere I expected anyone I knew to be able to visit. Yet here was a slide of Mary in her sunflower-yellow dress with her parents, smiling and squinting as they stood at the top of the Grand Canyon. That Mary should have gone there for a holiday was particularly galling as I fancied myself as something of an expert on ancient geology having watched David Attenborough trek down the Grand Canyon on *Life on Earth.* It was hard to know which I found more

9 **grudgingly** unwillingly – 18 **slide** a small piece of film in a frame for passing strong light through to show a picture – 22 **crucible** ['kru:sɪbl] melting pot – 23 **to spew** to come out in a rush or flood like for example lava – 27 **to squint** to partly close the eyes in order to see better – 29 **galling** ['gɔ:lɪŋ] annoying

astonishing: the awesome wonder of the Grand Canyon or the fact that Mary had actually been there.

Although I had always fancied America, after Mary's slide show I fell headlong in love with the country. On Saturdays when Navela would take me to Luton Central Library I would take out travel guides to New York and California and construct imaginary itineraries that traversed the length and breadth of the nation. I followed the American elections almost as avidly as the British ones and even compiled my own cuttings file on the 1984 Presidential campaign. When family friends came to visit my father would call me downstairs and ask me to tell the guests who the American President was. 'Ronald Reagan,' I would confirm before racing back upstairs to read *The Adventures of Tom Sawyer.*

To say I didn't excel at sports would be somewhat of an understatement. When we played football in PE I saw so little of the action that I would return to the changing rooms with my tracksuit as pristinely unmuddied as if it had been freshly laundered. In time I perfected a secret ritual of falling into the mud during PE so as to appear as if I had been in the heart of the sporting action. My lack of sporting prowess rarely concerned me most of the time. The only time I can remember wishing I was more gifted at football was when the Lea Manor football team, managed by Mr Moreton and named Moreton's Marauders in his honour, went to the United States to play against some American schools. They came back three weeks later feted as international sports stars and teenage ambassadors. It was a source of deep pain that, as with Mary and the Grand Canyon, I was reduced to reading books about America while Moreton's Marauders got to visit the real thing.

A year later I chose to study the assassination of John F. Kennedy for my high-school history project and wrote to

7 **itinerary** [aɪ'tɪnərərɪ] plan or route of a journey – 7 **to traverse** pass across – 8 **avidly** with extreme interest – 16 **PE** physical education – 18 **pristine** [prɪs'ti:n] pure, fresh and clean – 18 **unmuddied** without mud on it – 21 **prowess** ['praʊes] skill, ability – 25 **marauder** someone who goes around in search of sth to steal – 27 **to fete** [feɪt] to celebrate sb for their achievments

the John F. Kennedy library in Boston. They sent me a large parcel packed with information, booklets, photographs and photocopied articles about the life and death of the assassinated President. Even just receiving a package from the United States felt thrilling. I had an American penpal but after two letters my father started complaining about the strange letters with foreign stamps and told me to sever the correspondence.

The cinema had always been forbidden for our family; my parents were nervous about the consequences of allowing me to watch films alone in case it opened some moral floodgates they would be unable to block. It was Scott who suggested that we skip school one afternoon and go to the cinema. The plan was simple: we would go to school as usual in the morning but rather than returning for double English after lunch we would take the number 27 bus into town and go to the ABC. Eager to learn what it was that made my parents so nervous, I readily agreed.

I was fourteen years old the first time I bought a cinema ticket. It was 1985 and the film which popped my cinematic cherry was *Back to the Future.* Even now I remember the feeling of wonder and awe that surged through me as I sat in the darkened theatre. The knowledge my parents were unaware of what I was up to made the experience even more special; it was so liberating not to have to worry what my father might say should there be any kissing or nudity.

After *Back to the Future* I went back to the cinema and saw *Rocky IV.* Even though I went to an afternoon screening the cinema was completely packed. *Rocky IV* was even more thrilling than *Back to the Future* because during the fight scenes the entire cinema was cheering Rocky as if the fight

7 **to sever** [ˈsevə] to bring to an end, to break off – 26 **nudity** nakedness

was actually taking place in the cinema. For someone who had only ever watched films in silence at home this was an entirely novel experience. Over the next year Scott and I sneaked in to see *Rambo: First Blood part 2, Heartbreak Ridge, Over the Top* and *Crocodile Dundee.*

Meanwhile, after years of hiring video players, my father finally relented and bought a silver Panasonic VHS recorder which was mostly used to watch Bollywood films but when my parents were out and I had the house to myself I would watch other films. One of the boys in my school had a father who ran a pirate video store out of the front room of his council flat. Each film cost fifty pence to rent out; it was from that dingy backstreet video store that I first watched the films which defined my early teenage years: kung fu film classics like Jackie Chan's *Drunken Master* and Bruce Lee's *Way of the Dragon.*

If anyone wanted anything stronger they had to go to my friend Craig, the local supplier of video nasties. Thanks to some mysterious contacts, the precise nature of which he never divulged, Craig had a large selection of films which included the legendary *Driller Killer* and *I Spit on Your Grave.* These films were never as gory as their titles implied and the picture quality was as poor as the acting. When I complained to Craig he had already pocketed the money and was busy buying games for his Commodore 64.

Craig accidentally influenced me more than he intended on the evening he came to my house with a video cassette, breathlessly urging me that 'You have to see this film, mate, you're gonna love it.' He did not live far but it was rare for Craig to come to my house so this film had to be something extra special. 'It's called *The Breakfast Club,'* he told me.

The Breakfast Club was unlike any other film I had seen; it was also the film which convinced me that nothing could be

7 **to relent** to allow sth you had refused to allow before – 12 **dingy** dirty and dark – 17 **video nasty** film of bad taste usually including a lot of blood and violence – 19 **to divulge** to tell or make known (what has been secret) – 21 **gory** involving blood and violence

better than to be an American high-school student. After watching *The Breakfast Club* I began to borrow other John Hughes films. I saw *Ferris Bueller's Day Off, Pretty in Pink* and *Maybe Baby;* at the time I thought John Hughes was John Huston and could not believe that a man old enough to have directed *The African Queen* could have such a grasp of the preoccupations of the teenage mind.

After seeing *The Breakfast Club* I would fantasise that I was an American high-school student. I visualised having my own metal locker, imagined the pressure of prom night and speculated on what it might be like to date a cheerleader. In my daydreams, the possibility that my high-school experience might differ on account of not being white did not arise. I became so obsessed with the idea that on my weekend visits to Luton Library I began reading about exchange programmes that would let me spend a term at an American high school. It seems an absurd teenage fantasy but at the time I was deadly serious and truly believed that were it not for my obstructive parents I really could be an American high-school student.

I never actually raised the question of the US school exchange with my parents as I already knew what their response would be. I persuaded myself that if my parents were like those of my friend Terry, my life would be so much better. Terry was not like the rest of the Lea Manor rabble; not only was he the cleverest boy in our year but he walked as if encased in a perpetual Ready Brek glow, bounding along the corridors quoting lines from Monty Python the rest of us didn't understand. His white shirts were never less than dazzling and he had the hairstyle of a young Conservative. Terry and I became friends the day I saw him reading the latest issue of *Time* magazine and when I expressed interest he came to school the next day with a plastic bag full of old issues for me to read. His home was only yards

10 **prom night** a formal dance for American and Canadian high school students – 24 **rabble** a large and uncontrollable group of noisy people – 26 **Ready Brek** oat-based breakfast cereal – 28 **dazzling** extremely bright

from our school and I loved visiting his house because Terry's father Dave was obsessed with all things American.

Running and music were Dave's hobbies; his home housed the biggest collection of records I had seen. The living room had been converted into a music library where thousands of vinyl records were arranged alphabetically in wooden shelves that stretched from the floor to the ceiling. The room was a shrine to Americana; on the walls were vintage election posters of Franklin Roosevelt, an old Coca Cola sign hung above the door to the kitchen and a miniature black Cadillac rested on the bureau. Most impressive of all, Terry's father owned a jukebox. It was an original Wurlitzer from the fifties which he had restored and it took pride of place in the lounge. It was my first exposure to the music that existed beyond the current top forty; the music of Lou Reed, Neil Young and Tom Waits – Bruce Springsteen was still in my future. Visiting his home was as close as I had yet come to being in the USA.

The more bored I was with my life in Luton the more America appealed. All my hopes were encapsulated in the life I imagined was possible in the United States. Why had my father not landed at Ellis Island? We could have been living in Manhattan, not Marsh Farm. It wasn't that I was unaware the United States had its own race problems but even those seemed glamorous. I read about the black civil rights struggle, the bus strikes and Freedom Riders, I watched the television series *Eyes on the Prize* and saw white policemen firing water cannons at innocent blacks, and I read the collected speeches of Martin Luther King. I knew more about American black history than I did about the fight for civil rights in Britain. In the absence of British Pakistani role models I borrowed Martin Luther King and Malcolm X. For all my interest in the black struggle

11 **bureau** ['bjuːrəʊ] piece of furniture with a lid that you can open to write on *(Sekretär)* – 19 **to encapsulate** to express in a short form

I was not black, I had not read of any discrimination against Pakistanis in America and so the United States remained a place for second chances. Why would they care that I was Pakistani?

My first realistic opportunity to visit the United States came in my first term at university. It was autumn 1989, I had just seen *Field of Dreams* and *Dead Poets Society* at the cinema and I was scanning the notice board of the Student Union on Oxford Road in Manchester. One of the notices mentioned summer employment in America. It was selling encyclopedias door-to-door for six weeks and although the pay was commission only, the advertisement suggested the books practically sold themselves. Successful candidates would receive one week's training in Nashville before being stationed somewhere in America. I rang Amolak who was still studying in Luton, having failed his A levels. 'I think we should go for this,' I said.

'You sure about this, mate? You've never been on holiday and you want to piss off for three months? You think you'll manage?'

'I dunno, it just sounds like it could be really cool.'

'Have you asked your dad?'

'Not yet. I thought I'd apply, get the whole thing sorted and then see what he says. But I think if you go too he's less likely to go mental. Don't you think it would be so fucking cool if we both went!'

We carried on talking, me on the payphone at the end of the corridor on the second floor of Grosvenor House student accommodation in Manchester and Amolak in the hallway of his Luton home. I knew it was a crazy idea that would not go down well with my father but having moved away from home I was less worried about his reaction. Amolak was still living with his family and America seemed more distant to

24 **to go mental** to go crazy

him. 'Look, mate, if I go and send you a postcard from Asbury Park how fucked off are you going to be?' I asked Amolak. 'Go on, think about it, there I'll be, standing on the boardwalk in Asbury Park on my tod cos you couldn't be arsed to come with me. You telling me you won't be royally pissed off?'

'Listen, I gave you Bruce Springsteen,' Amolak reminded me yet again. 'You were listening to pop rubbish and chatting shit so don't be thinking you're going anywhere near New Jersey without me!'

'It's up to you, my friend. Like I said, I'm gonna go, you coming or what?'

'All right,' said Amolak finally. 'Stick my name down and see what happens.'

I rang the telephone number on the advertisement and was told to turn up the following week to speak to Andy, a company representative. With his spiky blond hair, square jaw and dimpled chin Andy looked like he had narrowly failed an audition for *Baywatch*. His voice had a relentless cheeriness which seemed out of place on a rainy Manchester evening. Andy told me the name of the company he worked for was Southwestern and that they had been selling books door-to-door for decades; apparently generations of Americans had worked for them and many had gone on to become champions of industry. The way he described it, working for Southwestern wasn't so much a job selling books as a holy rite of passage. 'So where exactly will I be working?' I asked him.

'I couldn't tell ya,' Andy replied, his eyes twinkling. 'It could be anywhere – we got students right now in Florida, in California and in Maine. You'll go where we send you. That's the deal.'

The alternative was to work in a factory in Dunstable that produced paint stripper; it wasn't frankly much of a choice. Andy wanted to know if I had what it took to sell books to

3 **boardwalk** path along a beach made of wooden boards – 4 **one one's tod** *inf* alone – 4 **to be arsed** *taboo* to be persuaded – 18 **cheeriness** positive expression – 25 **rite of passage** an event that marks an important stage in one's life, especially becoming an adult

strangers. I had never sold door-to-door but I told Andy that I had experience of telephone selling; while I was at sixth-form college I had had an evening job selling kitchens on the telephone. I told Andy I was not afraid of hard work and I told him about my father who had come to Britain because he wanted a better life. I wanted to go to America for the same reason.

'Competition is fierce for these jobs,' Andy said at the end of our conversation, 'but you know what? I'm gonna give you a shot, because if you can work half as hard as your father must have done then you and I will get along just fine.'

We shook hands and I told Andy I had a friend who was equally hard-working. Amolak travelled up to Manchester and was also interviewed and accepted. The first hurdle had been cleared, now we had to find the money for the flights. And tell our parents.

Each time I visited Luton I would tell myself this was the time to break the news and each time I would step back at the last minute. I tried to soften my father up by talking about how the modern employment market favoured candidates with proven work experience. Other times I would casually start discussing the brain drain and how the best minds and the best salaries were now to be found in the United States. When neither of these strategies seemed to be making much progress I decided to take the plunge. 'A lot of my friends are going to be spending the summer getting placements to help with their CV,' I told my father one morning as I had my cornflakes with hot milk.

'So long as you get money what does it matter what it is called: placement, work experience, job, who cares?' my father said.

22 **brain drain** metaphorical expression for the movement of large numbers of highly-skilled people from the country were they were trained to other countries were they can earn more money – 25 **to take the plunge** [plʌndʒ] decide to do sth after having delayed it through uncertainty or nervousness – 26 **placement** *Praktikum* – 26 **CV** curriuculum vitae *(Lebenslauf)*

'Well, I have been accepted on to a work placement,' I said slowly, trying not to sound nervous. 'It was very hard to get and it will be very useful. Amolak is going too.'

My father looked up from his newspaper. 'Going where?'

'America. The job is in America.'

'America? Why do you need to get a job in America? Have you heard this?' my father said to my mother.

I told him about the job and it was then that he exploded.

'Selling books door-to-door! Never. If it was something professional then maybe, but this? Never! Tell that Sikh boy you are not going.'

'Why not? It isn't going to cost you anything. I will pay for it myself and I will come back with money.'

'Have you not heard what I have said? Never. You are not going to America.'

The arguments continued for weeks. Amolak was having similar problems with his family. The company which had offered us jobs was pressing us to confirm that we were going and I was stalling them while hoping that my father would have a change of heart. Whenever I went home it was not long before the question of my summer plans arose. 'What I don't understand,' my father explained one afternoon as he was driving the family into town for shopping, 'is why do you need to go to America to earn money? If you go to America you have to pay for flights and accommodation but if you stay in Luton for the summer and work in a factory you have no costs and you can work overtime!'

I was tempted to remind my father that if I stayed at home I would not be seeing a penny of anything I earned but it was hard to explain to him that it was possible to aspire to more than working in a Luton factory over the summer. When he was in a more belligerent mood my father would interpret my

19 **to stall** *inf* to delay in order to gain time – 30 **to aspire** [ə'spaɪə] to direct one's hopes and efforts to some important aim – 32 **belligerent** [be'lɪdʒərənt] angry and ready to fight

desire to visit America as tantamount to a declaration of war. 'My son, it is very simple. They say this is a free country and it is. You have a choice. You can choose America or you can choose your family. But you cannot choose both.'

I tried to tell him that it was only for three months but he did not want to listen, for him the United States was everything he hated about Britain multiplied a hundredfold. 'Why do you want to go to America anyway? Americans are unclean, immoral, look at how little their girls wear.' I did not want to confess that was one of the reasons why I was so desperate to visit.

While my father remained hostile I tried to persuade the rest of my family. My mother's greatest concern was not cultural pollution but whether I would be safe. 'Look what happened when your brother went to America,' she said. 'Him and Zahid were like you and your Sikh friend and look what happened.'

My brother was also uneasy about me going. 'The roads are very dangerous,' he warned me. 'Even if you're not driving, someone else can just cut you up on those big highways. It's not worth the risk.'

The situation looked desperate and yet I could not bring myself to cast the plan aside. Seize the day, I told myself. Even if this tears me apart from my family I am going to do this. I could go for three months and even if my father did not talk to me for another six, he would eventually get over it; if I did not follow my dream I would never forgive myself. I told Amolak that come what may I was going to be in America that summer, with or without him, with or without my father's blessing.

Then, one day, as I was walking with my father along Old Bedford Road on our way into the town centre, he asked again about the proposed trip. 'So how long is it?'

'Three months.'

'And where will you be?'

1 **tantamount** having the same value or effect as – 22 **to seize** [si:z] to take and hold

'New York, Nashville and then a few months in California,' I answered.

I think he must have realised that I was going whether he approved or not. I never said as much but he must have noticed that I did not flinch or concede when he had warned me that I risked sacrificing my family for three months in the United States. We continued walking, my father taking short but purposeful strides while I shuffled along at his side. 'And you don't think you're better off trying to find work in Luton?'

'No, Dad, I don't.'

'How much is the flight to New York?'

'I'm not sure but I think it's about three hundred pounds.'

He stopped walking and, looking me in the eye, said, 'Let me pay.'

In the third week of June 1990, ten days after turning nineteen, I took the Intercity train from Manchester and arrived in Luton weighed down by a rucksack packed with clothes and a stuffed holdall. After saying goodbye to my family where only my mother reached out to hug me, my father drove me to Luton train station. I said goodbye to my father, made an attempt at hugging him, promised I would call as soon as I had arrived in the United States and bundled out of the Ford Cortina.

Amolak was waiting for me. He had already settled on the look he would sport for our American adventure: his head was covered by a Stars and Stripes bandanna, around his neck swung his dog tag and he was sporting a trimmed goatee. Under his faded denim jacket was a black T-shirt with an image from the cover of the live box set. I was also wearing a Springsteen T-shirt over which was a denim shirt with wing tips, a bootlace tie I had bought from a clothing store in Dunstable and a black waistcoat that was the best approximation Mr Byrite had for

5 **to flinch** to make a small movement because of pain or fear – 8 **to shuffle** to walk by dragging one's feet along instead of lifting them – 18 **holdall** large bag – 26 **to sport** to wear or show publicly and proudly – 29 **bootlace tie** tie that is as thin as a piece of string

the one that Bruce wore during the 'Tougher than the Rest' video.

'So this is it, buddy,' said my friend. 'We are on our way to the Yoo Nited States!'

We boarded the train from Luton, our rucksacks on our backs, and alighted at King's Cross before taking the Piccadilly line to Heathrow. The other students, the ones who were also spending the summer working in America, were already at the airline check-in desk. 'Do you realise that by the time we go to bed we are going to be in New York?' I said to Amolak as the girl at the check-in studied my passport.

The first time I saw America was through the window of the plane as it descended through the clouds towards the landing strip of the airport. It was past nine in the evening. I had spent the flight listening to music on my headphones while Amolak had been chatting up the two girls seated behind us. Outside the night sky had been as dark as ink when suddenly a collective hush of excitement spread throughout the cabin. I looked out of the window and saw the Manhattan skyline; at night the city seemed constructed from light. I had never seen anything like it and yet the view was completely familiar. I felt a long way from home.

The plane landed at JFK and a shuttle bus dropped us outside the Sloane House YMCA in midtown New York City. Amolak and I were given the keys to the room we would be sharing. The room had two bunk beds, a small wardrobe and tiny wash basin; the noise of traffic filled the room with honking horns and police sirens. We could not have imagined a more beautiful sound. I had brought a small pocket radio with me; I wanted to hear what New York radio sounded like. While Amolak stood at the basin splashing cold water on his face and spraying half a can of deodorant into his armpits I fiddled with the radio trying to locate any radio station. As I turned the dial

6 **to alight** to get off – 18 **hush** silence

I heard a familiar sound and a male voice singing: 'I got a wife and kids and Baltimore Jack, I went out for a ride and I never went back...'

'Hey, Amolak! Can you hear this?' I said, pointing the radio in his direction.

'Everybody's got a hungry heart, everybody's got a hungry heart...'

'You're fucking having me on!' my friend said, his face dripping with water. 'This is too much, mate: we're in New York and The Boss is playing on the fucking radio. It's just too fucking much!'

New York City in the summer of 1990 was a frightening place. A serial killer the newspapers had dubbed the Zodiac Killer was on the loose, murdering women according to their star sign. Every morning we would walk past the homeless pissing on the street and have breakfast at the Cheyenne Diner before spending the day exploring the city. Amolak bought a cheap stetson and I borrowed his bandanna; the two of us wandered through the city in the sweltering June sun, laughing in disbelief at our outrageous luck.

We bought postcards of the New York skyline but never found the time to mail them; when I rang home it was like being slapped hard by reality; the truth was all I wanted to know was that everyone was alive. I was having too much fun to miss my family and I didn't want to be brought back to earth with stories of what was going on back home. Amolak, however, seemed to feel differently and would ring home every day.

On our third day in the United States we walked to Penn Station and paid $11.95 for a round trip bus ride that took us to Asbury Park. The bus deposited us in an unpromising neighbourhood populated entirely by unsavoury-looking young men; as soon as we got there I wanted to return to the

13 **to dub** to name, call – 13 **zodiac** [ˈzəʊdɪæk] *Tierkreis* – 19 **sweltering** unpleasantly hot – 31 **unsavoury** unpleasant

relative safety of the big city. 'Just chill out, mate,' Amolak said. 'You've been watching too many cop shows.'

Still nervous, we followed the signs that led to the ocean. And then we saw it: the Asbury Park boardwalk. 'Holy fuck, can you believe we're here? Can you fucking believe it?' Amolak was yelling as we ran the length of the boardwalk past the dusty arcades with the Atlantic Ocean lapping a deserted beach.

'It's Madam Marie!' I shrieked when we passed a wooden booth upon which was painted a huge blue eye. Madam Marie had featured in a Bruce song.

Amolak kept running on the boardwalk but I began walking slowly and deliberately, staring hard at the wooden planks of the boardwalk, all the time whispering to myself, 'I am here, I am in Asbury Park, New Jersey.'

That afternoon we must have walked up and down the boardwalk a dozen times. We visited the Stone Pony, peered inside the Convention Center and saw the ruins of an amusement park. We tried to imagine what it must have been like when Springsteen himself visited those same haunts. It was high summer: the sky was cloudless and the sun was warm but the beach was empty, and we saw no one except two young French girls, sisters, who had also come to Asbury Park on a Springsteen pilgrimage. We knew they were hard-core fans as they wore home-made *Steel Mill* T-shirts. Meeting two French sisters, both Springsteen fans, in Asbury Park: it was perfect.

We spent five days in New York before travelling to Nashville on a Greyhound bus for sales training. We then took another Greyhound to California. Each time the bus made a stop I would step out and buy a postcard as a souvenir. It was the summer of Wilson Phillips's 'Hold On' and Roxette's 'It Must Have Been Love', two songs that seemed to be blasting out from every radio. I had my cassette player and Amolak and I would share headphones and listen to Springsteen. We crossed the Mississippi at midnight listening to 'Racing in the Street'.

19 **haunt** a place which a particular person visits frequently

The small Californian town of Yuba City was going to be our home for the summer, and the place where we would sell the encyclopedias. Amolak and I got off the bus and were met by Andy who shook us firmly by the hand before driving us to the apartment block where we would be living. The air was warm, the sky was blue and we were in California.

Kenny and Al, two American students who were also working for Southwestern and who we would be living with, were already settled into our new apartment. Kenny was from a small town called Floyd in Virginia, he had hair like Jackson Browne and drawled his words as if perpetually stoned. He was the first person I had met who used the word 'dude' without irony. Me and Amolak thought he was the coolest person we had ever met because nothing seemed to faze him. He was the most unlikely door-to-door salesman you could hope to encounter, the sort of person whose 'get up and go' had got up and gone. Al, on the other hand, was an archetypal nerd. He was from Wisconsin and wore thick-rimmed glasses, had a square-shaped head and a sensible hair cut. He looked like a cartoon drawing of a clean-cut young man.

When I had been told that Amolak and I were going to be living with Kenny and Al, I had been rather apprehensive about meeting them as they would be the first real-life Americans I was going to be spending time with. The teachers at the sales conference in Nashville had been American but most of the people I had actually spent time with had been other British students in the US for the summer. For all my love of everything American I knew I did not look how Americans imagined Brits looked and I was worried that something in my daily behaviour would expose me as not being quite British enough.

I should not have worried so much. Both Kenny and Al loved music; Al told me he had a subscription to *Rolling Stone* and that his father had been collecting issues since the sixties.

11 **to drawl** to speak slowly with long vowel sounds without separating the words clearly – 14 **to faze** *inf* to surprise or shock – 17 **nerd** foolish or useless person – 22 **apprehensive** worried – 32 **subscription** money you pay usually once a year to receive regular copies of a magazine

Both Americans were stunned that someone like myself, someone from England, could know quite so much about John Mellencamp, Tom Petty and, of course, Bruce Springsteen. They thought it hilarious how music they thought of as quintessentially American had somehow made such an impact on both me and Amolak.

It was this shared love of music that quickly helped me see Kenny and Al as friends first and Americans second. We were all, after all, employees of Southwestern and tasked with trying to persuade the good people of Yuba City to hand over their hard-earned money in exchange for a set of encyclopedias. On our first night in Yuba City Andy took Kenny, Al, Amolak and me to a local restaurant called Shoneys where he outlined our daily schedule. We would awake at six in the morning and have what he referred to as 'a shit, a shower and a shave'. We were expected to be out of the house by seven in the morning with our satchel of sample books and a map. The map would have the neighbourhood we were targeting circled on it.

Our week at the sales conference had taught us the pitch we were to use. I was to ring the bell and then stand back (so as not to frighten the homeowner or cause them to load their gun) and when someone answered I was to say brightly: 'Good morning/afternoon! I guess you've seen me around the neighbourhood and been wondering who I am? Well, let me introduce myself: my name is Steve…'

One of the strangest aspects to our week at the sales conference had been when Amolak and I were advised not to use our own names when selling books since our rather unusual names might puzzle possible book buyers. I was told to refer to myself as Steve while Amolak was to call himself Rupert, on account of his nickname Roops.

Once I had introduced myself as Steve I was to rattle off the rest of my pitch, pausing only to say: 'Gee, it's really hot out

1 **to stun** to surprise – 17 **satchel** a bag that you hang over your shoulder – 19 **pitch** the (sales) strategy how to persuade people to buy sth

here. Is there any chance I could get a glass of water?' at which point, hopefully, the owner of the house would invite me in and when they came back with my drink I would have my satchel open and begin dazzling them with the sheer variety and splendour of books contained inside.

It all sounded so simple. Unfortunately what Andy had not taken into account was that, having spent a year at university, I was unprepared for the cold reality of waking at the crack of dawn. Bleary-eyed, my head feeling like it was being pummelled by a wrecking ball, I would stand under a cold shower (the best way to start the day, we were advised) and wonder what on earth I had done to deserve such punishment. When it was time to leave the flat I found that my satchel weighed so much it felt like I was carrying the dismembered body parts of a particularly corpulent sumo wrestler. And then there was the heat. Yuba City during the summer of 1990 was scorchingly, head-poundingly hot. With a weighty bag over my shoulder it was unbearable.

On my first day knocking doors I was so unconfident with my delivery that no one invited me into their home. On the second day exactly the same happened, but I found myself spending an extended lunch break inside the air-conditioned rooms of a Taco Bell. By the third day I managed to persuade one woman to let me into her home but didn't manage to sell her anything. By now my American dream was beginning to fade fast. During the sales conference we had been taught that there was no room for negative thinking. If I had spent my day slogging and sweating from one no-sale to another the correct way to describe the day to my colleagues when I returned to the apartment was, 'Hey! I had a great day today! I learnt a lot!' I learnt a hell of a lot during my first two weeks.

Miserable as it was not to be selling any books, what made it partially better was having a chance to meet some normal

9 **bleary** ['blɪərɪ] red and unable to see well because of tiredness – 10 **to pummel** to hit repeatedly – 10 **wrecking ball** *Abrissbirne* – 28 **to slog** to do hard dull work without stopping

Americans. Having adjusted myself to the prospect of not selling any books ever, I decided I would try to enjoy myself by talking to interesting people instead. After knocking on door after door I found myself talking to a middle-aged woman who told me all about the time she was living in San Francisco during the summer of love. 'So you were a real-life hippie?' I asked her, my eyes filled with wonderment. I met a born-again Christian who invited me into his house and who made me iced tea while he prayed to Jesus to come and save this sinner, Steve. I knocked on another door and was met by a young brunette who invited me into her home. She told me her name was Zoe, she had brown curly hair, a face full of freckles and wore an MC Hammer T-shirt. I started with my preplanned script but stopped when I noticed her smile. Zoe told me she wasn't going to buy any books from me and, although this was the moment when I should have bid her goodbye and moved on, there was something in her open smile which kept me in her front room. 'Is that your Porsche outside?' I asked her.

'Yeah, my folks bought it for me for my birthday,' she told me.

'That's so cool,' I said enviously. 'It's bloody hard work slogging it out on the streets.'

'So what do you think of Yuba City?' she asked me. 'Bit different from England, huh?'

I told her I had not really seen much of Yuba City, all I had seen was the front doors of houses.

'You've not been to the park?' I told her I hadn't. 'Well, listen, if you wanna take a break from work I could always take you for a drive to the park.'

I was not experienced enough with American girls to know whether 'taking a drive to the park' was a euphemism for something else but this seemed as good a time as any to find out. Abandoning my selling strategy for the day, I clambered

31 **euphemism** ['ju:fəmɪzm] the use of a pleasanter name for something thought to be offensive or unpleasant – 33 **to clamber** to climb usually with difficulty

inside Zoe's scarlet Porsche. Three hours later, after a lovely afternoon sat in the park and a comprehensive drive around Yuba City, Zoe dropped me back at my apartment. I told the others I had learnt a lot that day.

One afternoon I was knocking on doors and an Asian woman answered. I started my spiel and I could tell from the warm smile on her face she recognised me as a fellow Asian. 'Do you speak Urdu?' she asked me.

'Yes, I do,' I replied in Urdu.

Then her husband appeared at the door. 'This young man is from England but he is Pakistani,' the woman told the man.

'Well, in that case come in, come in,' said the man, waving me into his house. I sat in their living room pleased to be out of the scorching heat.

'So where are you from?' asked the man.

'England,' I replied.

'No, I mean where are you really from?'

'Oh, Pakistan,' I said, correcting myself.

'Son, you misunderstand me. What I mean to ask is what village are you from?'

It never ceased to amuse me that whenever my father met another Pakistani one of the first questions he would ask was what village the man was from, as if the answer should mean anything now that both of them were five thousand miles from Pakistan. I had presumed this was merely small town backwardness but here I was in the United States of America, in California no less, thousands of miles from Luton and this man had asked me what village in Pakistan I was from. 'I'm not sure,' I said, 'I think it's near Lahore, I haven't been back for ages.'

'I bet you must be missing your mother's food,' the woman said kindly.

6 **spiel** fast talk, esp. intended to persuade

'I have to admit I am. It's been months since I've had a proper Pakistani meal…'

'Say no more – you can be our guest for lunch!'

That afternoon I sat with the couple and ate chapattis with mango pickle and yoghurt with slices of orange and mango. It was not quite like my mother's home-made yoghurt but it was closer than anything else I had enjoyed for months. As I was eating it struck me that for all my frustration about being Asian there were some unquestionably good things about it: perhaps my father had been right when he had talked about a shared sense of community, it was just that I needed to travel to the United States to witness it first-hand.

We spent so much time out on the streets that the only time I saw Amolak was in the evening when I was so exhausted I hardly had the energy to speak. I did notice how it didn't matter how early I returned home, Amolak was already there and when I asked him how his day had been it seemed to consist mostly of long lunches and hours spent writing letters back home. Early one afternoon I went back to change out of my sweaty T-shirt and found Amolak in the apartment. 'Hey, what the hell you doing here?' I asked him.

'I can't do this, mate,' Amolak told me sadly. 'Believe me I've tried, but I'm just so bloody homesick. I just miss my family too much.'

'Jesus, I didn't realise things were that bad,' I said, throwing my bag of sample books on to the sofa and sitting down next to my friend. 'So what do you want to do? You can't just leave now, it's only July and we're meant to be here until early September.'

Amolak looked at me with an expression that suggested guilt and relief. 'I've already rung Southwestern and, I'm really sorry, but they've agreed to let me go back early. I'm leaving at the end of this week.'

I had hardly thought about my family the whole time I had been there but the difference was that I had already left home. Amolak was still living with his family. 'You're sure about this?' I said. 'Think about it, mate: your parents will still be there in September. Why don't you just stick it out here, you'll regret it later.'

But there was no convincing him, he had loved the time in New York but the effort of rising at six in the morning to try and sell books to uninterested homeowners in smalltown California was beyond him. One July morning I shook him by the hand, gave him a hug and watched as his Greyhound bus vanished into the distance.

Saying goodbye to Amolak was the saddest day of that American summer and though there were happy times ahead it was not the same without my best friend. My favourite memory of Yuba City occurred in the week following Amolak's departure. It was another sweltering day and I had spent the morning standing in front of garden sprinklers to stay cool. Every door I had knocked on was slammed back in my face. I was hungry, hot and depressed. And I was missing my friend. I was standing outside a front door feeling thoroughly sorry for myself when I spotted a middle-aged woman waving at me from across the street. I had talked to her earlier that day. Although she had not bought anything she had been a great listener as I had poured my heart out to her about how much I was missing Amolak and how strange it felt to be so far from home. 'Hey, I have something for you,' she said as I wandered towards her. In her hands were a few boiled sweets. 'I saw you looking all down and I thought I'd give you some candy. You know, to keep your attitude sweet.'

I took the sweets and thanked her. As miserable as I was, I couldn't stop smiling. That this complete stranger should care enough about me to want to cheer me up was so heartwarming; it reminded me what I loved about America and Americans. And in a small way that woman helped remind me just how lucky I was.

With renewed motivation I set about knocking on more doors. Most people did not want to buy, but with enough persistence the sales began to come. With every week my sales tally increased, as did my commission. At the end of the summer I drove from California to Virginia with Kenny who was studying at Virginia Tech. While driving through Arizona I persuaded Kenny to take a detour and head to Flagstaff. He took a photograph of me standing at the lip of the Grand Canyon, smiling in a way not too dissimilar from that of a girl on a slide I had seen many years earlier. For two weeks I was Kenny's roommate at college, attending a few lectures, playing volleyball with his friends and hanging out with them in the evening.

There was a pizza joint in the town called Backstreets; all the employees wore fire-engine red T-shirts with the name emblazoned on the front. Since the restaurant shared its name with one of my most favourite Springsteen songs I managed to get a part-time job there just to get the T-shirt. One day, while Kenny was in classes I wandered into a local museum. I fell into conversation with a girl there and she asked me about my plans for the rest of my time in the United States. I told her that I only had a few weeks remaining but I was intending on returning to New York. 'Hey, you should stay with my brother,' she said. 'He's called Jason Snyder and he lives in Greenwich Village. You'll love him.' She wrote down his phone number and address.

After saying goodbye to Kenny I took a Greyhound bus to New York City which arrived late in the evening. I jumped into a taxi and headed towards West 11th Street. As the taxi

7 **persistence** steady effort – 8 **tally** a count of a number of things – 11 **Flagstaff** city located in northern Arizona

drew up outside the apartment, a man pulled the window of his apartment up and asked, 'Hey, are you Saf?' Jason, the girl's brother, turned out to be a lovely guy. During my week staying with him, my last week in the United States, I spent the days visiting galleries and the nights in bars. We went to the Metropolitan Museum of Art and MoMA, we wandered around Washington Square Park where I paid a dollar to hear a busker play 'Glory Days'. I walked past stores that offered piercings 'with or without pain' and T-shirts that said 'Welcome to New York: now learn English'. After a week sleeping on the couch in Jason's apartment I flew back to England. It was the first week of September 1990.

I kept returning to the United States. In my final year at university I took out a student loan and used it to fly to Los Angeles for two weeks. I dared not tell my family I had done anything quite so reckless; they suspected nothing although the next time I returned to Luton they did ask me how it was that I had developed such a deep suntan in the middle of January. Once I started working I thought nothing of flying to the United States three or four times a year. I would take off on my own and spend a week in Seattle, a long weekend in New York City, traverse the country by Amtrak to see America by rail. Each time Bruce Springsteen toured it was another excuse to go; I saw him in Pittsburgh on one tour and New Jersey, New York and Washington on another.

With each visit the less special travelling to the United States became; going to the country I had fantasised about for so long had become almost routine. It was never as viscerally thrilling, never as filled with wonderment and awe as it was during that first summer back when I was still a teenager. I never quite got the same sheer delight as during that first week exploring New York City with Amolak. My favourite memory is from that very

7 **busker** street musician – 14 **loan** money which is borrowed – 22 **Amtrak** National Railroad Passenger Corporation – 28 **viscerally** emotionally

first week. It was 21 June 1990, the longest day. I had read that Nelson Mandela was in New York and that there was to be a ticker-tape parade in his honour. Having decided we wanted to see the parade, we left the YMCA early in the morning and began walking downtown. The sun was beating hard, I had my shirt tied around my waist and Amolak was wearing sunglasses and his bandanna. The parade was in full swing by lunchtime, hawkers were selling commemorative T-shirts for five dollars each and medallions engraved with an image of Mandela for a buck apiece. Music was blaring from floats, ticker tape rained down from the sky and the streets were a throng of sweaty bodies.

'We got no chance of seeing him like this,' I shouted to Amolak above the din of the music.

'I know, this is a fucking nightmare.'

'Hey, I got an idea,' I said suddenly. 'Just follow me.'

I squeezed my way past some tourists. 'So, here's my idea,' I said. 'Instead of being with all these clowns on the street why not see the whole damn thing from high up?'

Amolak smiled.

It took more than an hour of walking in the sweltering heat before we reached our destination. 'Fuck me, they're tall bastards, aren't they?' said Amolak in wonder. 'There's no fucking way you're going to miss either of these fuckers.'

We walked through the magisterial entrance of the building, past the globe sculpture and lined up with the others to buy tickets to reach the top. The lift hurtled skywards like something from *Charlie and the Great Glass Elevator*. The doors opened and we walked out and on to the roof of the east tower of the World Trade Center. Amolak suffered from mild vertigo and started saying he wanted to leave as soon as

3 **ticker-tape** very long narrow lengths of paper on which information is printed and which is often thrown in the US to greet famous people who are visiting a town – 8 **hawker** someone who sells goods on the street – 10 **buck** *inf* dollar – 11 **throng** a large crowd – 14 **din** loud, continuous noise – 31 **vertigo** a feeling that you are loosing your balance when you look down from a high place

we had arrived. 'Mate, you got to look down,' I said, peering at the maze of streets and slashes of traffic. The rest of the group from the lift were over on one side of the roof, we joined them and looked down. Down below was the ticker-tape parade looking like a tiny snowstorm in a corner of the city. 'We got the best view in New York,' I told Amolak. From the top of the towers it was as if the entire world was within sight, not just the five boroughs of New York. Up to then, the tallest building I had ever visited was the fourteen-storey block of flats outside Waulud's Junior School; to be standing on the top of the tallest building in New York three days after landing in America was truly magical. I wanted to call everyone I knew and ask them if they could guess where I was. I was in the country I had always wanted to see, the city I had always wanted to visit and I was on top of the world.

Amolak took photographs of the city below while I slowly walked along the edge of the barriers trying to absorb the reality of where I was. I was in the country of Superman and Mr T, Rocky and Michael Knight, Bob Dylan and Bruce Springsteen. I did not yet know what the summer had in store but my mind was not on the months ahead but on the time past. I was thinking about Mary in the geography class and Craig giving me *The Breakfast Club*, I was thinking of the number of times I had heard 'Incident on 57th Street' and 'New York City Serenade', I was thinking that I was in a country where no one cared if I was Pakistani or Muslim. Standing in the baking heat on the longest day on the tallest building in New York, I was thinking that I had finally reached the promised land.

Factory

Some folks are born into a good life, other folks get it anyway anyhow.

'Darkness on the Edge of Town', Bruce Springsteen

My father began on the Vauxhall car production line in January 1971 – five months before I was born – and remained at the factory for fifteen years. I remember him leaving for work in the mornings, my mother filling his blue tiffin can with spicy dahl, folded chapattis and sliced tomatoes and cucumbers. We would not see him again until the evening when he would return home, tired and irritable. He'd eat in silence with the rest of the family with the black-and-white television on in the background. None of us knew exactly what he did at the factory, it didn't matter. He worked for the money, there was no satisfaction or pleasure in it; it was the price to be paid to ensure the family were clothed and fed. We did not know anyone who enjoyed their work and so it followed that I was raised to expect my eventual destiny to be a job I hated but which paid reasonably well.

The best way to ensure a well-paid job was to study hard and excel in education. The Pakistani parents who toiled in factories, drove taxis, assembled circuit boards and made dresses were solidly working class, but they had great ambitions for their children. When I was seven my mother would take me to Maidenhall Junior School, a few minutes' walk from my home. Maidenhall was in the heart of Bury Park and the children at my school were, like me, the sons and daughters

8 **tiffin** *old* a small meal taken around lunchtime – 21 **to toil** to work hard

of working-class immigrants. At the time, my mother had only two sets of clothes and the other Pakistani mothers would make barbed comments, saying: 'Sister, you must like that top a lot, don't you?' As they walked along Newark Road towards their terraced homes the conversations between the mothers would be full of confident predictions about the glittering careers their little boys would be following.

My best friend was Tanveer. Tanveer's father was so keen that his son have the best start in life that he insisted on speaking to him – and me – in English. This always made me feel uncomfortable as I had been taught to speak to my elders in Urdu, so when his father spoke to me in English I would nevertheless respond in Urdu.

Tanveer's mother was younger than her husband and also younger than my mother. She was a short, plump woman who favoured red lipstick and green eyeshadow, and her conversation would be an endless stream of praise for the wonder that was her darling son and the incredible success for which he was destined. Tanveer knew he was going to grow up to be a doctor, everyone in Bury Park knew: his mother told anyone who would listen that her little boy was going to be studying medicine.

Although they pretended to be friends my parents and Tanveer's parents were engaged in a lengthy war as to whose child was going to be more successful. When I visited his home in Bury Park there would be maths textbooks that he had taken out from the library which included extra tests that the teachers had not set. After he finished junior school his parents enrolled him in a school that was miles from where he lived which had brand-new facilities and virtually no other Asians. Anything and everything to ensure he excelled in his exams.

3 **barbed** sharp and unkind

On the night that our O level exam results were revealed I received a telephone call. It was the middle of August 1987. I had learnt earlier that day that I had passed ten subjects with a scattering of As, Bs and Cs. My parents had seemed reasonably satisfied and I had retired to bed feeling mightily relieved. That was before the telephone rang. I ran down the stairs. It was Tanveer. 'Hello, Sarfraz, how are you?'

It was past eleven and Tanveer never usually rang so I knew immediately that his mother and father had put him up to it. 'So how did your exams go?' he asked in a voice that made it clear he was only asking because he had been told to.

'Not too bad. Am quite pleased,' I told him honestly. 'Got ten, four As, four Bs and two Cs.'

He paused before saying, 'That's really good, your parents must be very pleased.'

'Yeah, they're all right, I think. What about you, how did you do?'

'I… they went well too…'

'Really? So, go on, what did you get then?'

'Err… well, I got twelve passes with eleven As and one B.'

I knew the instant Tanveer told me his results that I was in for a verbal battering from my father. 'Who was that?' asked my father.

'Tanveer,' I replied.

'Come here. What did he want?'

I told him Tanveer's results. It was not just my father who exploded with rage, my mother was also livid. 'So this is how you thank us,' screamed my father, 'making us look like fools in front of his mother and father? Do you know how hard they must be laughing at us in their house?'

22 **to batter** to hit sb/sth hard many times – 27 **livid** extremely angry

'We were told this was a bad school,' added my mother bitterly. 'All council house people. His parents took him to a good school in a private area.'

Tanveer's better grades meant that I had committed the worst of crimes: I had embarrassed my parents in front of others. I had let them down.

When I try to recall the atmosphere in our home the most overpowering memory is the urgent pressure we all felt to earn and save money. The sofa in our living room was golden velvet but in order to preserve its condition my mother had made a cotton cover that we stretched across the sofa and armchairs. The only time the cover was removed was when guests were coming; if someone unexpectedly came I would have to hurriedly whip the magnolia shroud off the three-piece suite. When we ate, my mother's constant refrain was 'You can eat as much as you like but finish everything in your plate.'

Nothing infuriated my father more than a light left on in an empty room; he would patrol the house in search of electrical appliances left switched on unnecessarily. We were constantly told we were living beyond our means, that all of us shared a responsibility towards contributing to the household. Before I was old enough for a part-time job I was dreaming up ways to make money. During the Rubik's Cube craze I would complete the cube in exchange for money. In order to preserve my secret technique I insisted on pocketing the cash and doing the cube in private. When I was safely in my bedroom I would use my mother's machine oil to grease the coloured stickers and reattach them so each side was a single colour. This ruse lasted a week before my friends began complaining that the coloured stickers were falling off their cubes.

14 **shroud** cloth for covering – 20 **means** income – 23 **Rubik's cube** *Zauberwürfel* – 23 **craze** extremely popular idea or fashion – 28 **ruse** trick to deceive someone

I also scoured the classified advertisements in the *Luton Herald* for items that I could buy and resell for a profit. My most spectacular deal was a 1955 edition of the *Guinness Book of Records* which I bought for fifty pence. It was the very first one so I thought it must be valuable. The man came to deliver it to our home, which must have meant he made absolutely nothing from the sale. The following week I placed a for sale advertisement in the paper. I did not put a price on the book but said that the highest offer would secure the sale. It eventually sold to a man who needed it to complete his collection. He paid fifteen pounds. The money went straight to my father.

Many of my schoolfriends already had Saturday jobs. Usually my father dismissed comparisons between me and my friends but when it came to work he was suddenly far more receptive. 'Look at your friends, they all work, time you started looking for work too,' he would tell me. 'Look at you, almost a man, you need to start behaving like one.' There was no purpose in pointing out that the reason my friends had jobs was because they were allowed to keep the money they earned.

At weekends I would take the bus into Luton town centre and try to find work. I would visit every store in the Arndale and on Leagrave Road. Friends would tell me that there was work available somewhere but when I turned up the vacancy would have disappeared.

I was in a newsagent asking the man behind the counter if he needed help when someone overheard me and asked if I was looking for work. He owned a store nearby and needed someone to help during the coming half-term holiday.

The shop was called The Door Store and, unsurprisingly, it was a store which sold doors. On my first morning I arrived

1 **to scour** ['skaʊə] to search every part of

half an hour earlier than the owner. 'So what they call you?' he asked brightly once he arrived.

'Sarfraz,' I told him.

'OK, so what do your friends call you?' he asked.

'They call me Saf,' I said hurriedly.

'Great stuff, Saf. OK, well, your first task of the week is to make a brew. Let me show you the kitchen. You make us both a cup of tea and then I'll run you through what I want you to do during the rest of the week.'

And with that he led me to the back of the shop and into a tiny kitchen. He pointed to the kettle before bounding into the store. It was not yet ten o'clock and the boss had asked me to do what he thought was a simple task, but already I was panic-stricken. I had never made tea using a kettle. When my mother made tea she boiled water in a pan, added tea bags, poured in milk and let the whole thing stew until a thin film formed on the surface. I filled the kettle with water, waited until it boiled and then added the tea bags. The owner walked in. 'What the hell are you doing?' he asked me. 'Don't tell me you don't even know how to make a cuppa?'

'I'm sorry, I just know how we make it at home.'

'All right, let me show you how we English make it. You take a mug and put a tea bag in it. You then fill the kettle and when it's boiled you pour the water into the mug. Then you stir and add milk. Got that?' I nodded my head. It seemed a bizarre way to make tea. 'So you sure you can do it next time? OK, what I need you to do now is help with this door.'

For the next five days I carried doors from the storage area at the back of the shop into the display at the front. No one bought a door in the time I was there; most of the time I minded the store and gave price details to anyone who asked. When I returned home in the evening after my first day of work my father treated me in a way he never had before and my mother had made keema aloo because she knew it was my favourite.

At six o'clock on the Friday afternoon, just as I was about to say goodbye and thank the owner for giving me work he put his hand into his pocket and drew out three ten-pound and one five-pound note. I had not discussed what I would be earning with the owner as I had been so relieved to be working at all.

As I took the number 27 bus back to Marsh Farm I held the thirty-five pounds in my hands, feeling the notes and thinking of what they could purchase. A Lyle & Scott sweater, maybe a pair of gleaming white Hi-Tec Capitol trainers. It was all fantasy, of course. When I got home I rang the doorbell and my mother answered. 'This is for you,' I told her, handing her the notes.

'There is no more beautiful thing that a son can do,' my father claimed later that evening, 'than to give his hard-earned money to his mother.'

I knew I should have agreed but the truth was I could think of plenty of beautiful things I could have done with the money instead. Even though I had not expected to keep the money I had earned working at The Door Store, handing it over to my mother still felt painful; if I could have had even a few pounds to myself it would have justified working the week but as it was, there was a shuddering anti-climax to my first experience of paid employment.

The following month Scott and I took the train to London to take part in Sport Aid's Run the World, a charity race organised by Bob Geldof. We had been training two times a week for the past three months and I had been persuading friends and teachers to sponsor me. I really wanted to take part because the previous year I had not been able to attend Live Aid. A

2 **keema aloo** traditional dish of South Asia, also known as potato and mince curry – 25 **anti-climax** sth unexciting, ordinary, or disappointing after sth important

boy in my class, a lanky lad called Paul Wilson, claimed to have tickets which he was willing to sell to me but my father had forbidden me from going. At the time I was crestfallen, so when Geldof announced Sport Aid I signed up even though it was not nearly so glamorous as the Wembley Stadium concert. The race was exhausting and the preparation we had done was wholly inadequate. The good news, however, was that both Scott and I did finish the race and the following week I set about collecting the sponsorship money. This amounted to over seventy pounds. Each night as I held the cash I promised myself I would mail the money to Sport Aid the following day but something always seemed to prevent me. This was money that my father knew nothing about, he had no stake in it. It was intended for the starving children of Africa, those desperate babies with the swollen bellies and huge sad eyes. I knew their need was greater than mine would ever be, I had cried when I saw The Cars perform 'Drive' on Live Aid. But the shameful truth is I never did send the money I raised to Sport Aid. I kept it and spent it on myself, being careful not to spend it on anything suspiciously expensive. I was not proud but the simple fact was that I had never been allowed to have so much money in my possession before and such a chance might never come again: the temptation was too great. And so, to my lasting shame, I kept the money intended for the hungry African children.

As I had proved I was able to find work at The Door Store, my father continued to push me to find work for when I left school. I was in my final year and trying to revise for my O level exams whilst looking for a summer job. The pressure to find work overwhelmed everything else; there were eight weeks between ending my exams and beginning at sixth form and I had to find a way to earn money. I wrote to the local radio station wondering if they might be looking for helpers, I wrote

1 **lanky** ungracefully tall and thin – 3 **crestfallen** deeply disappointed

to the local newspaper asking if they needed any assistance but both said there was nothing suitable. My father would search the *Herald* looking for possible jobs for me. One evening he noticed an advertisement for people to work in a factory which made sandwiches and he suggested I apply. There was the possibility of plenty of overtime. I applied and went for an interview where they asked me a few questions and handed me a small plastic cylinder into which I had to provide a stool sample, which I would then post to their laboratory to ensure I wasn't carrying any unpleasant diseases. Why could they not have provided a funnel to make it easier? I wondered in frustration as I valiantly tried to evacuate my bowels. Having failed to relax sufficently I was reduced to using a spatula to poke, scrape and deposit. My mother kept asking what was taking me so long in the bathroom but I was too embarrassed to explain.

I started work at the sandwich factory at the end of June 1987. On my first morning I was handed my uniform a white overcoat and hairnet – which all employees were obliged to wear. The factory floor was divided into half a dozen production lines. At the start of the line were dozens of loaves of sliced bread which would be fed to the start of the line. Hanging over the belt that drove the slices of bread along were large metal funnels that were filled with sliced tomatoes, cucumbers, eggs and so on. As the bread slid past, each worker would be tasked with adding a different filling. By the time the slices had reached the end of the line they had graduated into fully fledged sandwiches, packed into plastic cases and carted off for the nation to enjoy.

For the next twelve weeks I worked on the production line slicing eggs, adding tomatoes, spreading mayonnaise, opening loaves and other duties. The shift began at eight in the morning and ended at four in the afternoon; at around two the line manager would walk along the production line

8 **stool sample** *Stuhlprobe* – 11 **funnel** *Trichter* – 12 **valiantly** bravely – 27 **fully fledged** completely developed

offering overtime. I was instructed to accept any overtime offered which meant I usually didn't end the day until six in the evening. At weekends it was possible to sign up to two double shifts – two days starting at eight in the morning and ending at ten in the evening. The work was not physically gruelling but it was mind-crushingly dull. I perfected a technique of dividing the day into eighths, quarters and halves to try and hurry the hours along. After two hours I would tell myself I was a quarter of the way into the day; by four hours I would remind myself I had broken the back of the day and so on. The reward for my efforts came on Friday when the line manager handed me a small brown envelope with my printed payslip inside; after tax I was clearing over two hundred, sometimes three hundred, pounds a week.

Every Friday at lunchtime my father would wait for me, the golden Vauxhall Viva parked outside the factory. He would drive me along Leagrave Road and towards the Midland Bank in Bury Park where I had recently opened my bank account. The bank had expressed their gratitude at my banking with them by giving me a dictionary and official pen. My father was generous enough to allow me to keep both those items but insisted I withdraw my wages each week and hand them over. There were a couple of times when we left it a few weeks and I can still remember the excitement of holding a thousand pounds in my hands. Each time I gave the money to my father, I felt a little piece of me die. I knew it was the right thing to do but it frustrated me beyond words that my friends were seeing Madonna on the 'Who's that Girl?' tour at Wembley Stadium and, although I had earned the money, I was not able to go. I would often wonder why my father didn't give me even a fraction of what I had earned; it would have boosted my motivation and made me a less sullen presence at home. The truth was that he probably never contemplated it. All family

5 **gruelling** hard and tiring – 31 **fraction** small part *(Bruchteil)* – 32 **sullen** silently showing bad temper

income had to be pooled into a central bank from which he would then distribute to us according to our needs. When Uzma was in school she would ask my father for lunch money. Each time my father would apologise for having forgotten and then give her fifty pence. My sister did not have the heart to tell him that even a portion of chips cost sixty pence. He was not being miserly, he just had no idea how much things cost.

I grumbled and I sighed but mostly I was ignored and when I was noticed my father would say what he always said when any of his children voiced frustration about money. 'Do you think I spend your money on myself? Are my clothes any better than yours? When I eat do I eat any different, any better than you?' It was true too that my father cared nothing for material possessions for himself; wherever the money went it did not go on him. I only learnt later that my father sent money to his and my mother's relatives back in Pakistan. The pale-blue aero-gramme letters that regularly arrived from our uncles and aunts were filled with pleas for contributions to weddings and operations. They assumed that because he lived in England he was rolling in money. My father did not make a fuss about it but sent thousands of rupees back to Lahore and Karachi to help the relatives he left behind.

When I started sixth-form college I was allowed to choose the A levels I wanted to study and what degree topics I took was my decision. Not all Asians were so fortunate; at college many of those who studied the A level subjects that would get them into medical school did so under duress from their parents. While I was studying at college I was still unsure as to what career I was destined for. My father tried to assist. He would read the newspaper and if he read about a job that seemed lucrative he would call me into his room and suggest I pursue it. 'Have you thought about actuaries?' he once asked me.

7 **miserly** ['maɪzəlɪ] hating to spend money – 32 **actuary** ['æktjuərɪ] a person who calculates risks and tells insurance companies how much they should charge their customers

'Not recently,' I replied.

Another time he became convinced that I should study biochemistry as it was an emerging field.

My father had tried and failed to persuade me to aspire towards medicine. This was only because Tanveer's parents had already declared their little boy was going to medical school and my parents wanted me to keep up with their maniacal ambition. I, on the other hand, always knew that I could never be a doctor; I did not care enough about other people and could imagine few things more depressing than spending time with the ill and the infirm. One needed to have a calling to be a doctor and for me that call never came.

I knew I didn't want to be a doctor but I did not know where my employment future might lie. Amolak was the same. His father had worked for British Steel in Sheffield, then in a rubber factory in Letchworth and he was now in the building trade. He had almost single-handedly built the extension on his house. My friend had spent his teenage years assisting his father on building sites across Luton but he was not going to be a builder just as I knew I would not work on a production line. On Saturday afternoons Amolak and I would sit in Greenfields in the Arndale Centre fantasising over the teenage waitresses who seemed only interested in bringing us our pots of tea and wonder what would happen to us once we left sixth-form college. 'I'd quite like to do law,' I once said to him. 'It must be really cool, to actually make a difference in someone's life, you know what I mean?' Ever since I had been at school teachers had said my argumentative nature made me a natural lawyer and every time I watched *LA Law* it reignited my interest.

'Wake up, mate,' said Amolak incredulously. 'The fact is the only law us lot get a look in on is immigration law. None of that high-class corporate tax shit. No. It's Mr Shah wants to bring his missus from Bangladesh. That's it.' I sat gloomily staring at

7 **maniacal** [mənˈaɪekl] wild and exaggerated – 29 **to reignite** [ˈriːɪgnaɪt] to start (burning) again

my cup of tea. 'Thing is, mate,' continued Amolak, 'if you want to make some serious cash you gotta either go it alone or get into the City. No other way. Look at all the fellas with cash and carrys in Bury Park. They're building fucking mansions back home.'

'It's not just about the cash though, is it?' I said. 'It's what you get to do with it. It's like with my dad, he's totally obsessed with money but hates spending it! He loves chasing it but wouldn't know what to do with it if he had it. You get me?'

'Yeah, that's Asian dads for you though, isn't it,' replied Amolak, leaning back. 'My dad works like a bastard but does he spend any money? Does he, fuck! It's Poundstretcher all the way.'

When I had lived in Luton I had collected live concert tapes of Bruce Springsteen shows; on one of those tapes Springsteen told the audience that 'it's easy to let the best of yourself slip away'. Graduating from university in the summer of 1992 and floundering while friends began graduate trainee schemes, I thought about those words. What not letting the best of yourself slip away meant. After graduating I applied to an accountancy firm and found myself at the final interview stage. Ahead of the interview the company invited me to an open evening, a chance to meet other employees in a relaxed environment. The dress code for the evening was 'casual and relaxed'. That evening I took the bus from west Didsbury into Manchester city centre dressed in my western-style denim shirt and jeans. When I arrived at the open evening I looked around and saw that every single man was wearing a suit, apart from me. I walked around for thirty minutes trying not to be self conscious and discussed tax law and corporate accountancy with the other applicants. Inside me a voice was screaming that this was everything I did not want from my life. Look around you, I

3 **cash and carry** a type of warehouse for various goods that is operated on a self-service basis – 12 **poundstretcher** person who hates spending money – 18 **to flounder** to struggle not knowing what to do – 29 **self conscious** uncomfortable because you wonder what people might think about you

said to myself, is this what you want to become? The truth was that if I had been offered and taken that job I knew it would have left me unsatisfied; it would have meant that I had let the best of myself slip away.

* * *

I didn't want to leave Manchester after I graduated. What I was going to do with my life was still a mystery but while I pondered the big question I signed up with some temping agencies and was offered work as a directory enquiries operator and then sorting mail for the British Council. I found I had a knack for being fired; I didn't care about the work I was doing and I wasn't a good enough liar to convince my employers I respected them. When I was not working, there was no money. I was living in a rented house in south Manchester, and when times were truly desperate I would call my brother. However bad my relations were with my father, I could at least count on Sohail who without any fuss would send me cash in the post once or twice a month. Without his help I might have been forced to consider a return to Luton but thanks to my brother I was always able to pay my rent and have money for food, even if it was only a few pounds for the week. Some weeks my daily diet was nothing except a pint of full-fat milk and a Mars bar. Meanwhile, Amolak had graduated and landed an amazing job at a leading investment bank almost immediately. He would be earning more money than either of us could imagine and still I had no clue where my life was going. When I returned home at the weekends my father would ask what I was doing for work and when I told him he would reply with silence.

I worked in Manchester for almost three years; the work was menial, the pay pitiful, the prospects lousy and yet I had never been happier. When I had money it was mine to spend

7 **to ponder** to think about – 7 **temping agency** agency for temporary work (esp. in offices) while someone is absent – 10 **knack** [næk] *inf* special skill, talent – 29 **menial** ['miːnɪəl] not interesting or skilled

as I wished; I spent it on attending concerts and buying records. In the evenings I was out clubbing every other night and my dreadlocks ensured I was more desirable to girls than I had ever been before. Manchester was the place to be in the early nineties and I was right in the centre of it all. Because I did not drink, music and dancing were how I lost myself; while the out-of-towners took coaches into Manchester to visit the Hacienda, my friends and I would be at 42nd Street, Discoteque Royale, the Ritz with its bouncing dance floor and, our favourite, the Brickhouse. Every night it was another club. Sometimes I was with friends, other times I'd go on my own but I'd always see familiar faces singing along to the Stone Roses, Happy Mondays and Blur. I had virtually no money and each time I went back to Luton I was reminded of how bad relations between my family and me were, but for the rest of the time I did not think about it. I was only twenty-three and I assumed that somehow things would work themselves out. Meanwhile I had great friends, girls were throwing themselves at me and I was living in the hippest city in the world. Work and the future could wait.

While my father had been alive I had always known a safety net existed; I knew that even if I did not have a career I would always have a home and something to eat. When he died I felt the safety net that had protected me throughout my life fall from under me. I was shaken out of my complacency. Once I had been naive enough to imagine that if you went through school and college and university, somehow you fell into a career. It was startling to realise that if you did nothing about it then nothing happened; that you did not get something simply because it was deserved.

On the same day that he suffered the heart attack that was to kill him, my father was painting the house he was buying for my younger sister. He worked all day, came home and had

25 **complacency** [kəm'pleɪsənsɪ] feeling of satisfaction with oneself without good reason

a heart attack. Having become more committed to Islam he told my mother he wanted to visit Mecca and talked about seeing India. The plan was to do it later, but for my father it was always later: work today, save the money, forgo what makes you happy now and at some point in the future you can do what you please. That point never came for my father; at the age when he was almost ready to start living his life as he wanted and not for his children, his life was taken away. If his death taught me anything it was to value the life we have. The trouble with waiting till later is sometimes it's too late.

It had always been my dream to have a job that was creative but the only Asians I had heard about who were even vaguely doing what I wanted were Salman Rushdie and Hanif Kureishi. Years later I grew to respect and admire both writers but neither penetrated my teenage consciousness. I was not into mainstream pop culture and these were literary writers, both Asian but from a very different background to mine and so for someone like myself who was not born into wealth and did not have a mixed-race heritage there were no role models. I didn't know if the things I wanted for my life were possible for someone like me.

Ahead of the interview for a master's degree in documentary production I contacted someone who had already completed the course for advice about what to say. Her name was Charlotte and we met in a bar called The Nose in west Didsbury. It was local to where I lived and had been somewhere I went almost every night; returning there in the aftermath of my father's death was unnerving: everything looked precisely as it had before and yet my world had been comprehensively devastated.

Charlotte had completed the course earlier in the summer and was now searching for work as a television researcher. She

4 **to forgo** to not do sth that is a pleasure – 13 **Salman Rushdie** British-Indian novelist – 13 **Hanif Kureishi** English playwright, screenwriter, novelist and filmmaker whose father was from Pakistan

told me I had done very well to be considered for an interview since the course was highly competitive; those offered a place had an excellent chance of employment in the media since the course enjoyed a good reputation. She asked why I wanted to do the course and I explained how much I had wanted to work in a job that was interesting, how much television had meant to me when I was younger and how I had always been fascinated by politics. And then I told her about my father. The words tumbled from my mouth. This poor girl who knew nothing about me and had agreed out of simple generosity to meet me had to listen as I poured out my heart. I told Charlotte how my father's death had robbed me of any sense of security and protection and how my family were in danger of disintegrating. I told her how guilty I felt about returning to Manchester while the others were still suffering in Luton and I told her how my brother and mother had encouraged me to apply for the course and promised they would look after the household. Charlotte looked rather embarrassed by my candour. I asked her if she thought I had what it took to be accepted. 'Oh, you'll get it, no doubt about it,' she said to me. I asked her what made her so sure. 'Well, just listening to you right now,' she replied, 'seems to me you don't have any choice – you can't afford not to get it.'

I got into the course which started three months after my father's death. It was the autumn of the O. J. Simpson trial which I followed after my lectures in the history of documentary film making. In the spring of 1996 as the course was reaching its conclusion I saw an advertisement in the *Guardian* for graduate trainees at ITN. Whilst I had been studying for my master's I had also been working unpaid in the newsroom at Granada for one day a week. Working in a newsroom seemed the best of all possible worlds: it was not as unstable as the

9 **to tumble** to fall suddenly or helplessly – 13 **to disintegrate** to fall apart – 18 **candour** quality of being honest and truthful – 24 **O. J. Simpson** former US football player who was accused of double murder – 29 **newsroom** office in a newspaper or broadcasting station where the news are collected and prepared for presentation

freelance hell of trying to get into documentaries, it would be a staff position that paid regularly and it was journalism – something that had always been an obsession of my father and mine. I applied for one of the four jobs alongside five thousand other applicants. I did not apply for anything else. I decided I stood more chance if I applied only for the jobs I truly wanted. That way I would not have to lie to the interviewer or myself.

The first interview was with a senior ITN editor called Robin Elias and the head of human resources. Robin, a grey-haired man with friendly eyes and a militarily clipped moustache, asked the questions while the head of human resources scribbled notes. I left the interview unsure how well I had performed, but then a few weeks later a letter arrived informing me I was being invited for a second and final interview. This was, I realised, the most important interview of my life. Getting this job would completely change my life; more importantly, if I did not get the job I had no plan B.

That evening I met up with Amolak for a drink in the town centre; he was wearing a suit, his hair tied into a ponytail, and he was full of confidence. 'Don't you worry about it, mate, the job is yours,' said Amolak. 'Think about it, you got the knowledge, you got the ethnic thing going, plus you're a cocky bastard. It's gonna be fucking wicked, ain't it? Mr Bank sahib and Mr Journalist sahib! Who'd have thought two fools from Luton would get this far?'

'God, I hope I get this, mate,' I told him. 'Things are so bloody rough at home: Mum crying every day, my brother's trying to take over from Dad, his wife's got a baby on the way. Jesus, I need something good to happen in my life, mate… I really do.'

'You got to have faith, dude,' said Amolak. 'Your family has been through shit but you guys are stronger than you think. Trust me.'

1 **freelance** selling your services to several organizations without being firmly employed by a single company *(freiberuflich)* – 22 **cocky** self-confident in an unpleasant way – 23 **wicked** *inf* excellent

The morning of my final interview I woke early, ironed my white shirt and the black suit I had bought from Top Man especially for the interview. My mother asked me if I wanted chapattis but I was too nervous to eat. Before I left the house I asked my mother for her blessing. I hadn't asked her for anything like that since I was eight years old, unable to sleep and needing my mother to read me some verses from the Koran to ease me into slumber.

'Go, go with Allah's blessing,' said my mother, stroking the top of my head. 'Remember, son, everything that happens is Allah's will, He is very powerful, when you walk with Allah there is nothing that is out of reach. Go, son.'

The letter informing me that I had got the job arrived in the week before the first anniversary of my father's death. The family had been dreading the anniversary, it would mark twelve months of pain. We had all been fearing for our mother who was still not coping well and since my father's death our family had been aching for some good news, for something positive that would make life feel less grim. That was why the job was so critical because finally there was something I could say to my mother that would make her happy.

I rang Amolak to let him know the good news. He wanted to know when I was due to start work. I told him my first day in my brand-new job was 23 September. Bruce Springsteen's birthday.

I returned to Maidenhall Primary School for the first time in almost thirty years in the winter of 2006. The headmaster of the school had contacted me some months earlier to tell me that the school had recently been modernised. The headmaster wanted to know if I would be interested in officially opening the newly renovated Maidenhall Primary School. I called my mother to tell her about the conversation; after I had explained

8 **slumber** sleep – 15 **to dread** to fear

the gist of what the headmaster had told me I asked her if she understood the significance of what it meant to officially open the school. 'You do know what I mean, don't you?' I asked her in Urdu. 'It's a really big thing – to be asked to open the school I attended?'

'Yes, son, I understand,' she replied.

I attended the opening with Uzma and my mother. They sat at the front of the main hall which was filled with more than six hundred pupils, parents and teachers. I sat on the platform alongside the mayor of Luton and the chairman of the school governors. As the children began singing 'He's Got the Whole World in His Hands', the chairman, a middle-aged Asian man, asked me how my father was.

'How do you know my father?' I asked.

'Everyone knows your father,' the man replied. 'He is very active in the community but I have not seen him for a few years now.'

I explained that my father had died eleven years earlier.

The headmaster made his speech about the brand-new facilities at Maidenhall Primary School. The headmaster introduced me as their special guest and I stood up and gave a short speech about how this was my first school, the one my mother had taken me to in the summer of 1978 when she walked with me on our way back to our Bury Park home. My mother and sister listened as I told the parents and children that the only reason I was standing in front of them was because of the hard work of my mother and father and how the children in the hall now had so much more available to them than my generation. 'You can do anything you want in this world,' I urged them. 'You just need to work hard and dare to want more from life.'

1 **gist** [dʒɪst] the main points or general idea

With the speech over the headmaster invited me to cut the ribbon and officially open the school. They had prepared a special brass plaque on which my name had been engraved. I cut the ribbon, the schoolchildren cheered and I could see my mother smiling broadly.

In the end, the only thing parents want from their children is for them to do them proud. I knew my mother was proud but it was impossible not to think about the man who was not there to see the journey reach full circle. I know it would have made my father hugely proud to have seen me open my old school but he would have been equally proud, I think, of how the rest of the family had transformed their lives in the years since his passing. My mother had warned us that when a parent dies it can be the catalyst for family meltdown; in our family the loss of our father galvanised us, brought us closer together and drove us to work harder to make something of our lives. It was his labour, determination, desire and work which had made it all possible. We were the beneficiaries of his dream to ensure his children did not, like him, have to work in the factory.

- comparison between S. and the son of the OKO family
- looks for an job => Door Shop
  ↳ handed out the money to his mother
- charity race => never sent the money away
- starts working in the sandwich factory
- did not know what to study firstly - sth. creative

2 **ribbon** small and narrow band – 14 **catalyst** *here* person that causes changes to happen – 15 **to galvanise** to shock into sudden action – 18 **beneficiary** [benəˈfɪʃərɪ] someone who has the advantage of sth

has a new job => journalist at television

opens a new school

meanings of marriages

Better Days

I'm just a scared and lonely rider but I gotta find out how it feels.
I want to know if love is wild, girl I want to know if love is real.

'Born to Run', Bruce Springsteen

Everything I knew about marriage I learnt from my parents. When my mother arrived in Britain in the spring of 1974 she had been married to my father for fourteen years but they had never lived alone together. After eleven years apart, my parents can't have been much more than strangers to each other. Those years apart shaped their years together; whatever feelings my parents had for each other were not expressed in tactile terms. I never once saw my parents hold hands or each other; even on the day my mother first arrived in Britain my father acknowledged her with only a nod. They did not use each other's first names when speaking to each other and if my mother wanted to refer to my father when speaking to someone else she would call him 'the father of Sarfraz'. In other couples this might have been explained away as the inevitable evolution of a relationship, the lack of demonstrative affection merely the result of overfamiliarity. But my parents never had the opportunity and, perhaps, the inclination to become physically comfortable around each other. When I was growing up I assumed that was what all marriages were like: arrangements, businesslike affairs. Love had very little to do with any of it.

There is no photograph of my parents on their wedding day. This used to puzzle me when I was a young boy. Weddings were meant to be the most important day of one's life but there was no visual record of my parents' wedding day. And yet there

12 **tactile** able to be felt by the sense of touch

were photographs of my mother and father taken separately, there were even a few photographs of my brother and sister when they were small children. When I was a child my parents rarely talked about their wedding day, to this day I do not know the actual date they were married.

Every Thursday our local newspaper the *Luton Herald* would fall through the letterbox and after I had studied the property section and scanned the television listings I always made a point of examining the weddings page which would be filled with small photographs of smiling couples. I would particularly be on the lookout for photographs where one of the couple was not white; occasionally there would be black men and white women but I never saw an Asian man with a white bride.

When I was eleven years old it was girls that really interested me but in my family such curiosity had to be explored in secret. When I went to school Scott, Craig and the others would be talking about having seen films called *Porkys* and *Risky Business*. Someone would claim they saw their dad's blue movie and I would laugh along while secretly wondering whether a blue movie was a film that made you cry and if so why my friend William was so pleased to have seen it.

During the early eighties, before my family had its own video recorder, my father would rent a machine from the ABC store in Bury Park. On the weekends that we had the player in our home my father would bring home three or four Bollywood films which we would watch over the course of the weekend. Among my father's friends there was one man called Munir who worked with my father at Vauxhall while his wife assembled circuit boards at home. He was a small very dark man with a pockmarked face and greasy hair whom we always enjoyed visiting as he had his own video player.

One Sunday afternoon we had taken a taxi into Bury Park to visit Munir and were sitting on his chocolate-brown, fake

19 **blue movie** pornographic film

visiting Munir, watching films, looking for some magazines

velvet sofa drinking tea, into which was stirred two teaspoons of ghee. Nearby was a table with a mosaic of the Taj Mahal. On one of the walls in the living room hung a large prayer mat, on another were two plaques upon which were written in ornate Arabic some quotations from the Koran. The third wall had a large photograph of a scene from the Hajj.

Most times we visited Munir there would be some conversation and then he would put on an Amitabh Bachchan film and everyone would be happy. This particular afternoon he decided to play an old black-and-white film from the forties which my parents appreciated but which bored me senseless. I slipped out of the living room and wandered into the sitting room. Here was a large wooden table on which were soldering irons, screwdrivers and electrical wires. In one corner of the room were two large cardboard boxes. Inside each box was a stack of old issues of the *Sun*. I pulled the top one out and studied the headlines before turning the page. Staring back at me was a young woman with long curly dark hair, wearing a dazzling smile and almost nothing else. I stared intently at the photograph trying to soak up its potency as speedily as I could in case anyone stumbled in and caught me. No one came. Another newspaper, and another girl with another smile and another pair of breasts. Two boxes filled with newspapers. My mind could not calculate how many naked girls the boxes contained but I had to see every single one. I knew this was risky, any second now someone could walk through the door and catch me, but something inside me compelled me to methodically and systematically go through every single issue of the *Sun*. By the time I had almost finished with the second box my heart was beating so fast I thought it would punch its way out of my chest. 'Where did you go?' I turned round to see Navela. 'What are you doing?'

2 **ghee** a type of clear butter used in South Asian cooking – 8 **Amitabh Bachchan** very popular Indian film actor – 13 **soldering iron** *Lötkolben* – 20 **potency** power

watching naked models in magazines

I could feel the blood rushing into my face. 'Nothing, nothing,' I stammered, 'just been reading the newspaper.'

My sister looked puzzled. 'Reading the newspaper? Let me see.' She lifted the flaps of the cardboard box and peered inside. 'But these are old! What are you reading them for?' I offered no explanation. 'Look, the others were asking about you. That film is almost over and Munir says he has an Amitabh film you've not seen.' Heart pumping, I hurried back into the other room.

My parents never learned the truth of what I was doing while they were watching their classic movie just as they did not know why I was so pleased when the Freemans catalogue arrived in our home. As soon as it came through the letterbox I would dash upstairs into my bedroom, close the door and sit tightly on the other side so I would know instantly if anyone tried to come into my room. The two sections I studied most intently were the underwear pages and the shower sections. I would forensically study the photographs, trying to discern the merest hint of a nipple behind the soapy suds. Sometimes I used a magnifying glass.

I remained on a diet of catalogue models until I discovered *Amateur Photography,* which could be found at the Purley Centre library. The library was on the way to school and almost every afternoon I would stop by there on my way home, usually to read the newspaper or borrow a *Dr Who* novel. Once I had discovered *Amateur Photography* the magazine became part of my library ritual. I would sit by the reference section where the old issues were stored and methodically skip past the articles about lenses and wildlife photography until I reached the colour photographs of nude models. Every issue had them, and I made sure I saw every issue.

Scott lived not far from me. During lunchtime the pair of us would run out of the school gates and race each other home. My mother would already have my chapattis and curry on the

17 **forensic** scientific methods of examining objects that are involved in crime – 17 **to discern** [dɪ'sɜːn] recognize – 18 **suds** small bubbles

Scott told S. about porns and old magazines

table and once I had wolfed them down I would hurry out of the front door and race towards Scott's home. We would spend the rest of the lunch break playing cricket, or sometimes tennis, out on the street. One after noon while I was gently lobbing the cricket ball towards him I mentioned my visits to the Purley Centre library. 'They have this magazine there,' I told him, trying to be casual. 'It's meant to be about photography.'

'Yeah, the ones with the girls showing their boobs?' asked Scott breezily.

'You know about it?' I asked, stunned into pausing with my bowling action.

'Yeah, Robert told me about them,' he replied airily. 'They only show tits. Just tits?'

'Well, yeah,' I said, rather put out that he wasn't as impressed as I thought he would be.

'That's nothing.'

I said nothing.

'Hey, Saf,' Scott said, 'you know the woods near your place?'

By our house there was a small wood through which a path led to Limbury Mead and the newsagent's where we bought our papers. 'Richard told me that he was out there one time and he found an old porn mag!'

'No!' I felt gutted that I had not been told this before.

'You don't believe me? I can show you if you like?'

We still had half an hour before we had to be at school. Seeing the look on my face, Scott dropped his bat and the two of us raced to the wood and began rummaging in the grass. Twisting between the branches and obscured in the grass were pages from *Mayfair* and *Escort* that some kind-hearted reader had discarded on the bushes. It was never the whole magazine, just random sheets of creased shiny paper that we would carefully pick out from the branches and unfold so that the delectable cover girl was displayed in all her naked glory. Each

9 **breezy** cheerful, in a light-hearted manner – 27 **to rummage** to look very carefully for something – 33 **delectable** beautiful

breathe => read more often the
believe Koran
every night watching TV => nudity

time I found a new page a surge of electric pleasure would pass through me.

While I spent my afternoons poring over discarded porn magazines or browsing the videos on the top shelf of the video store in the Purley Centre, I spent my evenings reading the Koran. My mother had taught me that Allah saw and knew everything. This meant that He had seen me in the library, in the woods and in the video store. I vowed to read the Koran more often and hoped that my teenage curiosity did not make me a bad Muslim. Was I going to suffer in Hell because I had lingered too long on the underwear models in the catalogue?

Watching television with my family was a minefield. I lived in constant fear that someone on screen might kiss another character or, even worse, jump into bed with them. The safest television was news and current affairs, which my father was addicted to, and tame British situation comedies like *George and Mildred* and *Terry and June* where there was little danger of seeing anything offensive. It was rare to be able to watch an entire episode of anything else without there being a scene that would have me squirming with embarrassment. If two characters were kissing we would all at first pretend it was not happening, I would start flicking through whatever book I might have had with me, my father would spontaneously start a conversation. The longer and more intense the kiss, the more discomforting it was for my family; my father would start grumbling and my mother would be murmuring about how whites were lacking in all shame.

It was only late at night that I could watch television more freely and even then it would not be long before my mother would call out to ask what I was doing downstairs. I would say I was watching the snooker but in fact would be viewing some impenetrable foreign film on Channel 4 in the hope it might

16 **tame** *here* harmless – 20 **to squirm** to make small twisting movements because of nervousness or embarrassment

never had a girlfriend in school / does not want to

include some nudity. During the eighties Channel 4 broadcast a series of 'red triangle' films; the red triangle was intended to inform viewers the films would have sexual content. I was surely not the only teenage boy who struggled manfully with obscure films like *Themroc* in the hope that at some point I was going to see a bare breast or two.

When I saw *Tarzan the Ape Man* I was convinced Bo Derek was the most beautiful woman I had ever seen. Her eyes, smile, delicate bone structure – not to mention her body – all seemed to my fourteen-year-old eyes to be the epitome of perfection. Why I thought Bo Derek would in any way be interested in hearing from a skinny teenage Pakistani boy from Luton I'm not certain but I wrote her a letter outlining just how much I liked her. She didn't write back.

While I was writing to American film stars and poring over old issues of *Amateur Photography* my friends at school had real girlfriends. This was never a realistic option for me. I knew my parents expected me to have an arranged marriage and anyway none of the girls at school fancied me. This was one of the cruellest consequences of being an Asian at a predominantly white school. When I was at high school, a fanciable Asian was an oxymoron. I had to make do with unrequited crushes on girls. The only relationships I had back then were in my head; I would fantasise about Colette, a pint-sized Bardot with dirty-blonde hair and bee-stung lips. I would construct elaborate fantasies in which we would be thrown together by fate. I imagined our next-door neighbours selling their house and Colette's parents buying it. Every morning we would walk to school together and we would get closer and closer until she would finally realise just how deep my feelings were for her. Naturally the next-door neighbours remained resolutely where they were and I remained invisible

10 **epitome** [ɪ'pɪtəmɪ] perfect example – 22 **oxymoron** stylistic device characterized by the combination of two contradictory words – 23 **unrequited** [ʌn'rɪkwaɪtɪd] not felt in the same way by the other person – 23 **crush** strong but short-lived feeling of love – 25 **pint-sized** *inf* small

does not know what love means

and asexual to Colette and all the other girls in my school. I was the funny one who did well in tests; I wasn't someone who was allowed to have sexual desires. If any such feelings were revealed it was bound to cause mirth and mayhem in school with jokes about kisses smelling of curry. Some girls enjoyed teasing me in class by calling my name and when I turned to face them they would smile seductively at me. It only took a few seconds before I would divert my eyes, my head hot with embarrassment. Once one of the girls knew she could produce such a delicious display of humiliation she would pass this knowledge to the others and soon enough half a dozen girls would be calling my name intent on attracting my attention.

As frustrating as it was to be ignored by girls at my high school it was also something of a relief because if a girl had fancied me I would have been able to do nothing about it. Falling in love would have been deeply inconvenient as it would have involved my parents disowning me and throwing me out of their home. I didn't know what love felt like but according to the songs I was listening to when I was fourteen, it was overpowering, and its power overwhelming. When you fell in love it seemed you no longer had control over your emotions and you became a slave to your desires. This scared me. The most frightening description of love was in the Pet Shop Boys' song 'Love Comes Quickly'. The way they described it was almost as if you had control over falling in love; walk down a street or turn a corner and bam! that was it, you were in love.

That's all well and good, I remember thinking, but what happens if the girl you love doesn't love you back or doesn't even know you exist? What happens if love comes quickly and you can't do anything about it?

My father treated the concept of love with a withering mixture of contempt and pity. 'What is love, anyway?' he would ask. 'Love is childish, anyone can fall in love, a ten-year-old

4 **mirth** [mɜːθ] laughter – 4 **mayhem** great disorder – 17 **to disown** to say that one has no connection with – 31 **withering** intended to make one feel ashamed

can say they are in love but can you trust a ten-year-old to stay with the same person for forty years? That is what is wrong with the white people: they put their faith in the heart rather than the head.' There was an uncomfortable disparity between the world view of my parents and the universe of my friends. The films I watched and the music I listened to were filled with the magic and wonder of romantic love and yet at home it was continually being made clear to me that I would never know what love was. Love was futile and foolish, marriage was sensible, solid and stable. Naive individuals fell in love, good sons got married.

I was in my third year at high school the first time I attended a wedding. It was held, as all Pakistani weddings in Luton were during the eighties, in a recreation centre that was hired for the day. Pakistani social life revolved around attending weddings and once we were living in Marsh Farm it was the one time when I was in the company of a large number of other Pakistanis. My family would hire a taxi to drive us to the venue, making sure we had not eaten beforehand. We would all have dressed specially for the occasion, my mother wearing a dozen gold bangles on each wrist, my sisters in new outfits and me in my imitation Farah trousers and shoes with tiny tassels. In the main hall traditional Pakistani wedding songs would blast from speakers, there would be rows of tables and chairs and on the tables were gigantic pots with steaming hot pilau rice, chicken curry, tandoori chapattis and other dishes that we would scoop on to paper plates and eat with plastic cutlery.

Seated together at the front of the hall would be the new husband and wife, the man wearing an elaborate golden turban and ornate kurta pyjama while his bride would be obscured under layers of garish make-up and mountains of gold jewellery. What I remember most vividly was the looks on the

9 **futile** ['fju:taɪl] useless – 22 **tassels** bunch of threads tied together as a decoration – 26 **to scoop on** to put on – 31 **garish** unpleasantly bright

expected to marry a strange

faces of the bride and groom. They always looked miserable. I later learnt that it was the custom that the girl should not appear to be enjoying herself. At the time, however, whenever I looked at the married couple I would feel a stabbing fear: was this to be my fate too? Everyone stuffing their faces with free food while two strangers looked into each other's eyes and wondered what on earth they had agreed to?

The most important duty for Pakistani parents was to successfully marry off their children, they did not believe themselves to be good parents until they had fulfilled this responsibility so, for them, this was their happiest day. It was inevitable that sometime during the afternoon someone would nudge my father or mother and say, 'and when will it be time for your younger one?' It was a joke and my parents would treat it as such but it turned my blood cold. It reminded me that some day I would be expected to marry a stranger.

My father began openly discussing my marriage when I was fifteen. He would be reading the newspaper or watching television and all it took was a reference to divorce for him to start in on me. On Christmas Day 1986 the whole family were watching *East Enders*. Den had only just presented Angie with divorce papers. 'You know why she is getting divorced?' Dad asked me. 'It is because these whites don't believe in marriage, for them it is just a game. There is no commitment any more. Get bored of one person, just find another. That's their style. Have you seen the figures? One marriage in three ends in divorce.'

'Maybe it's a good thing?' I said suddenly.

'A good thing!' my father said, sounding shocked. 'How can it be a good thing?'

'Well, maybe their relationship is over,' I said slowly, 'and being married does not make them happy…'

24 **commitment** the willingness to fulfill a promise

'Being happy?' retorted my father. 'You think that's what marriage is about? Marriage is about commitment and family and having someone to look after you when you get old. Being happy! Look at me and your mum. If it was about "being happy" do you think I would have worked like a donkey to bring your mother and you children to England when I could have married someone from here? The problem with people from here is that all they think about is being happy for now. That's why they have girlfriends and boyfriends, all that rubbish. They get married at sixteen, move out of their parents' home and then two years later they are divorced. All because they wanted to "be happy".'

'Yes but not everyone gets divorced at that age…' I protested.

'You don't have to believe me, just look at the statistics! Have you ever heard of anyone from Pakistan getting divorced? It's impossible. We have more respect and we know that when you get married it is for the long term. When English people get married all they are thinking about is themselves but when Pakistanis get married they are thinking of their families and they are thinking of honour.'

Honour: the shame of letting down people who I did not know or care about. The terror that my behaviour might reflect badly on my family consumed my father. I could not believe that other people spent their time thinking about me or the rest of my family, and if they did that simply made them tragically sad, so either way I could not care less about what they, these unidentified others, thought of what I did. Nonetheless my parents appeared to live their lives in perpetual fear about what 'the community' might think.

In the same way as I was brought up to believe love and marriage were entirely distinct, I was also raised to understand that parental approval was conditional. When he talked about

22 **to let down** to disappoint somebody's expectations – 29 **perpetual** endless – 32 **distinct** separate

consequences if S. wants to be like white people

marriage my father framed it as a choice. 'It's up to you,' he would say. 'You can marry anyone you like; do what your friends will do and have girlfriends and live with them. This is England, I cannot make you do anything you do not want to do. But I can tell you what I want you to do: find some respectable girl from back home, someone who is a good Muslim, who will look after you and your mother and who you know will be there for you in good times and bad. Now of course, if you were to take the first choice, if you wanted to be like your English friends, there would be consequences. I will not tolerate anyone bringing this name into disrepute. So if you want to do your own thing, that is fine, but you cannot expect to live under this roof. You will be like your English friends: on your own.'

'I never said I wanted to be like them,' I would mumble in protest, the prospect of being booted out of my bedroom filling me with alarm.

'You don't need to say anything: I know the films and television you watch, the music you listen to. But you must remember: you are not like them, you have your own culture and your traditions. Look at Benazir Bhutto: she was the daughter of a prime minister, educated at Oxford and yet she had an arranged marriage. Do you think you are better than her?'

My father often cited the example of Benazir Bhutto since she was a hugely successful and well-known woman. 'No, I've never said anything about not wanting an arranged marriage.'

'So tell me what your intentions are? How old are you now? Fifteen? You need to start thinking about the future and what you want to do. If you want to go down the honourable route, these things take time. The best girls are snapped up quickly. I need to know that you are serious.'

'It's not that I don't want to, it's just that it feels too soon. I don't think I am ready for marriage.'

1 **to frame** to express – 15 **to boot out** to kick out – 20 **Benazir Bhutto** former Prime Minister (1988-1990) of Pakistan and the first woman elected to lead a Muslim state

cannot sleep thinking about the arranged marriage

'Marriage is not something you are ready for, son, it is something that you say yes to and then you become ready for it. Education, work, these things will happen anyway but marriage you have to plan for.'

'Can I think about it?'

'You can think about it, there is no hurry but remember: I will not have anyone in my family bringing dishonour to my name.'

After these conversations I would not be able to sleep. I would toss and turn in my bed, plotting ways that I could avoid further discussions. Sometimes Navela would come to my room when she saw my bedroom light was still on. 'What's the matter?' she'd ask. She was much closer to being married than I was, my father had even visited Pakistan seeking potential husbands for her and yet she did not seem panic-stricken by the prospect. 'I know it's a bit strange but you're not the only one who it's going to happen to,' she would tell me. 'It's just the way it is. It happens to everyone.' Navela would then recite a verse from the Koran, and after she had finished, she would blow gently on my face and sweep her hand across my face. 'That will help you sleep,' she would say. 'Do you want to try sleeping with the lights out?'

'No, leave them as they are,' I would reply, crawling under my blanket.

* * *

The two things everyone knew about Muslims was that we did not drink and we had arranged marriages. Throughout my teenage years I was relentlessly quizzed on both topics, and the biggest question of them all was would I really be having an arranged marriage? I didn't know the answer to that, and I didn't know if it would even be up to me so eventually I settled on an answer: 'I think my parents would like me to have one,' I

does not want to marry a Pakistani girl

would say, 'and I think it would really be so much easier if I did, but I don't know whether I will or not and if I met someone I really liked I would probably just go for it.'

One evening I was at Scott's house. We had just played on his Astro Wars and were about to play a few frames of snooker. I had given my stock response to his mother but she still wanted to know more. 'Do you think it would matter if the girl you fell in love with was white?' She asked the question innocently enough but it was an explosive enquiry.

'Well, I think that would be a bit of a problem,' I said with massive understatement.

My father never explicitly said anything against dating or marrying a white girl but all his talk about bringing shame to the family, not letting the family down, not blackening the name of the family amounted to him saying 'keep your hands off white girls'. This was, at the time, a distressingly simple task.

'Well, I know you've explained it all before but it still sounds very peculiar to me,' said Scott's mother.

You and me both, I said to myself.

'Leave it out, Mum!' interjected Scott. 'He's not going to have an arranged marriage. Saf's English like me – he's not going to marry someone he doesn't know!'

He was right of course. Even when I gave my stock answer I knew I was lying through my teeth. Everything about an arranged marriage felt wrong.

The immediate future involved Navela whom my parents were becoming increasingly keen to see married. My father went with my sister to Pakistan in search of a potential husband. Navela had spent the first ten years of her life in Pakistan but it still shocked me that she was so unconcerned about marrying someone she didn't know. 'Just so long as he's not shorter than me,' was her main stipulation.

6 **stock response** standard answer – 33 **stipulation** statement of conditions

I had slightly higher expectations. I wanted a girl who was like Molly Ringwald in *The Breakfast Club* or Diane Keaton in *Annie Hall,* I wanted someone who would make me feel like Lionel Ritchie felt when he sang 'Hello' or to whom I could play Phil Oakey and Giorgio Moroder's 'Together in Electric Dreams'. Instead the song which most resonated with me, which accurately described the state of my heart, was Foreigner's 'I Want to Know What Love is'.

For all the years that I had been listening to and loving pop music I had been aware that it was a chaste obsession; it was a love affair without the sex. I hadn't been in love, hadn't met anyone who felt about me anything close to what those pop songs were about. The girls at my school had been fanciable but they had hardly noticed I existed.

It was not until I started a summer job making sandwiches where I met Laila that all my suppressed yearnings found their focus. We began work on the same day. There were other Asian girls in our group but I could not stop looking at Laila, at her huge eyes, long straight black hair streaked with red highlights, her floaty black gypsy skirt which hung about her ankles. When she told me later that she wrote short stories and poems and wanted to be a writer I asked her, 'Is there any point in you even going to college when you gonna have to marry someone from a village in Pakistan?'

'Like hell I am!' she shot back. 'I'm getting the fuck out of this shit-hole town first chance I get. You think I'm sticking around to study in Luton with its bloody college of higher bloody education? God Almighty!' She laughed. Laila had the filthiest laugh I had ever heard. It was a laugh you'd expect to come from a saucy barmaid, a big bold bawdy laugh which was all the more shocking coming from a sixteen-year-old Pakistani girl.

10 **chaste** [tʃeɪst] not taking part in sexual activity *(keusch)* – 16 **yearning** strong desire – 28 **filthy** dirty – 30 **saucy** producing sexual interest in an amusing way – 30 **bawdy** loud and dealing with sex in a humorous way

wants to meet Laila at his house

Laila became the reason I came to work. In my evenings, those hours when I was not speaking to her, I would hold imaginary conversations with her. Nothing in my life so far had prepared me for the churning stomach, the leaping bounds of my heart when I knew I would see her soon at work, nor the gloom that filled me on the weekends.

One weekend my family were due to go to Nottingham to see my brother. There were few times in my life when my home was mine alone and so I made my excuses. I began hatching a plan: why not take advantage of my family's absence and invite Laila home? We could maybe watch a video of one of those films that she had been telling me I needed to watch – *Billy Liar* or A *Matter of Life and Death*.

'Where do you live again?' she asked when I brought the topic up as I was delivering more sliced loaves to her to spread on to the moving platform.

'Marsh Farm,' I replied.

'And when are they going?'

'Saturday. Go on, it'll be really fun. Just for a few hours.'

'But we talk all the time anyway.'

'I know we do but I want you to see my house. I can even show you where Lea Manor is.'

'Sounds great.'

'OK, we don't have to see Lea Manor but honestly don't you think it could be fun? We can hang out.'

She didn't say anything. It felt like I was asking her out which of course I was.

'Yeah, OK' she said finally. 'I'll give you my phone number at lunchtime.'

I wanted to offer her mine, but there was no way that a girl could call me. The subsequent questions and shouting from my parents made that a non-starter. But Laila's parents were, I assumed, far more liberal and understanding.

4 **to churn** to move about violently – 6 **gloom** feeling of deep sadness – 31 **subsequent** ['sʌbsɪkwənt] following

told her dad
cos
→ never seen her again

'Hello, is Laila there?' I had finally summoned the courage to call the number.

'Who is speaking, please?' The man had a rough accent; I had imagined her father to be an educated, soft-spoken man.

'I'm a friend of Laila's. She is meant to be coming to my house.'

'Who is speaking? Laila coming to your house?'

'Yes, my name is Sarfraz. I work with Laila. She was meant to be coming round to see me today.' I was repeating myself because I did not know what else to say. This was not what I had been expecting.

'Your name Sarfraz? Laila not here. Goodbye.'

The phone went dead.

I saw Laila the following week. 'What the hell happened to you? I thought we were meant to be meeting up.'

'Yeah, and that's what would have happened if you hadn't blathered on to my dad!' Laila snapped. 'What were you thinking telling my dad I was going to see you?'

'I thought he would have known,' I said weakly.

'Think about it, Sherlock. Me telling Dad that I was going to see a boy at his house would have gone down like a bucket of cold sick. Honestly!'

'I'm sorry,' I offered.

'Yeah, well, kiss goodbye to me ever coming to your house. Kiss goodbye to me being allowed out of the fucking front door this decade! You know what, in a way you did me a favour. Because you reminded me just how much I hate my stinking life and this stinking town and my stinking family! I wish I could just tell them all to leave me the fuck alone so I could just vanish out on my own. That's what I want.'

That was the last time I ever saw Laila. I found out later that her father had demanded she leave the job in the sandwich factory.

1 **to summon** to collect with an effort – 17 **to blather** *inf* to talk foolishly for a long time

I had known her for only three weeks but Laila changed what I expected from my life. I had always suspected there was more than the kind of marriage my parents and everyone they knew had. I had crushes in the past but I had a deeper connection with Laila. So long as there were girls like her in the world it seemed insanity to accept my parents' demands that I marry someone from the villages of Pakistan.

I left Luton for Manchester and hoped that during my time at university I might meet a girl who would rescue me from having to contemplate an arranged marriage. I now had the freedom I had craved and I could be as debauched as I wished. However, even though I had put two hundred miles between me and my hometown, I could not so easily put my past behind me. Lacking in confidence, shy around pretty girls, hating my body and convinced no girl could see me as anything more than a friend, I was a troubled undergraduate. It was not until I decided to have dreadlocks that my self-esteem improved. As much fun as it was, the girls I met were always white, which meant that although I liked them it seemed unlikely they could be the one. I needed to meet a girl who was a Pakistani Muslim, someone my parents would approve of. But I rarely met another Asian. All my friends, male and female, were white. I sometimes wondered if perhaps the price of having gone to school and grown up with whites was that it was only going to be white girls to whom I would be attracted and who would like me. The only Asian girl I had liked was Laila and I had managed to ruin her summer, if not her life.

While I remained in Manchester I was protected from having to hear the complaints of my parents that I was becoming an embarrassment. All the other Pakistanis of my age had accepted their parents' wishes; my parents wanted to know how long I would continue to deny them their right to see me

6 **insanity** madness – 10 **to contemplate** to think (about) deeply – 11 **debauched** [dɪˈbɔːtʃt] behaving badly, especially in relation to sex and alcohol

S → 25 years
↳ should marry

married. Each time they bowled the question I batted it away. 'None of my friends are married,' I would say. 'All your friends are white,' my father would reply. 'Is that who you want to compare yourself to?' I endured the lectures and returned to Manchester and the lifestyle I was not yet willing to relinquish. At the Brickhouse, dancing to the Stone Roses and chatting up pretty young girls, the world my parents represented seemed very distant.

After my father died Navela came to our home and urged my mother to marry off both me and my sister. We hardly saw her, but she felt it was her duty as the eldest to set us straight. Now we were without a father we were not as attractive a proposition to any family looking for a match. The longer we left it the more desperate our plight would become. Uzma was nineteen and I was twenty-four. 'You don't want to be the last one left on the shelf,' Navela warned. 'What father is going to give you his daughter if he thinks our family won't be able to look after her?'

'But what about the girl!' I would shout back in irritation. 'What about the actual girl? Why does it have to be about money and status, why can't it just be about two people liking each other?'

Navela looked blankly back at me. I had hoped my sister and brother would have a more enlightened view, they seemed loath to offer me the freedom they had not enjoyed.

When I was twenty-five and had landed my job at ITN, I knew that yet another excuse had gone. So I did what I always did when the pressure became too much: I ran away.

I moved to London so my family could not continually hound me about marriage. My career began to take off, but the only news that would have pleased my mother was an announcement of marriage. However well I did at work it

1 **to bowl** to throw the ball (cricket) – 1 **to bat** to hit the ball with a (cricket) bat – 5 **to relinquish** to give up – 14 **plight** sad condition or situation – 23 **blankly** emptily, showing no understanding – 25 **loath** unwilling

was impossible for me to feel successful because each time I returned home I was left feeling like I had failed my family. It made for an intensely schizophrenic life.

'Don't make a mistake you will regret later, son,' my mother would say to me. 'One day you will realise that we were right all along but by then it will be too late. I just want to know you will be all right.'

'But I am all right, Mum,' I would tell her. 'Life is good! I am doing well. You don't have to worry about me.'

But she would worry. 'Who cooks for you?' she would ask and when I replied that I cooked for myself she would shake her head sadly. 'You need someone to take care of you,' she would urge. 'Do you not get bored of being on your own?'

'But I'm not on my own! I have lots of friends.'

'Aren't there any nice girls in your workplace?'

'No Pakistani girls,' I'd reply.

The wedding invitations continued to arrive at our home but I refused to attend. My appearance would only provoke embarrassment for my mother.

'I can't even walk to Bury Park now,' she would claim as she soaked scraps of old chapattis in water before feeding them to the birds. 'Everyone wants to know what is wrong with Mr Manzoor's children. Some even tell me that I am blind, they say you must have a girl in London. And how can I tell them they are wrong? How do I know I am not being made a fool? Aren't parents always the last to know?

You could be drinking, you could be with some *ghori* you are hiding from us. That is what they tell me and I smile at them and say, not my son, but what do I know? Son, you don't talk to me any more. I am just your dumb illiterate mother, the one who gave birth to you, and now when I want to talk to you you say not a word. Not a word. And so I yak away like an idiot to myself. That is my kismet.'

32 **to yak** *sl* to talk continuously about unimportant things – 33 **kismet** fate

It hurt me to hear her but I did not know what the compromise was, what I was meant to say that would make her feel better without me sacrificing my hard-won freedom.

Among the Asians at my sixth form college, some had married after their exams, others waited until after graduating from university; by the time I was thirty there was only Amolak and I who were still single. Neither of us wanted to sacrifice what we had achieved to marry a stranger. Amolak's parents were even more direct with him than my family were, they would insist he meet prospective brides who would arrive from Leicester, Leeds and Bedford with hopeful parents keen for their daughter to marry a wealthy banker. His strategy was to behave as if he was the most arrogant and obnoxious person on the planet. It would take no more than ten minutes before the girl would be led out of the house by her horrified parents while Amolak's father tried to apologise for his son's behaviour. When his father tried to reprimand him my friend would tell him he was not yet ready to think about marriage and when he was he would let him know. 'I'm just not ready to give up my Saturday nights out with the boys,' Amolak would tell me. 'You know as well as I do that as soon as you got that fucking ring on your finger that's it, say goodbye to the good times and hello B and fucking Q. I ain't ready for that shit.' Amolak claimed he was already resigned to his first marriage failing. 'The way I see it there's only so long the two of us can stop the inevitable. So basically, if you assume in a couple of years you'll get married, that will go to pot when the fact that you've got nothing in common starts becoming an issue. So by then you're in your mid-to late-thirties, you're a free agent and you've still got time to find The One.'

13 **obnoxious** very unpleasant and offensive – 17 **to reprimand** to express strong disapproval – 22 **hello B and fucking Q** refers to the B & Q stores where people can buy all sorts of houshold appliances – 25 **inevitable** [ɪnˈevɪtəbl] unable to be avoided

'So you're telling me you've factored in your first marriage breaking up?' I asked him.

'It stands to reason: the first one will be for my parents and the second one will be for me.'

Both of us knew what we wanted – a girl who would understand us – but the chances of such a girl existing and also being the correct race and religion seemed negligible.

When I had heard 'Born to Run' it had seemed the most romantic song I had ever heard; the girl I wanted to spend the rest of my life with was someone to whom I could say the lines that Bruce sings to Wendy in that song: 'we'll live with the sadness and I will love you with all the madness in my soul.' I was not going to be able to say that to some girl from a Pakistani village whom my parents had imported into the country.

Each time a Springsteen tour came round we told each other we were obliged to see as many shows as possible because who knew when the next time might be and whether we would be able to attend. We disregarded the countless number of married couples we met at concerts, that was not going to be our fate. 'Enjoy it while we can, mate,' Amolak would say as we boarded the plane or the Eurostar, heading to yet another concert. 'It ain't gonna be going on for ever. Next time the man comes round who knows where we'll be.'

As long as there was another Bruce Springsteen concert I could put aside the big questions about what I was doing with my life. So long as there was Bruce to love I could try to forget that there was no one to love me. And yet as the number of concerts I attended continued to rise, the gnawing sense that I was letting myself down remained. Listening to Springsteen had never been about the cold accumulation of concert tickets; if I measured my devotion only in how far I travelled or how many concerts I attended, how did that make me any

1 **to factor in** to include in a calculation

have no expectations in love

different from a fan of Barry Manilow? The true fans of Bruce Springsteen were those who had absorbed the wisdom in his songs, who saw him not only as a musician but as a role model, someone who had married a woman he loved and did a job he enjoyed surrounded by some of his best friends. Neither Amolak nor I had love in our lives, we only had friendship and fear. Once it had been the fear of an arranged marriage, but by the time we were in our early thirties that fear had been replaced by another: the fear of being alone.

Since the death of my father my brother had become head of the family; with that status came the task of discussing marriage. The most frustrating thing about listening to my brother was that as much as I disagreed with some of what he said, I had no practical alternatives. If he had been in an unhappy marriage I could argue that I was unwilling to repeat the same mistakes he had made. The truth, however, was that his marriage was astoundingly successful. In the years that Nazia had been in Luton she had learned perfect English, had passed her driving test, was an equal partner in the family property business and had also had two gorgeous children. She was not the stereotyped, subservient Pakistani village girl; in fact, I had more fun talking to her than with my own family. Driving around town in their people carrier, dressed in jeans and stylish tops, my sister-in-law was a strong argument in favour of arranged marriage. It was not surprising my brother believed marrying his wife had been the best decision he had ever made; it probably was. And yet as happy as I was for him I was still certain I did not want an old-style arranged marriage. Why? I blamed Bruce Springsteen.

Listening to Bruce had ruined my love life. All those songs about love had affected my expectations. If not for Bruce, I might have grown up and settled for the love of a sensible girl.

17 **astoundingly** surprisingly – 21 **subservient** willing to do what others want

'think you are going to stay young for ever'

Instead, I knew my ideal girl would be someone to whom I could play 'Born to Run', 'Backstreets' and 'Racing in the Street' and who would get it. There wasn't a chance I was going to find that amongst any Pakistani girls – it wasn't that likely around English girls – and yet, in hoping for the kind of love found in the songs of Bruce Springsteen, at the age of thirty-three I found myself single and alone: a rebel without a clue.

It was about this time that *Friends* ended its long run on television. It may have been just a TV show, but its demise threw me into a crisis. *Friends* legitimised singledom, it promoted friendship over love and so long as Ross, Rachel and others were living the single life in Manhattan I felt I had permission to live the single life in London. So when Ross and Rachel and Monica and Chandler and Phoebe and Mike all found each other, it couldn't help but force me to think about my own life and concede the most important thing was missing.

My single white friends were either spending hours on the telephone complaining about how hard it was to meet anyone or they were out speed-dating and bar-hopping. And for me the years of freedom in Manchester and London had not led to The One. What was so different, I began to wonder, about meeting a girl through speed-dating and being introduced to someone through the family? In both cases you would be meeting a stranger with a view to a possible relationship. Both situations were contrived, what made one socially acceptable and the other not?

'You know what the trouble with you is?' Sohail said to me one evening when I was sitting in his front room. 'You think you are going to stay young for ever. You don't know how quickly time goes. And when time starts going, so does your body. You need to think about who is going to be around for you when you can't manage living on your own.'

7 **rebel without a clue** (usually) rebel without a cause – 9 **demise** [dɪˈmaɪz] the end of sth important or powerful – 16 **to concede** to admit as true – 25 **contrived** [kənˈtraɪvd] artificial

telephone calls for Sarfraz for marriage

These were questions I had been asking myself and I did not know what the answer was. My brother was the one with the supportive wife. I had my logically worked out arguments and cleverly constructed responses, but I was alone.

'You know how embarrassed Mum is,' continued my brother. 'She says she is scared of going down to Bury Park in case anyone asks about you and Uzma. As far as I am concerned you can do what you like but now that Dad isn't around it's up to me to tell you what Mum is thinking and she wants you to think about getting married.'

'So what does she want me to do?' I said slowly.

'She just wants to have permission to spread the word her son is looking, that's all,' he replied. 'There won't be any pressure, she just wants you to meet some girls.'

'All right,' I said. 'If Mum wants to let people know about me that's fine, but on one condition: I am not meeting any parents. If there's a girl who you think might have potential, she has to call me or give me her number and I will talk to her one to one. I don't want any of this parents talking to parents and the people don't even chat crap.'

Each time I returned to Luton the phone would ring. 'Is your mother there?' the woman would ask in Urdu.

'Yes, can I ask who it is?' I would reply.

'Yes, it is about a girl for you,' the woman would answer.

'In that case you can speak to me, auntie.'

'All right, son. Tell me how tall are you?'

'Five ten.'

'And what is your monthly wage?'

'Auntie, it is not polite to ask about money.'

'And how old are you?'

'Let me get my mother.'

My mother would scurry downstairs and I would hear her answering the questions coming from the other end of the telephone. 'Yes, of course he works... he is a journalist... Yes, thanks to Allah he does have a full head of hair... no, he doesn't have a car... age? Sister, he is thirty-three but you know with the young people these days they do not want to get married young like we did and he spent so much time making his career... By all means you can come but he is very busy, he works in London, you understand... And about your daughter? I'm sure she is very successful... So you will give our number to her? Very good, sister... Goodbye.'

When I came back to Luton at weekends there would be a notepad next to the phone upon which would be written telephone numbers and one-word descriptions: insurance, computers, dentist. Often I had no idea of even the names of the girls. I was tempted to throw them away but the nagging possibility that the numbers might lead me to The One forced me to keep them in my back pocket.

All I knew about one girl was that she had studied at Cambridge. This seemed promising. I assumed the girl must have something to her, it was worth at least a phone call. I dialled the number. 'Hello, this is Sarfraz, your mum gave my mum your number.'

'Oh hi, yes, hello...' said a voice on the other end.

'I don't know anything about you but I thought, what the hell, I might as well give you a call. If you went to Cambridge University you must be worth talking to!'

'I see...' said the girl, her voice trailing off, '... but I went to a college in Cambridge, not the university.'

I tried to mask my disappointment and we talked about what each of us did and films we liked. It was clear I had nothing in common with this girl but I didn't want to be rude in case she was beautiful. 'It's a bit strange not knowing what you look like,

1 **to scurry** to move hastily

Talking with a special girl => wants to see her

isn't it?' I said to her. 'I tell you what, why don't I email you a pic and you can email me something too… Don't worry,' I joked. 'I'm not gross or anything… but don't expect someone fucking gorgeous either!'

'I hope you don't mind me saying this but I really don't approve of foul language,' said the girl.

'Oh right, well, I'm sorry about that,' I said. 'So, can you send me a picture?'

'Yes, I can, but I wear a hijab so you won't see all that much.'

'You wear a hijab?' I repeated.

'Yes, didn't my mother tell you that?'

'No, she didn't,' I replied.

That was the trouble with asking parents to find girls: they did not have a clue. How had it ever occurred to them that a God-fearing, super-Muslim was going to be my ideal bride? 'Listen, to be honest, I'm not sure there's much point in us exchanging pics,' I told the girl. 'The fact is I'm just not going to be a good enough Muslim for you.'

'I'm sure that's not true,' she replied.

'It is true. I'm really shallow, I don't drink but I do like to have a good time and I just get the feeling we won't have anything in common.'

'How can you say that? We've only been talking for a few minutes,' she said.

'OK, let me ask you something,' I said in one last-ditch attempt to salvage something from the wreckage of the phone call, 'do you like Bruce Springsteen?'

'Bruce Springsteen?'

'Yeah, the singer, do you like him, have you ever heard anything by him?'

'Oh, I'm sorry, I don't really like English music.'

As I feared, when it came to suitable girls my mother was almost comically clueless. The promised dentist would turn out

3 **gross** fat and ugly – 20 **shallow** not deep, lacking seriousness – 25 **last-ditch** made after many failures and with little hope for success – 26 **to salvage** save from loss or damage

 said no to every girl

to be a dietician, the biochemist would be working at Boots; everyone seemed a little too into religion; none sounded like they might actually be a laugh. Where were the sexy Pakistani girls? I wondered. Where were the passionate ones? Perhaps it was too optimistic to have hoped my mother would have had access to them. When I reported back to Amolak he was not surprised, it had been a similar experience for him meeting girls who were better on paper than in the flesh. 'Time's running out for us, dude,' he'd say to me gloomily, 'soon it's only gonna be the divorcee market left.'

Having initially been delighted by my willingness to meet some prospective wives, my mother began to complain that I was not taking the enterprise seriously. 'This is not some game that you can meet all these girls and keep turning them down,' she warned me. 'These families have their honour, what do you think they must feel when you tell them their daughter is not good enough? Say no to one girl, fine, two or even three girls. But if you keep refusing everyone you talk to this is not good.'

It was not good for me either; I had naively hoped to find someone, a girl whom I could love with all the madness in my soul.

When I was asked to present *Luton Actually* I agreed but on one condition: I was not, on any account, going to talk about love and relationships. The official reason I gave was that I felt uncomfortable discussing such things in public when I had failed to discuss them in private. That was not the whole truth; I was reluctant to talk about love because I had nothing to say. In matters of the heart I was a failure, I could talk about politics and identity and religion endlessly but ask me about love and I would fall silent. The longer I remained without it the less

1 **dietician** [daɪəˈtɪʃn] sb who professionally advises people about food and eating habits

Concentrate on career

confident I became that I would ever know what love truly was and the more I buried myself in work.

Following the broadcast of the documentary Sohail and my mother stopped harassing me about getting married. The programme had penetrated my brother's consciousness; he no longer considered me a failure. 'You need to concentrate on your career,' he began urging. In the past when I had suggested to my family that the right girl for me was unlikely to come from a rural village in Pakistan they had accused me of arrogance, now my mother seemed more relaxed about me following my own path in life. I felt liberated from family expectations and more confident than I had ever been before that when the right girl did come into my life, my family would no longer stand in the way of my happiness.

My life had been a journey from fear. Ever since I was little I had been frightened of the future. When I was young I had been frightened of the future as it might have meant being alone. Now at the age of thirty-five I was no longer afraid. I did not know what the future might bring but, finally, it offered the promise of better days.

- about the meanings of love/marriage
- doing some boys stuff / watching films / reading magazines
- arranged (families) marriages
- in high school times: he never had a girlfriend
  ↳ does not know how to show feelings / what's love / ⇒ father explains
- → thinking about his own marriage
  ↳ explained by the father (honour, no divorces)
- met Laila ⇒ ruined her life/relationship
  ↳ a lot of calls for Sarfraz for a marriage

can't believe that he is a Muslim

Reason to Believe

God have mercy on the man who doubts what he's sure of
'Brilliant Disguise', Bruce Springsteen

I cried the first time I realised that I was a Muslim. It was Christmas 1977 and I was six years old. The most important thing in my world at the time was convincing my father to buy me an acoustic guitar so I could copy the bearded man on television who sang 'Mull of Kintyre'. Religion meant little to me. At school assemblies I would be with all the other Pakistani boys and girls singing 'Lord of the Dance' and 'Once in Royal David's City'; my best friend Tanveer and I both had small parts in our school production of *Joseph and the Amazing Technicolor Dreamcoat.* They were great songs and fabulous stories, I accepted them like I had the commemorative Silver Jubilee medallion and tangerine during that special assembly earlier in the year.

By the seventies Bury Park was already overwhelmingly Pakistani, and the halal butchers, sari centres and carpet stores did not shut down for Christmas. When men like my father went to buy their bags of chapatti flour and cans of ghee it was not the plight of Mr Callaghan that they discussed but the military coup in Pakistan which had brought General Zia to power.

At Eid my father would buy live chickens from the local farm and sacrifice them in the back yard, throwing their heads into the fireplace as my mother starting plucking them. My father did not work on Eid, but Christmas was an opportunity for him to earn double time while the whites ate turkey and watched

12 **Joseph and the Amazing Technicolor Dreamcoat** musical based on motifs from the Christian Bible – 21 **James Callaghan** Prime Minister of the United Kingdom between 1976 and 1979 – 22 **General Zia** Muhammad Zia-ul-Haq sixth president of Pakistan

Mike Yarwood on television. While he was working the rest of us remained bored at home.

During one Christmas week, while the rest of the family were busy, two-year-old Uzma and I watched television and that was how I came to see *Jesus of Nazareth*. As a six-year-old I did not appreciate the religious significance of the series; to me Jesus was just another superhero like Spider-Man, Steve Austin and the Incredible Hulk. I might not have known much about religion but I knew that superheroes did not die, which was why I burst into a flood of tears when at the end of *Jesus of Nazareth* Robert Powell was hung from a cross, his face bleeding from his crown of thorns. My tears made Uzma wail too. My mother came running in. 'Why are you crying?' she asked when we both rushed into her arms.

'They've killed Jesus!' I explained as the tears kept streaming down my face.

'What did you say? Who killed Jesus?' said my mother drying my eyes with her dupatta.

'The Romans,' I said, pointing at the screen. 'It was on television.'

Hearing my explanation, my mother stopped drying my tears. She looked me in the eyes and said, 'So that's why you're crying? Son, we are Muslims. It is the Christians who cry about Jesus.'

That made no sense to me. An innocent man had just been crucified and my mother was telling me I was not allowed to be upset. I started crying again. I wanted to be able to feel sorry for Jesus, I was not sure I wanted to be a Muslim.

When my family moved to Marsh Farm in the autumn of 1979 I was placed in a school where I was the only Muslim in the class. The boys I had been friends with at Maidenhall were starting

1 **Mike Yarwood** English comedian and TV star who was very popular in the 1960s and 1970s – 12 **to wail** to cry with a long sound of grief or pain

explanation about their religion

to attend daily after-school Koran classes but I lived too far to join them. In Maidenhall my friends had names like Haroon, Ali and Tanveer, in Wauluds my new friends were called Scott, Robert and Craig. After first agreeing that I could attend assembly so long as I only mouthed the hymns and did not actually sing them, my father changed his mind and requested that I be taken out of morning assembly. Each morning while my friends were singing hymns I would be drawing with Jason, the Jehovah's Witness, whose parents had also demanded he be exempted from the assembly.

It was during the first Christmas in Marsh Farm that I began to resent that I was Muslim. In the week before the holidays, normal lessons were suspended. Instead, our teachers asked us to bring in packets of biscuits, cans of soup and other non-perishable foods which we would then deliver to the elderly. By way of reward, once the hampers had been dispatched we were allowed to bring in toys from home for a week of officially sanctioned fun. Scott brought Ker-Plunk, Robert had a game called Buzz, which involved passing a metal loop around a wavy course, and Craig casually walked in with a pool table under his arms. I was forced to play with my friends' toys without offering anything in return. When they asked why I did not have any of my own, I replied that toys were against my religion.

If I complained about that, my father would answer, 'Why are you trying to copy them when you have your own religion?' As if to remind me, above the sofa was a framed photograph of Mecca at the time of the Hajj pilgrimage. On either side of the photograph were two bronze-coloured plaques with quotations from the Koran in Arabic. My mother had told me that the quotations said that there was no God but Allah and that Mohammed was his messenger but I did not then

10 **to exempt** to excuse sb from a duty or service – 12 **to resent** to feel anger and dislike about – 14 **non-perishable food** food that can be kept long – 16 **hamper** large basket with a lid

Start reading the Koran → Allah is always watching.

understand their significance. Islam was like those plaques: hanging over me, significant but indecipherable. Both Sohail and Navela had read the Koran, taught by my mother at home and Uzma and I both knew our time was coming.

The Koran that my brother and sister had read had its own section in the display cabinet. It had been brought to England by my father when he had left Pakistan in the early sixties and it had remained with him throughout the decade as he moved jobs and homes. There was a rigid code of behaviour relating to the Koran: while it was in the cabinet we could not turn our back to it, point our feet in its direction or hold it without first washing our hands. Even before I had started reading it, the Koran exerted a potent power over me, continually reminding me that I was not a good Muslim. The quotations on the wall and the Koran in the cabinet gave the impression that Allah was always watching me, aware of every lapse into sinfulness. Apparently there were people who had memorised the entire Koran; there were special schools back in Pakistan where young boys would spend hours studying the text. Those who succeeded in committing the entire volume to memory were rewarded by Allah with an automatic place in Heaven. When she told me this my mother presumed this would motivate me to learn Arabic. To my young mind this offer of a guaranteed place in Heaven seemed like a free ticket to commit any and every sort of sin. Each time I thought this it made me realise how far I had still to go to be a good Muslim.

I began learning Arabic in the same week that The Police were number one with 'Don't Stand So Close to Me' and seven Irish prisoners began a hunger strike. Each evening I would watch the news, eat my chapattis and read *The Guinness Book of Astronomy,* fantasising about what it might be like to own a telescope. Then my father would ask, 'Have you read your Arabic today?' The television was switched off and Uzma and I

2 indecipherable [ɪndɪˈsaɪfrəbl] impossible to be read or understood

would sit with my mother at the dining table. My mother would start by saying a letter of the alphabet and we would repeat it. She would then say the next letter and we would repeat that. After five letters she would say them again in sequence and we would say them back to her.

Once we had mastered the alphabet she read us stories in Urdu that we then read back to her; both Urdu and Arabic used the same alphabet so my sister and I learnt both languages simultaneously. There were differences: in Arabic there were symbols that indicated how letters would be pronounced but in Urdu we just had to guess. Then again,

In Urdu I knew what the words meant; although I was pronouncing my Arabic correctly I had no idea what I was saying. 'Don't worry if you can't understand the words,' my mother would say reassuringly. 'Allah is very pleased with anyone who reads the Koran, you will be blessed with good fortune for reading it.' Although it was relatively straightforward to read the words from the page it was not making me feel any closer to Islam; the Arabic words I would read out loud made a pleasant sound but that was all they were: pleasant sounds.

My task was to complete the entire Koran. Every evening I would go to the bathroom and wash myself in the manner that my mother had taught me. First the hands, then my arms up to the elbows and then my face including ears and neck. Finally I would place my feet in the bathtub and splash cold water on them and my ankles. Only then would I take the Koran from the display cabinet into my parents' bedroom, lay it flat on my mother's pillow, put on a white cotton cap and, sitting cross-legged, start reading. I wrote the page number I had reached each night on a green piece of card. Once I had read out loud for thirty minutes I would write down the new page number and close the Koran.

praying to the Koran for wishes / health
thinking of angels

I had a ritual once I had finished for the evening. I would kiss the Koran on the front and back and all four sides, having a silent conversation with Allah, and make six wishes, one for each kiss. Please can you persuade my father to buy me a ZX Spectrum. Please can you persuade my father to take me to London Zoo. Please could you persuade my father to buy me a telescope. Please can you make me less skinny. Please can you make us really rich. Please can you make sure that my mother and father never die. I would say out loud: 'Please, Allah, don't let anything happen to Mum or Dad.' We did not have any other relatives in this country and one of my greatest fears was that if something happened to my parents I would be left alone.

My mother loved telling me stories about Islam and the Prophet. When I came home at lunchtimes she would sit with me in the lounge and tell me about the origins of Islamic festivals. In the evenings when she was pickling peppers or preparing to make yoghurt she would tell me about the angel Gabriel who had brought Allah's words to the Prophet. I was a reluctant audience but my mother was so passionate in her telling that despite myself I would find myself captivated. She told me about the two angels who watched everything I did. 'One writes down the good deeds and the other writes down the bad deeds. We cannot see these angels because they are made of things our human eyes cannot see but they are there all the same.' She told me that on the Day of Judgement each man would have to account for his sins and if the good deeds outweighed the bad he would be admitted to Heaven. My first impulse after hearing this was that I had to tell my schoolfriends about the angels. They needed to have the chance to get into Heaven.

4 **ZX Spectrum** personal home computer – 17 **peppers** *Paprika* – 20 **reluctant** unwilling – 21 **to captivate** to keep sb's attention by being interesting

parents are proud
↳ finished reading the Koran

We were playing football in the courtyard outside school when Scott asked me what I had done the previous night. I told him I had been reading the Koran and related the tale of the angels. 'Say something Koranic,' he said.

'It's not Koranic, it's Arabic,' I explained, 'and I don't want to. Didn't you hear what I just said about the angels and how they know everything?'

'Go on! Say hello or something.'

'I don't know how to say hello, I just know stuff that's in the Koran.'

'Say that then.'

I had by now learnt some passages by heart and was secretly quite proud of this. I quoted a few sentences in Arabic. Within seconds a crowd had gathered around me, listening to what I had just said. 'Do it again! Do it again!' I felt like Paul Daniels or Doug Henning being asked to repeat a particular trick. I quoted another passage from the Koran. Again, pandemonium in the courtyard, the football game was abandoned and I found myself surrounded by cheering boys. It was as if I had scored the winning goal for our school. Even the tough boys, the ones we were all scared of, could not hide their curiosity at my special talent. As I went into school I could not wait to get home and learn more from the Koran. I hoped that the morning's events were recorded by the good angel.

I finally completed the Koran seven months after I started. This delighted my parents who happily rang their friends to tell them the good news. 'Not even nine years old and he has read it,' my mother would say down the telephone, 'and I taught him at home, just like his brother and sister.' Secretly, I had hoped for something amazing to occur in the instant that I finished the last page of the Koran, perhaps not a miracle but at least a sense of well-being, a spiritual glow that might briefly

17 **pandemonium** a state of wild and noisy disorder

Koran reading afternoons at the age of 9

envelop me and make me feel connected to my religion. But I felt nothing. I had not understood a single word I had spent the past seven months reading and when I asked my mother what I was expected to do on completion she answered that I had to read the whole thing again. 'And soon you can start learning how to pray too.'

Great.

Once every few months my mother would organise a Koran reading afternoon where she would invite other Pakistani women and some of their children to our home. These events were usually held on Sunday afternoons. In the morning we would take the bus to Bury Park to buy food that we carried home in plastic bags which had photographs of baskets of fruit printed on them. While my mother bought meat and rice and bottles of Tibet cream, I would buy the latest edition of *Stardust*, which was a magazine devoted to the Bollywood film industry. We would return home and an old bed sheet would be spread on the floor of the lounge and my mother would begin preparing food. On the bed sheet was the Koran, not the blue volume but one bought from Pakistan which was divided into thirty separate sparas or chapters. Once everyone had arrived, they would sit cross-legged on the sheet, take a spara and start reading. Having completed the Koran, both my sister and I took part. When the women saw that we would also be reading, they congratulated my mother. 'What good children you have, to have read the Koran at such a tender age and at home! Allah will be sure to reward them for their good hearts.'

My father excused himself from those Koran reading afternoons. He was more political than religious, more Pakistani than Muslim. Naturally he wanted his children to have read the Koran and learn how to pray but that desire was as much about preserving culture as exploring Islam.

starts going to mosque

Eid was the best part of being Muslim. On the morning of Eid my father would wake me at seven and I would stumble half asleep into the bathroom where I would do what were apparently called 'absolutions'. After a quick mug of tea my father and I would go to the mosque for morning prayers. In the first few years that we lived in Marsh Farm there was no purpose-built mosque in Luton; instead we would all gather in a converted terraced house in Bury Park. Dozens of Pakistanis and Bengalis would meet and file into the living room, a mountain of shoes piled in the back garden as the white neighbours occasionally peered from behind the curtains.

By the time I started at Lea Manor High School a brand-new purpose-built mosque had opened in the heart of Bury Park. It was built from red stone and at the top of its minaret was a crescent moon, which was the highest point in Bury Park. Wherever you walked in the area the minaret was visible.

In the first week that it was opened, racists hung a pig's head from the crescent moon. The search for the culprits lasted months but no one was ever caught. For my father it was just more proof that we would never be welcome in this country. 'Those dogs who did this. They must have known that the pig is an unclean animal but you see how much effort they went to? That is how much they hate us.'

As much as I loved Eid – the new clothes, the ten-pound notes from my parents' friends when they visited, the pilau rice and visits to the Ambala Sweet Centre – visiting the mosque was deeply embarrassing. It would start with my father and I sitting cross-legged with hundreds of others. The men in the mosque were of all ages. Old men with pointed silk prayer caps, henna beards and dyed hair, their children with freshly greased side partings concealed by white cotton prayer hats. My father dressed for once not in his suit but in a traditional

4 **absolution** forgiveness for a sin – 18 **crescent moon** ['kresnt] the curved shape of the moon when it forms less than half a circle – 18 **culprit** person guilty of a crime – 30 **to dye** to give a different colour – 31 **side parting** *Seitenscheitel*

pray in the mosque with his father

kurta pyjama, immaculately pressed and smelling of Brut aftershave.

The imam sat at the front and spoke in an Urdu that was so ornate I could barely understand a word. From what I could gather the imam rarely deviated from two themes: the need to get closer to Allah, and the related theme which suggested that the best way to get closer to Allah was to donate some money to the mosque. 'They've built their mosque why is there still a cash fund?' my father would grumble as the imam pleaded for us to dig deep into our hearts and pockets.

Following his pleas two men would walk past each row of worshippers with an outstretched bed sheet. As they walked past men would delve into their pockets and throw five-, ten- and twenty-pound notes on to the sheet. Just before the men with the bed sheet came towards us my father would slip me a five-pound note which I would then toss in with the rest of the donations. It was then that things became most uncomfortable. With the donations collected the imam would stand up and lead the rest of us in prayers. Having not learnt how to pray, I was forced to just ape the men around me: when they stood up I would stand up, when they turned their head left so would I and when they knelt and touched the ground with their foreheads I would do the same. I had no idea what I was doing. When my mother had tried to teach me the rituals I had not paid much attention so the symbolism of each action passed me by; as the prayers continued I would be consumed by a paranoia that everyone in the mosque realised that I was a fake. I followed each gesture terrified of getting it wrong.

After the imam had led the prayers, everyone read out loud some verses from the Koran. Each man had his head bowed and he said the prayers to himself quietly, but speedily. The entire mosque would hum with the prayers of the worshippers. My father and I were the only ones who didn't seem to know

4 **ornate** not simple, having a great deal of decoration – 5 **to deviate** to move away from – 13 **to delve** to search digging deeply – 27 **paranoia** fear that one is hated and mistreated

Ramadan
fasting when he is older

what to say. The prayers would end, each man would turn and hug the person on either side and wish them 'Eid Mubarak' and slowly file out of the central mosque. My father and I would collect our shoes and head towards the sweet centre to buy barfi and ludoos for the family. Returning home, the feeling that I was a fraud would not leave me alone.

With each year at high school being a Muslim became increasingly frustrating; when I had been younger it had meant reading the Koran, going occasionally to the mosque and tolerating the boys who would knock on our door to sing Christmas carols on Eid 'because you told us it was your Christmas'. In the spring of 1980, a television drama called *Death of a Princess* had featured the beheading of a Saudi princess. At school I had been taunted with comments like: 'So do they chop your arms off in Pakistan if you steal anything? Do they cut your willy off if you cheat?' but this didn't last for long.

By high school my friends were starting to drink and I was starting to fast. 'Fasting is how we show what we are prepared to do for Allah,' my mother explained. By not eating I would be able to spend more time contemplating my faith, I would be cleansed and spiritually nourished. At the start of Ramadan my mother would take out a special calendar which had details of what time the sun rose and set. If the sun rose at 4.16 in the morning, that was the time for the fast to start. I would be awoken at four, and after weakly splashing cold water on my face I would attempt to eat the hot chapattis that had already been prepared. Even though I knew I would not be eating for many hours it was hard to eat at that time in the morning. For the rest of the day there was no food or drink consumed. When I was at high school Ramadan seemed to land in the heart of summer; athletics, cricket and exams were all confronted

6 **fraud** [frɔːd] someone who is not what he claims

father does not fast
blood pressure

on an empty stomach. My head would be throbbing by the time I returned home. The most I could do was to head to my bedroom and climb under the blanket and hope to sleep away the final few hours of the fast. Navela and my mother were the only other ones fasting and they were both busy working; I would be too weak to move. In the evening before breaking the fast we would sit around the chrome- and smoked-glass dining table. The minute that the fast ended, each of us would pop a date into our mouths. 'Shaabash, my son. Well done!' my father would exclaim. 'Now eat. Eat whatever you like.'

As I attempted to wolf down the pakoras and samosas I couldn't help noting that while my father was the strongest champion of Ramadan I couldn't remember him ever fasting. 'Don't you think I would like to fast?' he would protest when anyone pointed out this contradiction. 'But what can I do? I am not a well man and Allah says that if you are sick you are free of the obligation of the fast.'

'And what is wrong with you?' I would enquire.

'You even have to ask? I am a sick man! Your mother has to make me special food, I have to watch my blood pressure, diabetes.' Considering his myriad illnesses my father looked quite well.

It might not have been so bad if I had felt some emotional release at the end of the fast. What made Ramadan so disappointing was that my faith was not rewarded; the longed-for flash of revelation, something magical and profound to overcome me the moment I started chewing on the date did not arrive. There was only a dull headache.

Having spent my high-school years surrounded by white friends and far from the Bury Park Muslims it was startling to begin sixth-form college in the autumn of 1987 and find the place seemingly over-run with Asians. They spoke in a strange

9 **date** sweet fruit growing on some palm trees *(Dattel)* – 21 **myriad** ['mɪriəd] a very large number

tradition and rules of being Muslim
=> Bruce is his religion

patois, they did not share any of my music and film tastes; they were Muslims like me but I had nothing in common with them. The only Asian who became my friend was Amolak and he was Sikh and like me he was not a typical Asian. His father was an elder at the local Sikh temple but Amolak was a huge fan of Islamic qawwali music. I had grown up listening to men like Nusrat Fateh Ali Khan and Aziz Mian, their religious devotional music was the Islamic equivalent to gospel music and it was one of the few things I could say made me truly proud to be Pakistani and Muslim.

By college I was no longer fasting during Ramadan, and had to be practically dragged to the mosque at Eid. The older I became the less sense religion seemed to make; Islam, as my parents taught it, seemed to be about rules and obedience. Not thinking for yourself but trusting the words written down hundreds of years ago; I found that an unsatisfying way to live. If religion was about answering the profound questions of how to live, I found that Bruce Springsteen gave me more persuasive answers than Islam. At college Amolak and I went around referring to ourselves as disciples of Bruce, arguing to anyone who would listen that the man was nothing less than a prophet. We called Dave Marsh's biography of Springsteen 'the holy book' and quoted Springsteen lyrics as if they were psalms. We planned on forming our band which was going to be named 'Yasser Arafat and the Ayatollahs of Love'. None of this delighted my parents. My mother would forever be goading me to take my posters off the wall; two years earlier I had come home from my summer job at the sandwich factory to find that she had taken down all my Madonna posters. The Springsteen posters, being less suggestive, lasted longer but whenever the conversation turned to how I had given up on my religion the good name of Springsteen would be used in vain.

1 **patois** ['pætwɑː] dialect – 19 **persuasive** having the power to influence others – 25 **Yasser Arafat** former leader of the Palestine Liberation Organisation (PLO) who died in 2004 – 26 **to goad** to make sb do sth by constantly annoying them

Comparison between Whites and Muslims

To be a good Muslim seemed to demand that you blindly follow the rules, repeat the rituals time and time again and never think for yourself. It was only many years later that I realised it was not Islam I was reacting against, it was the cultural values of my parents' generation. At the time I could not make the distinction between religion and culture; there seemed to be certain things you had to love and hate to be Muslim. You were meant to dislike Jews. My father's attitude towards Jews was that of an uneasy admiration. 'Look at what they have suffered and yet they own the world,' he would say. 'Do you see Jews going to pubs and drinking like the whites? No, they know about hard work. They are tough people. Like the Hindus. Very clever. Look at the corner shops: all Indian. Big companies: all Jews. And us Pakistanis? All we have are the taxis.'

You only had to watch the news during the eighties, or read about Sabra and Chatila or hear other Muslims discussing Israel to know that it was the role of every good Muslim to defend the rights of Palestine and hate all Jews. I had a problem with this. For one thing I was something of a Second World War obsessive and had read too much about what the Jews had endured to be able to hate them. Reading *The Diary of Anne Frank* had inspired me to write my own diary; during junior school I had loved *When Hitler Stole Pink Rabbit* and *I am David*. And then later I read William Shirer's book about the Third Reich and watched the harrowing documentary, *Kitty Goes to Auschwitz*. By the time I was in my teens I had also discovered Bob Dylan and Woody Allen. Having seen *Annie Hall* made me feel I had more in common with Woody Allen than I did with the bearded men at the local mosque.

* * *

17 **Sabra and Chatila** names of two refugee camps in the south of Beirut where a massacre of Palestinian and Lebanese civilians was carried out in 1982 – 26 **harrowing** extremely upsetting

 Rushdie

On Valentine's Day 1989 the Ayatollah of Iran issued a fatwa on the British Muslim author Salman Rushdie. *The Satanic Verses* had been published the previous year. In Bradford Muslims had set alight copies of *The Satanic Verses* and I had seen Rushdie appear on television defending the book and arguing that it was not intended to offend Muslims. We discussed the controversy in my A level politics class; it was assumed that because I was Muslim I automatically wanted Rushdie dead. The truth was I was simply not as furious as I was supposed to be. The more the Rushdie affair dominated the news the more I realised just how little I had in common with the Muslims who were meant to be speaking for me. Not once did anyone who visited us during that time raise the subject of Rushdie; the men we knew were pragmatic Muslims who believed in their religion enough to pray and fast but were too busy fiddling the social security to have time to demonstrate against a book they would never read. Watching angry Muslims was alienating; I couldn't understand their anger. Perhaps real Muslims were meant to be furious but I knew that I was more offended and scared by the protestors. If they were prepared to get this upset about a book what else might they get angry about? What else might they be prepared to do?

To be a Muslim as a teenager seemed to involve not being able to do things: not being able to have Christmas presents, not eating during Ramadan and not being able to drink. Everyone knew that Muslims didn't drink. By my final year of high school most of my friends had started visiting pubs; the following morning Scott and the others would report back on the night. I didn't resent not drinking; having grown up in a Muslim family it had never occurred to me that I would ever touch alcohol.

1 **fatwa** a statement or order concerning Islamic law issued by an Islamic scholar –
17 **to alienate** ['eɪlɪəneɪt] to make someone feel they are different

In the first week that I arrived at university I was invited to have a drink. I was living in university accommodation, a block of flats called Grosvenor House, which came with its own pub. Fifteen freshers walked into the pub, unappetisingly called The Grot, and lined up at the bar. 'So, what you drinking, mate?' asked a ginger-haired Bradford lad whose name I had already forgotten.

Looking around I could see bottles of Newcastle Ale, Guinness and cans of Stella. Black Box's 'Ride on Time' was playing on the jukebox. 'Just a mineral water for me please,' I said finally.

'You don't drink?' a girl named Sophie asked.

'No, Muslim and all that, y' know,' I answered, trying not to look into her huge brown eyes.

'But the Muslims I know are the biggest pissheads going,' said the Bradford boy.

'Really? Yeah, well, I just never have, y' know.'

'Fucking hell. So you mean to tell me that you have never touched a drop in your life?'

'Nope.'

'You've never been tempted?'

It wasn't peculiar that my university friends wanted to know why I did not drink; what is far stranger is that I was not tempted. In the six years I lived in Manchester I went through three years of university life during a time when the city was one of the hippest places on the planet. I started university in Madchester's heyday, when the Stone Roses, Happy Mondays and Inspiral Carpets were all exporting the baggy sound to the world; I went to the Hacienda nightclub, saw Oasis in the week that their first record came out and I did it all stone cold sober. I lived two hundred miles from home, surrounded by amateur alcoholics. I understood that if I was to join in with the drinking I would probably have more success with girls

27 **heyday** the time of greatest success and popularity

discussing:
no alcool | no girlfriend

(less success was not mathematically possible) and yet I did not touch a drop.

If anyone asked why I did not drink I would reply that I was a Muslim. 'So, are you quite religious then?'

'No, I don't drink and I don't eat meat that is not halal.'

'But do you believe in the religion?'

'Err, well…'

'What's the difference between a vegetarian teetotaller who is not a Muslim and you?'

If pushed I would usually answer that I did not drink because I didn't want to disappoint my parents; the cliché of the Muslim who goes mental at university was all too familiar. Years later I met other Muslims whose university and work lives were double existences riddled with lies and deceit; they were one way in front of their parents and entirely another when around friends. I didn't want to be like that. I only half succeeded: although I never touched alcohol my mother was convinced that I was secretly drinking. 'You come home smelling of cigarettes, far from home with all those white boys going to pubs. How can I believe you don't drink?' she would ask me when I returned to Luton.

'But I don't join in when they drink!' I would protest.

'And what am I supposed to believe that you drink? Water? You probably have some white girl up there in Manchester too, is that why you don't come to Luton very much?'

'I don't drink and I don't have a girlfriend!' I would reply, disappointed at the truth of the last part of that statement.

Religion is a powerful thing; some of my earliest memories are of my mother describing Hell. It was a place of eternal fire and torture; as a young boy I would imagine how it might feel on Judgement Day knowing that until the end of time you would be burning in Hell, all for not having lived a better life when you had the chance. Some of that fear abated with time

8 **teetotaller** a person who never drinks alcohol – 14 **riddled with** full of

fathers dead

-> crisis => go back to the Islam Religion

but some remained. 'The greatest sin in the eyes of Allah is to have learnt Arabic and to have forgotten,' my mother would tell me and even as an intelligent university graduate those words pierced through me. I had largely forgotten Arabic and the guilt for having lost the faith remained. Even if I didn't believe in Heaven and Hell I did want peace of mind on Earth; I envied those whose faith gave their lives meaning. Atheism is a cold and soulless road to travel; I wanted to believe and I hoped that by not drinking the possibility of a return to Islam still existed. So long as I did not touch alcohol then I could say I was a Muslim. It was not much of an identity but it was the only one that could not be denied to me. I was a Muslim. I just did not know what that meant.

Losing my father threw me into a crisis; it seemed so pointless to live, struggle, dream and achieve and yet at the end to die. Could it really be as brutal as that? It was in the months after his death that I most envied those who had faith; for all the tears my mother shed and the nights when she could not sleep, she did not once express any anger that her husband was gone. She was distraught, but even in the depths of her darkness she was able to say: 'It was Allah's will, he gives us life and he can take it away as he chooses, it is not our life but His.' One part of me wanted to scream, 'Where was Allah in the hospital room when you begged him to give you your husband back?' but another part wanted to say, 'I want to believe like you do.' I wanted so much to believe that my father was not actually gone but had simply passed on to some other plane but the feelings never came.

When I was young my mother had told me that every Thursday the spirits of the dead return to the homes of their living relatives. If their family still remembers them they return to Heaven but those who have been forgotten are punished.

20 **distraught** extremely upset

Collecting money for funeral

Each Thursday after my father died, my mother would prepare some food: two chapattis, some curry and salad, and a glass of water. She would place them on the dining table and then recite a prayer from the Koran. During the time the television would be switched off and the rest of us would be silent. On every anniversary of my father's death we would contribute a few thousand rupees which my mother would collect and send to an orphanage in Pakistan. The orphans would then devote themselves to reading the Koran, reciting it day and night until it had been read twenty or thirty times. The more times it was read the sweeter the blessings for those in the afterworld. I did not know if these blessings ever reached my father but it was reassuring to know he was not forgotten.

Losing my father did not make me more religious but it did remind me that I was a Muslim. Sohail was also spurred into learning more about Islam. 'What you have to remember,' he said to me some months after my father's death, 'is that you might not think about your religion most of the time but there are times when it is shameful to not know the basics. You remember Dad's funeral? We did not know the correct prayers to say. We had to get someone to come over and say them. That is embarrassing! We should know these things, how to pray, what to say when someone dies, even if we never think about it, we should all know what to do.'

It seemed a reasonable suggestion; it is only in those life-changing moments of birth, marriage and death that we tend to ask the truly significant questions. For all my protestations that I was not a Muslim my religion was continuing to shape who I was; it was the reason why thinking about relationships and marriage was such a fraught business.

I moved from Luton to London and found myself making excuses for why I could not come home for Eid. With my father no longer around, Eid was not what it was. At the age of thirty

8 **orphanage** ['ɔːfənɪdʒ] place where children live whose parents are dead – 15 **to spur** [spɜː] to urge or encourage – 30 **fraught** causing extreme worry

I was comfortably British, occasionally Pakistani, and only technically Muslim. This was the twenty-first century after all. What did religion matter?

It was almost two in the afternoon when my mobile phone rang. It was a clear bright Tuesday in the second week of September 2001. I was heading back home to Luton; today was a rare day off and I had promised that I would spend it with my family. I answered the phone. It was Amolak. 'Hey, mate, have you heard anything about a plane hitting the World Trade Center?' As I worked in journalism friends would often run rumours and conspiracy theories past me; on this occasion I told Amolak that I knew nothing. We had been to the top of the World Trade Center some years earlier; the idea that a small plane might have accidentally crashed into it seemed plausible. I rang work to ask if they knew anything more.

'Sorry, not a good time to talk,' was all they could say before hanging up. I contemplated going into work. As a journalist the first impulse on hearing breaking news is to call in and offer to help; no one wants to miss out on the story of the decade. I sensed that something might have happened in New York but it did not yet seem worth sacrificing a day off and disappointing my family who already complained that I did not spend enough time at home.

Minutes after boarding the train the phone rang again. It was Uzma. 'Are you watching the television?'

For the next forty minutes as the Thameslink train sped northwards to Luton phone calls and text messages described what the rest of the world was watching on television. It was too soon to know who might be responsible for smashing two passenger planes into the twin towers but I had my fears.

An hour later I was in the living room of my mother's house eating keema aloo with chapattis and watching the second tower collapse in a mountain of dust. My mother was crying. ‘Those poor people, all they were doing was going to work,’ she said. ‘Going to earn money for their families, why did they deserve to die? Who would do such a thing?’ I continued eating and said nothing. Since she did not speak English my mother would often ask me to translate what she was hearing into Urdu. ‘Who are the idiots that would take innocent lives?’ she continued. ‘Do they not have a conscience? Taking fathers from children? What are they saying? Do they know who did this?’ I looked up from my food and said, ‘They’re saying it was Muslims.’

Osama bin Laden changed my life. For the first thirty years of my life I had been running away from my religion but on 9/11 my religion caught up with me. There was nowhere left to hide. A few days after the attacks on the World Trade Center I was having a drink with Amolak in Luton town centre. ‘You realise what this means, don’t you?’ my friend asked me. ‘It means that America isn’t ours any more.’

I said nothing but understood.

‘Me and you, Sarfraz, we always thought, fuck this country; if Britain doesn’t want us we always have America. Not any more, mate, now we are going to have to do what we can in this here country because you know that the second you try to land at JFK they are going to haul your arse into jail. They’re not going to bother with questions. My friend, we are fucked.’

‘You know I’m supposed to be going to New York next week, don’t you?’ I said. I had booked a short holiday to the United States, a treat for having worked through summer without a break.

‘You seriously thinking of going?’

‘Yeah, I’m still going to go.’

‘Mate, listen to me. Don’t go on that bloody flight. Are you fucking daft? Cancel the flight. Do you think they will even

33 **daft** [dɑ:ft] stupid or silly

let you on the plane looking like you do? It's going to be hard enough walking through the Arndale without being frisked.'

Earlier that summer there had been rioting in three British towns. At the time the disturbances in Bradford, Burnley and Oldham had been described as 'race riots' between Asian or Pakistani youths and the police. After 9/11 it was no longer about Pakistanis, Indians and Bengalis but Muslims, Hindus and Sikhs. And there was no doubting who was public enemy number one. Flying into New York was always a tense experience, the thin-lipped airport security staff seemed to enjoy taking extra care in studying my passport photograph. I dreaded to think what arriving in JFK might be like following the attacks; the newspaper reports of innocent Asians being detained for questioning and then slung back to Britain confirmed Amolak's grim theory that the United States was no longer our promised land. I cancelled my flight. It took a few days for me to notice the irony: I was scared of flying because I was scared that others would be scared of me not because I was frightened of terrorism.

It was a year after the 11 September attacks that I felt confident enough to visit the United States. Bruce Springsteen had reunited the E Street Band and had released an album, *The Rising*, that was being seen as his response to 9/11. One of the songs on that album, 'Worlds Apart', featured the Pakistani qawwali singer Rahat Ali Khan. To hear a Pakistani Muslim musician performing with Springsteen was an intensely emotional experience; for so long I had heard my parents condemn my music tastes by telling me: 'Why do you like their music when you have your own?' and here was the evidence that both worlds could exist together in one song.

When it was announced that Springsteen and the E Street Band would be playing in New Jersey, I knew I had to go.

2 **to frisk** to search for hidden weapons, goods etc. – 14 **to detain** to prevent a person from leaving a police station or prison for a certain time

Amolak could not get time off from his work so I found myself buying a single concert ticket and booking a seat to JFK. Before I left I packed photocopies of newspaper articles that I had written. If the immigration officials wanted evidence that I was the journalist I claimed to be, I would have it available.

In the line at JFK I sucked hard on a mint and tried to remember to breathe deeply and look relaxed. I had not done anything wrong, I told myself, there was no reason to be anxious. I could feel my heart pounding. I was motioned to approach the immigration officer. He was a large man with a ruddy face and furry moustache. 'Passport,' he said. I handed it to him. 'What is the purpose of your visit?' he asked.

It was interesting how immigration officials could ask the same question to different people and apply varying levels of menace; if it was a pretty young girl the same questions would be asked as if they were just a formality but when they were directed at me it was as if I was in a court of law fighting to stay out of the electric chair. 'I'm here to see Bruce Springsteen,' I told him.

The man stopped what he was doing and looked up at me. 'You're here to see Bruce? And you've come all the way from England?'

'Yes, and it's not the first time either,' I explained. 'I'm a hardcore fan. Saw him in Barcelona when the tour started.'

'Hey, Danny, this fella is seeing Bruce at Meadowlands,' the man said, talking to his friend on another booth.

'No kidding. That's great, man. Bruce is the best. A real working-class guy, y'know.'

'Yeah, I know, I've met him actually and he's a really nice person too.'

'Wait a second, you've met him!'

'Yup.'

11 **ruddy** red – 15 **menace** threat – 26 **booth** small enclosed place for one person

The paperwork was completed. 'Well, let me tell you something: there is no better reason to come to the United States than to see Bruce Springsteen. You take your passport and have a great time at the gig, you hear.'

The biggest lie that I was told when I was growing up was that there was only one way to be a Muslim. That way was to be obedient, deferential and unquestioning; it was to reject pleasure and embrace duty, to renounce sensuality and to never ever ask why. Even as a young boy this did not appeal and so I spent my life thinking that I was a bad Muslim. The irony was that for all the temptations I never actually did anything too bad: I did not drink, I did not renounce my parents, I did not become involved with any extremist groups. I kept believing in an Islam which was more tolerant, which did not take itself so seriously that it burnt the books of those it did not approve of. I wanted to be a Muslim like Philip Roth was a Jew or Bruce Springsteen was Catholic. When I was young, that did not seem possible, and so I ran away from my religion. But, eventually, it caught up with me. I still hope to find my reason to believe.

- explanation of his religion / beliefs from his family, especially his father
- Starts learning Arabic
  ↳ praying with the Koran => said wishes to Allah
- finished reading the Koran at the age of 9 => Koran reading afternoons
- tradition => fasting

7 **deferential** showing respect to others – 8 **to renounce** to state publicly that you no longer have a particular belief or connection or are no longer going to keep a title, position or privilege

always surrounded by Pakistani

Land of Hope and Dreams

Everybody needs a place to rest, everybody wants to have a home.

'Hungry Heart', Bruce Springsteen

I was the only boy in my school who wanted Argentina to win the World Cup and the Falklands War. It was early 1982, I was eleven years old and in my last year at junior school. In many ways I was no different from the other children in my class. I excused myself from school for Eid, but still handed out Christmas cards. At home I read the Koran and learnt Arabic but at school I talked about *The Young Ones* and *The A Team*. It was easy to believe I was just like everyone else; my father, however, believed otherwise.

My father left Pakistan when he was twenty-nine but he never stopped being Pakistani. He came to Britain for economic reasons and his relationship to this country remained rooted in financial pragmatism rather than emotional attachment. 'This is not your country,' he would tell me, 'you have your own country, your own language.' I was brought up to believe that Pakistan was our true home and Britain merely where we happened to live. When we lived in Bury Park it was an easy distinction to maintain; we lived around mostly Pakistanis, I went to a school that was mostly Pakistani and the only people who ever visited our home were Pakistanis. When we moved to Marsh Farm that all changed. At school I was just another schoolboy collecting Panini football stickers and stealing peeks at the girls doing handsprings in the playground in the hope

6 **Falklands War** war between the United Kingdom and Argentina over the disputed islands in the South Atlantic Ocean south of Argentinia – 11 **The Young Ones and The A Team** popular TV series – 26 **to steal peeks** to take a quick look at something when one should not – 27 **handsprings** *Handstandüberschlag*

daily morning production

of seeing a glimpse of their knickers, but at home my parents were constantly reminding me I was Pakistani and different from my friends.

My father was an extravagant farter and he farted without shame or warning. If he was in bed he would turn his body and lift one cheek so it was at an angle before letting rip with both methane-fuelled barrels. He seemed able to vary the sounds of his farts; some were rapid and high-pitched while others were blustery movements in three elongated parts. His explosive farts were rivalled only by the noises he produced when he was washing his face in the morning. The routine began with a comprehensive drenching of his face in water followed by repeated gurgling of the mouth. After that came the most distressing part. From the furthest reaches of his body my father would summon up phlegm. Clearing his throat does not adequately describe the enormous effort involved; it sounded as if the phlegm was being dragged out from the ends of his toes, from the tips of his fingers, phlegm that was not coaxed but rather threatened out. After twenty minutes of this dramatic throat clearing and spitting he would emerge as if none of us had heard the sounds that had been coming out of the bathroom. It might seem as if talking about my father's farting and expectorations is tasteless and pointless but both were indicative of something else. I suppressed my farts, I squeezed my legs tight and hoped they would be silent; my father positively celebrated his. He farted like a proud Pakistani and I as an embarrassed Brit.

When the first newsflash came on television in the spring of 1982 announcing that Argentina had invaded the Falkland Islands, I didn't pay any attention and continued with reading my computer magazines. Within weeks, Mrs Thatcher had dispatched the British Navy to the South Atlantic and the whole

1 **knickers** ['nɪkəz] underpants worn by women and girls – 4 **to fart** to let air from the bowels come out noisily – 9 **blustery** very windy – 9 **movement** one of the main parts of a piece of classical music *(Satz)* – 15 **phlegm** [flem] the thick jelly-like substance produced in the nose and the throat, esp. when one has a cold

father's proud of being Pakistani

country had become experts on the history of the Falklands. In the evenings when the family sat together to watch television the news was filled with pictures from Southampton and Dover with thousands of people waving flags and watching the ships set off to defend the islands. Harrier jets rocketing towards the skies from enormous aircraft carriers and the daily press conferences from the Ministry of Defence where a funereal spokesman would deliver the latest news became addictive rituals. The Union flag was flying everywhere, the whole country was gripped by patriotism. International politics did not usually interest the pupils at Waulds Junior School but the Falklands War reached even us. In the playground when we played football it was no longer Manchester United against Tottenham but the Argies against the Brits. Everyone hated the Argies and everyone wanted the Falklands to remain British. Everyone except my family.

'Those thieving English bastards,' my father would mutter as we watched the news from the South Atlantic. 'So arrogant. Those islands; what have they got to do with England? They are thousands of miles away from this country, they are next to Argentina, but Thatcher tells us they are hers! The arrogance of these people!'

My father cared little about Argentina, for him the Falklands conflict was just another example of the British acting like they owned the world. Any incident, sporting or political, where the English were the losers delighted him. 'Do you know how excited they got when one of their boxers fought Ali,' my father asked us one evening, laughing at the memory. 'Cooper. He was going to beat Muhammad Ali they said! By the time Ali had finished with him, their man Cooper was ready to convert to Islam!' We all laughed at the silly Englishman who thought he could beat the Muslim.

7 **funereal** [fju'nɪərɪəl] heavy and sad, suitable for a funeral

'You know what the trouble with this country is?' he would say. 'It was built on theft. Have you heard of the Koh-i-noor diamond? One of the most beautiful and biggest diamonds in history. And you know where it comes from? Lahore. But it was stolen by Queen Victoria for her crown. That's what these people do. They take everything from other countries and claim it as theirs and then tell the world they are better than everyone else. And whenever anyone rises up against them they always seem shocked. Like we should have been grateful that they were stealing our country! And now this general says he wants his islands back and they are shocked again. I tell you I hope he gives Thatcher a good beating. I would love that.'

For us the Falklands War was David and Goliath in the South Atlantic and it was blindingly obvious that we should support the Argentines. Not everyone at my school agreed. One afternoon the teacher was showing us where the Falklands were on the map. After she had pointed them out I put my hand up. 'Miss, you know how the Falklands are eight thousand miles away? Don't the Argentines have a right to say that they belong to them?'

Mrs Abbott was not impressed. 'The thing is, Sarfraz,' she said slowly as if I had learning difficulties, 'countries are not meant to invade other countries. That is wrong, and that is why we are at war with Argentina.'

Mrs Abbott wasn't really a geography teacher. She actually taught PE and she would teach geography in tracksuit bottoms and top. I suspected she did not know much more about the subject than I did. 'But Britain invaded countries all over the world, how come that was right?'

'This is geography, not history. If you want answers to that you should talk to Mr Morrison at your next history lesson. We need to move on.'

At the end of the lesson I was surrounded by pupils. 'Do you really support the Argies then?' asked Stephen. Any fears

26 **PE** Physical Education

surrounded by people who wants to know his opinion

that I was about to be given a hard time abated when I saw his expression. He was not angry, just confused and, perhaps, slightly impressed at my rebellion.

'I just think that Argentina has more right on the islands than Britain does.'

'So you want the Argies to win then?' It was Michael. He had never spoken to me before then and although he was shorter than me and had a cherubic, deceptively innocent face I was frightened by him. Michael was a dangerous combination – a quick-witted bully – and he could tell that I was nervous in his presence.

'I don't want the Argies to win,' I said slowly. 'It's just I don't understand why it's worth trying to hold on to something that doesn't really belong to this country.'

Michael's cheeks were reddening. I could tell my argument hadn't won him over. 'It's what my dad told me anyway,' I added weakly.

'Yeah, well, your dad is a Paki just like you, ain't he? And *my* dad says you can't trust the lot of you.'

Another reason why I wanted Argentina to win the football was because Ossie Ardiles and Ricardo Villa played for them and they also played for Spurs who were my team. I also wanted them to win because I felt sorry they had lost the Falklands War; the World Cup had started the day after the Argentines had surrendered.

Why did I not want England to win? My father had taught me there were two choices: I could be British or Pakistani. I did not feel British, I did not even know what it meant. But the trouble was that I did not feel wholly Pakistani either. It wasn't much fun being Pakistani during the eighties. There were no sexy Pakistanis I could fancy, no creative Pakistanis I could admire, no successful Pakistanis I could respect. On television Pakistanis, and Asians in general, were almost invisible. When a programme did feature Asian characters – such as *Mind*

8 **cherubic** [tʃeˈruːbɪk] like a little angel – 22 **Spurs** Tottenham Hotspurs; English football club located in North London

parents to Pakistan
↳ bringing clothes
+ cricket stuff

Your Language or *It Ain't Half Hot Mum* – we overlooked its offensiveness since we were so grateful to see someone who looked like us on television.

In the summer of 1983 my parents went to Pakistan. It was the first time for my mother since arriving nine years earlier and my father had not been since 1973. My parents loaded their luggage with old clothes for the relatives: shirts and sweaters that were too small for me and jackets I had outgrown. Most of the luggage that was packed was to be given away.

My parents returned from Pakistan with a cricket set, complete with full-size stumps, batting pads, gloves and cricket bat. They also bought me a tracksuit top and jogging bottoms. Both had sporting stripes running down the side and the number 9 on the chest and the hips. The next time I was playing cricket with my friends I made sure to wear my new sports kit. As I emerged from the front door of my house and began jogging towards the field, I noticed everyone laughing. 'What are you wearing your pyjamas for?' asked Scott.

I looked down at my clothes. They were made of light cotton but I was sure he was mistaken. 'No, these are sports clothes.'

Richard, Robert, Craig and the others continued shrieking with laughter.

'You idiot, you're wearing pyjamas!' said Richard.

I was sure they were wrong but the truth was I had no idea what pyjamas looked like. 'No, *you're* wrong,' I told the others. 'This is a *Pakistani-style* tracksuit.'

The visit to Pakistan gave my father new ammunition in his battle to rescue me from becoming too well-adjusted. 'You should have seen those boys,' he would say to me. 'So obedient and hard-working! Every night I would go to bed and my bedclothes would be freshly washed and ironed. In the morning, breakfast was on the table.' My sister and I would

11 **stump** (cricket) any of the three upright pieces of wood at which the ball is thrown

whole family is flying to Pakistan

listen glumly. 'I tell you the truth. My heart wanted to give one of those boys a chance to come to this country. All they need is that chance. They have no chance in Pakistan but with their attitude they could do very well here.' The threat now was not only that we would be sent to Pakistan but someone else would take our place.

Almost as soon as they returned from Lahore my parents began planning on taking the entire family there. Such visits were expensive and it was another two years before we had saved up the money. I would come home from school and notice new luggage in the living room, huge brown suitcases with large straps and buckles piled one on top of the other. Navela and my parents were excited by the prospect but Uzma and I were deeply sceptical. In the evenings my ten-year-old sister would sit with me in my bedroom and we would try to construct coping strategies for the weeks ahead. 'They won't even know who I am,' she would complain. 'They'll probably think I'm really weird because I'm not like them.'

'It's going to be a nightmare,' I agreed. 'We just have to remember it's only for three weeks, I mean, think about some of Dad's mates – they send their kids over for three months!' We would both shudder at the very idea.

Two weeks before we were due to fly I bought a pack of ten blank cassettes and asked Navela to fill the cassettes with recordings of the *Steve Wright in the Afternoon* radio show. Each afternoon I would race upstairs to ensure that she had taped the programme. The show would stretch out over two cassettes, which I would neatly label. I was careful not to listen to them. By the time that we were due to fly I had more than a week's worth of unheard Steve Wright shows. It might have seemed a bizarre project but just in the same way that we all had to have injections to inoculate ourselves against TB and malaria the cassette tapes were my way of protecting myself

1 **glumly** unhappily and quietly – 23 **due** expected – 32 **to inoculate** to give a weak form of a disease to someone to make the body resistant to the disease

arriving in poor Pakistan => uncle

from feeling completely alienated and alone in a strange place far away from home.

The small dark-skinned man who came to meet us at Lahore airport looked familiar. He came charging towards us with a large toothy grin as we emerged from the arrivals hall. It was only when he hugged my father that I noticed how they shared the same hair, lips and jawline. 'And where is Sarfraz? Is this Sarfraz? Son, come here and give your uncle a hug,' the short man said to me, lunging in my direction. I didn't know how to respond, and so I stood motionless and let the man who was my uncle hug me. Soon we were racing out of the airport and squeezing into his Honda, two large suitcases strapped to the roof and six people packed inside. Even as the car started to move it was surrounded by beggars. One had no legs and was crawling on the dusty floor, there was a tiny birdlike woman with missing teeth, wearing a tattered dupatta on her head and holding a baby in one arm and extending the other into my face. 'Please sister, please brother. I am very poor, you are rich,' she moaned. 'Allah rewards those who think of others.' Outstretched hands were thrust in our faces. 'Please, we have only just arrived,' said my mother patiently.

'Don't pay any attention to them. Get out of our way,' said my uncle crossly. 'Rude bastards. Never seen anything like this before, have you?' My uncle had got that right.

On day one our uncle took us to his house where we sat on a simple cane bed, drank cold lassi and handed out clothes to his children. Despite the sweltering heat, my father always dressed in a pale-grey suit, white shirt with silver cufflinks and tie. At the time I thought he dressed that way because of his natural fastidiousness, but now I think it was his way of reminding himself – and those around him – that he had moved on. From

26 **cane** stem of certain plants such as bamboo – 26 **lassi** popular yogurt-based drink in India and Pakistan – 28 **cufflinks** *Manschettenknöpfe* – 30 **fastidiousness** carefulness that every detail is correct and clean *('Pingeligkeit')*

racism

education, and a disdain for excessive emoting. The English might have been a nation of thieves but they were successful thieves, and more than anything my father respected success.

I came home a few shades darker and a few pounds lighter. I had been apprehensive about visiting Pakistan but I had also secretly hoped that in the instant I landed in Pakistan I might feel a sense of home. No such emotions were forthcoming; all the relatives I had met had referred to me as English: the door towards feeling Pakistani had slammed in my face.

On the way to Lea Manor there was a subway where a gang of skinheads would hang out. They looked like glue sniffers and I knew they were trouble: a Sikh boy called Rupinder who was one year below me at school had told me of how the boys had spat at him as he tried to walk through the underpass. After he told me this story I was always nervous about seeing the skinheads and changed my route to school. Not all racists were so easily identifiable. When I asked someone, for example, where the nearest bus stop was and the lad pointed me in the wrong direction, I would know he was a racist: racists loved giving bad directions.

At Lea Manor there were very few Asian pupils and only one Asian teacher. His name was Mr Judge and he taught maths. Mr Judge was a short, plump, middle-aged man who wore a large turban, thick glasses and dressed in a brown suit, usually over a patterned sweater. Mr Judge's maths lessons were anarchic; each time he turned his back towards us there would be a flurry of conkers hurled towards him. He tried vainly to discipline us, but his thick Asian accent meant no one took him seriously. Those of us who obeyed Mr Judge did so as much out of sympathy as respect. Whenever he tried to discipline anyone he would start spluttering, 'Hey, what you doing? Hey,

1 **disdain** not worth one's respect – 1 **to emote** to openly show emotion – 27 **conker** *Kastanie* – 31 **to splutter** to talk quicky and in a confused way

no respect towards Pa.

you listen to me!' Most of the class would fall about laughing at him.

'I will inform your parents about your unacceptable behaviour!' he once shouted to Jason Fairclough.

'Yeah, well, my dad hates Pakis!' fired back Jason.

Mr Judge walked up to Jason. What did you say? Repeat what you said!'

'You touch me,' said Jason, 'and my dad will beat the shit out of you!'

'Get out of my class! I will not tolerate this! Get out now!'

Such scenes were repeated weekly, and each time someone threw a conker which was aimed at his turban but which bounced off his suit or each time one of the girls innocently asked him: 'Sir, why do you smell?' I felt a stab of sympathy for poor Mr Judge. To be humiliated so regularly by teenagers when all he was trying to do was introduce us to algebra.

As we all filed out of the room at the end of our maths lesson I would see him tidying up his papers and rubbing the equations from the blackboard in advance of another class and, most likely, another gruelling hour and I used to wonder what it must have been like to be Mr Judge. But it wasn't only pupils who could be hurtful. In woodwork, if I got my measurements wrong, the teacher would say, 'I said five centimetres not five chapattis.'

Another teacher, who I was convinced was racist, began one lesson with a discussion about how words could be abbreviated. 'So, for example, you, Sarfraz,' he said, turning to me. I immediately began to feel the tingle of unwanted attention. 'Now, you are Pakistani, are you not?'

'Yes, sir,' I replied.

14 **stab** a sudden feeling – 19 **equation** a statement that two quantities are equal (*Gleichung*) – 28 **tingle** stinging sensation

'So if someone was to call you a Paki, and the term is a common shorthand for Pakistani, then it would be true to say you are a Paki, would it not?'

I could hear tittering in the class.

'Yes, but no, sir… it's not just a shorter word, is it, sir…' I said, trying to make my point.

'All I'm saying, Sarfraz, is that technically, and only technically, mind, you are a Paki… would you agree?'

I looked straight at him. The more smug he looked, the more I hated him. 'Yes sir,' I replied finally.

It is not easy to convey the impact of such incidents. They were happening at the same time as I was reading newspaper stories about racist attacks on homes and children. One story which affected me very deeply was the killing of Ahmed Ullah, an Asian schoolboy stabbed to death in Manchester by a white boy, Darren Coulborn, who later confessed that he had 'killed a Paki'. Ahmed was about my age. Everything he ever was and everything he would ever be had been stolen from him by someone who hated him simply because of the colour of his skin. This was the world outside my home, a world where people like me were hated for things we could not change.

'What you have to remember,' my father would tell me, 'is that the whites don't actually want you in this country. You do understand that, don't you? Remember Enoch Powell? I was in this country when he was speaking. The reason I say to you to speak Urdu and not forget you are Pakistani is that you never know when we might have to leave. It could happen. And if it does what will you do? If the Tories say they want to throw us all out, send us back home as they say, what will you do? Do you think your friends Scott or Richard will stand up for you? Take you into their home? Of course they won't. That's why I still keep our house in Pakistan. Open your ears when I tell you

4 **to titter** laugh quietly and and in a nervous way – 9 **smug** [smʌg] pleased with oneself – 24 **Enoch Powell** conservative politician and Member of Parliament who delivered a speech in 1968 ("Rivers of blood") in opposition to mass immigration to Britain

only has his parents

this: Pakistan is the only country that will never deny you. It is the only country that you can always say is your home.'

My father was always dismissive of my friends, I'm not sure he even believed it was possible to be friends with a white person. But I knew differently. Scott was my best friend and he was white. One afternoon, when I was about twelve, I was walking home from school with him and I asked him what he thought would happen if there was an accident.

'What do you mean accident?' Scott asked.

'You know,' I said, walking more slowly, noticing a small pebble on the road and pausing before booting it ten yards. 'What do you think would happen if there was, like, a car accident and my mum and dad died. What do you think would happen to me?'

'That's a bit of a stupid question,' Scott replied.

'No, it's not, it's OK for you cos you have your uncle and your grandparents and all that. So if anything happened to your mum or dad you got people who would look after you. I don't have anyone!'

'Yeah, but it's still a stupid question,' continued Scott. 'Because if anything happened to your parents, all that would happen is my parents would adopt you and then we would become brothers.'

I wished me and Scott could have been actual brothers. If I could have summoned a genie who could have rubbed my brownness off, the shameful truth is that I would have been elated. As that was impossible, I settled on being invisible. That was how I felt being Pakistani during the eighties: I wanted to be invisible and anonymous so that no one could point at me and say: 'You are different and you do not belong.'

This country didn't seem to accept me as one of its own, and yet where else did I have that I could call home? Not Pakistan,

3 **dismissive** considering not worthy of attention or respect – 25 **genie** ['ʤi:nɪ] a magical spirit in Arab fairy tales – 27 **elated** extremely happy

which had felt completely alien to me. I didn't seem to belong anywhere. And so when England played Argentina in the World Cup quarter finals in 1986 it was not really surprising that I wanted Argentina to win. This was the infamous match in which Diego Maradona scored two goals. When the replays proved the first goal ought to have been disqualified, newspapers and television declared that Argentina had cheated and the result was a travesty. My father found the entire matter hilarious. 'They've spent the past two hundred years cheating the rest of the world and now when they get a taste of their own medicine they complain!' he would say.

I agreed. I had not wanted England to win and the fact that the humiliation was partly because of cunning as well as skill only made their defeat sweeter as far as I was concerned.

And as I grew older I still did not feel any loyally towards Britain; when Norman Tebbit coined the 'cricket test' in April 1990 I had no qualms about failing it. It was his government after all that had been in power throughout my childhood and who had contributed to my lack of patriotism. Even before she was Prime Minister, Margaret Thatcher had spoken about this country being 'swamped' by immigrants, and my local MP was so right-wing that he supported the pro-apartheid government in South Africa. It was because of Margaret Thatcher and John Major that I had never felt the right to call myself British. Each year I would watch the Conservative party conferences and see the pink-faced delegates waving the Union flag and singing 'Land of Hope and Glory' as if it was the last night of the Proms. It made me feel like this was not my country.

* * *

4 **infamous** [ˈɪnfəməs] well known for sth bad – 8 **travesty** sth that completely misrepresents the true and real thing – 16 **cricket test** Tebbit said in an interview that many immigrants would fail the test because they didn't cheer for the England cricket team – 17 **qualm** [kwɑːm] feeling of uncertainty

In 1997 Labour won the general election and Tony Blair became the first Labour Prime Minister in eighteen years. When Labour came to power the *Observer* newspaper had a front-page headline which read 'Goodbye Xenophobia', and that was how it felt.

The people in power resembled human beings; Tony Blair had chosen a Bruce Springsteen song as one of his Desert Island Discs and he had even invited Noel Gallagher to Downing Street. The 'Cool Britannia' New Labour ushered in was a far more welcoming concept than the land of hope and glory of the Conservatives that had left me feeling alienated.

It was not only in politics that Britain seemed to be changing. Two years earlier when I had been living in Manchester and Britain had hosted Euro '96, I had noticed how many flags of St George were being flown. In the past, the English flag had filled me with fear as it contained so many deep, racist resonances, but during Euro '96 I found myself feeling less frightened by the flag. The television screens showed images of young Asian boys with their faces painted white and red and wearing England shirts; perhaps it was possible to be patriotic and Pakistani. Four months before the start of the 1998 World Cup championships I had been in a London nightclub and the DJ had played 'Brimful of Asha' by the Asian band Cornershop. All around me I could see white boys and girls singing and dancing along to this song about a Bollywood playback singer. I should have been joining them but I preferred to watch. If someone had told me fourteen years earlier, when I had been watching Indian films with my family on our rented video player, that there would be a time when Asha Bhosle would feature in a number one hit single, I would have considered them insane. It was as insane as a group of British Asians becoming pop stars. As unlikely as the thought that being

4 **xenophobia** [zenə'fəʊbɪə] unreasonable fear of foreign people – 8 **Noel Gallagher** English musician and former member of the English rock band Oasis – 9 **to usher something in** ['ʌʃə] to start a new period with important changes

Asian might be considered cool, that white people might pay to watch a film about a Pakistani family growing up in the seventies or read a book about a Bangladeshi woman or laugh at a comedy sketch where the joke was on them and not the Asians performing the skit. During the nineties I could sense Britain was changing and with that I found my own feelings evolving. I still loved America, but following my father's death I knew it was no longer available as a place to which to run; I needed to be near my family. Pakistan was where I was from but not where I was at; that only left Britain.

'The thing is,' I told Amolak when we discussed it one afternoon while wandering through the Arndale Centre in Luton, 'you know how I've always supported any other team against England? I've started thinking it's not like the Australians have done anything for me, have they?'

'Damn right they haven't,' confirmed my friend. 'Racist fuckers. Think about what they did to the Aborgines.'

'Exactly, the way I see it it's a bit stupid to be supporting France – bunch of racist National Front-voting bastards – or Australia when it's Britain that's given us the chances we've had.'

'I hear you, mate,' replied Amolak.

'I mean, you've got a fantastic job in the City earning a ton of money. Who gave you that job? It was an English person, yeah? And me, I'm doing all right and it's only because a British person took a chance on me. Wasn't anyone Pakistani.'

'Hey, if it'd been up to an Asian, you know what our lot are like,' added Amolak. 'Climb up the ladder and then pull it up behind them as fast as they bloody can.'

'Exactly, and then you think about your dad and mine, all that work they've done, it's all been for this country.'

5 **skit** character who is made fun of – 7 **to evolve** to develop gradually – 19 **National Front** right wing party

does not know who to support

'So you're gonna support England then?' Amolak asked me. 'Doesn't that stick in your throat a bit?'

'So, who you gonna support?' I asked him.

'To be honest, I don't give a fuck about football but probably Iraq because you know if they lose they ain't gonna have any legs in the morning.'

I saw England play Argentina on 22 June 1998 with my family. We were in my mother's house. She was in the kitchen making popcorn and the sound and the smell of the corn popping drifted into the living room. Having spent my life wanting England to lose I now wanted them to win. I was not the only one in my family now supporting England, Sohail was too. 'All these people who go on about Pakistan this and that,' Sohail told me as his two-year-old son Omar sat on his lap, 'they haven't spent any time there. There's a reason why our dad left Pakistan. You know, all you can do is try and keep some of the past,' my brother continued, 'but in the end it's all going to go. You do what you can but my kids aren't growing up any differently from the white kids.'

My father had voiced similar sentiments when he had been alive but for him the prospect that we would forget our past was a source of fear. Now my brother was accepting that raising his children in this country did imply they would not be Pakistanis, but for him it did not seem a terrible loss.

Four years later England met Argentina again in the 2002 World Cup championships. It was the summer of the Queen's Golden Jubilee, and the World Cup had begun in the same week I turned thirty-one. I took the train from London to Luton to watch the England match with my family. In the taxi on my way to my mother's house I saw Luton was awash with flags of St George sprouting from taxis and cars, on bedroom windows and on top of hats. Maybe some of those sporting the flags were racists, but perhaps they were simply proud to

30 **awash with** full of

call Britain their home; I no longer felt a reflexive repulsion on seeing the flag. The match against Argentina was critical and when David Beckham scored the winning penalty our house erupted with laughter and applause. Even my mother joined in with the cheering.

When the match was over I took a bus into the town centre. I was feeling euphoric; if I had drunk alcohol I would have happily spent the afternoon getting drunk. Walking through the town centre, I ran into groups of England fans singing and cheering. In the past it might have been a frightening sight, but now I wanted to join them. As I passed a menswear store I noticed a black T-shirt with an England flag on it, the flag was modestly sized and the design understated. It was the type of T-shirt I could imagine wearing; I wanted to proclaim my pride in the England performance. Three times I walked past the store and picked up the shirt and imagined wearing it and each time something stopped me from buying it. I was worried that others might question my right to wear the flag of St George. In frustration I called a friend. 'What are you ringing me for?' she asked. 'Of course you can bloody well wear that T-shirt!' Emboldened by the conversation, I bought the T-shirt and spent the rest of the afternoon proudly walking around town with the flag of St George on my chest. That evening I met up with Amolak and Sanjay in town. Amolak was wearing an England badge and Sanjay had a plastic bowler hat in red and white on his head. When 'Three Lions' began playing on the jukebox the entire bar, packed with whites, blacks and Asians, sang along. I sang too, with as much passion as I could muster. The louder I sang the more confident I felt in wearing the flag of St George; it felt like it was my flag too. The search for an identity I could feel comfortable with had, I believed, reached its destination. I was wrong.

1 **repulsion** very strong dislike – 28 **to muster** to produce

On the morning of 7 July 2005, I was in my flat in London. I awoke and stumbled into the kitchen to make myself a coffee before going into my study and turning on my laptop to check my emails. I had set the BBC news website as my internet homepage, and the top story said that there were some severe power cuts on the London Underground that were causing chaos for morning commuters. One of the greatest pleasures of working from home was the smugness I felt on days when Underground workers went on strike or when signalling failures crippled the tube. It felt so liberating to not have to worry about how to get to work.

Leaving my computer on, I went to my living room and turned on Sky News. They reported that the problems on the Underground were not to do with power cuts, as had been first thought, but were something far more serious. The same sick feeling I had felt four years earlier when I had heard about the attack on the twin towers returned, the same silent pleading that this would not have been perpetrated by Muslims, not again.

When the details began to emerge, it was even worse than I had feared. Four British Muslims, three of them Pakistani, had become Britain's first domestic suicide bombers and they had set off to London from Luton train station. The same train station that I used every time I came home to see my family, the same train station my father had dropped me at the last time I had seen him alive. The photograph that the newspapers printed that week of the four bombers with their explosive rucksacks on their backs was taken at Luton train station as they were about to board the Thameslink train to King's Cross. I knew intimately the route the four men had taken. And, yet again, it was my hometown that was in the news for all the wrong reasons.

18 **to perpetrate** to commit a crime

drives home
not sure if the bombers are really Muslim

What was it about Luton? When I had been growing up there the town had been something of a national joke, but recently it had been inextricably linked with Islamic radicalism. Only a few years earlier a young British Pakistani, also from Luton and also called Manzoor, had been caught fighting against the British in Afghanistan, and more recently there were regular police raids on suspected extremists in my hometown. When friends asked me whether Luton was as bad as the media portrayed, I would strongly defend its reputation. That was why I had been so pleased that with *Luton Actually* I could present a more positive depiction of Luton, and yet now the worst terrorist atrocity on British soil had been committed by four British Muslims who had chosen Luton to begin their journey to mass murder.

I returned home on the first weekend after the bombing. It was a tense time. Police were patrolling the Underground and stopping and searching anyone whom they thought looked suspicious. As I boarded the train at King's Cross I made sure I left my holdall unzipped so that anyone suspecting me could see that I only had some clothes, my iPod and my copy of the *New Yorker* inside. I felt I had to prove that I was not a 'bad Muslim'.

When I arrived at Luton train station I jumped into a taxi to take me to my mother's home. I asked the taxi driver how things were in Luton following the bombings. 'See, me personally, I don't think they did it,' the taxi driver said.

'What, you mean, you don't think it was those four Muslims?' I asked.

'No way, I reckon it was the Jews who did it to make us Muslims look bad. Same as with 9/11.'

3 **inextricably** [ɪnɪksˈtrɪkəblɪ] from which it is impossible to get free – 12 **atrocity** [əˈtrɒsɪtɪ] act of great cruelty

I would hear such claims on a depressingly regular basis. Sometimes I would try arguing back, but eventually it was easier to try to circumvent the conversation altogether. For my brother, the negative publicity around Luton was damaging for his property business. 'Do you want to know who's to blame? It's these bloody Arabs and North Africans,' he told me as we sat in his living room. 'Algerians and Moroccans and all that lot. They've got war in their blood and they come into our communities and start spreading it around. Most Pakistanis just want to be left alone to live their lives.'

It was true that the Pakistanis I knew in Luton, the ones who came to our home to drink tea and gossip with my mother couldn't care less about international politics or foreign policy. But there were others, the ones who lurked outside the central mosque handing out leaflets, who did not feel the same. These were the Muslims who grabbed the headlines with their anger and their hatred. They were the Muslims who were the most visible. Why were they so angry and why did they hate this country so much? As someone who was also from Luton and who shared the same religion and nationality as these alienated and angry men, it sometimes felt in the days and weeks after 7/7 as if I was expected to speak for the bombers and in some way explain why they had bombed the tube. But in fact, when I heard those young British Muslims speak so contemptuously about living in this country, my reaction was one of anger, confusion and betrayal. What they felt and what they preached was not in my name.

That Saturday afternoon I met up with Amolak to have tea at Greenfields in the Arndale Centre. 'So, it's your lot again then, hey?' were his opening words. 'It's the same old, same old, innit. Muslims blow things up and us Sikhs get mashed up by some fucking drunken muppets who don't know any better.'

3 **to circumvent** to avoid – 14 **to lurk** to wait or move in a secret way, as if intending to do sth wrong – 31 **to mash up** to crush into a soft substance

'Mate, what's up with these people?' I asked my friend. 'I honestly don't get what's going on in their heads.'

'Fuck all, that's what's going on,' Amolak replied. 'Look. Read any paper and you got some bearded fool yapping on about Iraq, but if you ask me that's not what's the root cause of all this shit. It's this next lot, these teenagers. They're fucking ungrateful bastards, that's what. Plain and fucking simple.'

Amolak was upset for the same reason as I was: everything that we had worked for in our lives and all that our parents had striven to build was now being threatened. When my father had come to Britain in the sixties he had come as a Pakistani and he had died as a Pakistani; he had never wanted to be British. I had grown up in this country wanting to be British but I had never really felt as if I truly belonged here. But this next generation, the teenagers and twentysomethings who had been brought up to take for granted everything that we had to fight for, they were telling us they did not want to be part of this thing called Britain. And not only did they not want to be part of it, they actively wanted to bring it down.

'I tell you, mate, it's not looking good right now,' Amolak said gloomily. 'I mean, let's be honest, it is kinda taking the piss, isn't it? How long you think the white man is going to take this shit? If it was some English geezers kicking off like this in Pakistan what do you think would happen to them? Summary fucking justice and no questions asked.'

'If it was up to me you know what I would say to them,' I told my friend, 'I'd say, if you hate this country so much, why don't you just fuck off to somewhere that's Muslim enough for you. If an English person says it everyone turns round and calls him a racist but I know plenty of Asian folk who think exactly the same.'

'Mate, everyone we know thinks that,' added Amolak, 'course they do. Fact is, it used to be the white man who made our lives shit. Now it's the Muslims.'

What most maddened me about the attention given to these Muslim extremists was the feeling that my claim on this country, my right to call myself British, was being wrenched from me. And yet I was never convinced that there really was a clash of civilisations between Muslims and the rest of the world; the clash was between people of all religions – those who were moderate and reasonable – and extremists. How did one person become a moderate and another extremist? The most common explanation was that the policies of the British and American governments has helped radicalise a generation of young British Muslims. But if that was true, why were there not Pakistani Americans exploding bombs on the New York subway?

Some weeks later I sat with my family as we ate in the living room of my mother's home. It was rare for our family to discuss politics, but since the London bombings there had been a sombre atmosphere in Luton, and it had infected our house. Even Nazia who had a resolutely sunny disposition was quiet; none of us knew where all of this was heading.

'What do they want? These people who did this?' asked my mother as she tore off a piece of chapatti and dipped it into saag aloo. 'Those poor parents,' she continued. 'You give your life to your children and they do this! What must they be going through?'

My mother saw the human tragedy rather than the political context; she was imagining the shame and disappointment the mothers of those boys must have felt, and she empathised with them. As I tried to imagine those parents' emotions it made me

6 **to wrench** [rentʃ] to pull and twist away – 20 **sombre** ['sɒmbə] serious and sad

reflect on how I had been raised. My mother and father took great pride in being Pakistani, but I was brought up in a largely white environment. Had my parents never left Bury Park, and forced me to attend mosque after school each night, there is no question that I would have turned out a very different person. I doubt I would have ever grown up to become an extremist; those of us who grew up in the eighties were still struggling to be accepted as British – we didn't have the luxury of being able to reject the term. When Navela started high school she had to fight to have the right to wear trousers, today Muslim students have the legal right to wear the hijab. There were no faith schools for my parents' generation to send their children to, and so we managed, and muddled our way through the state system.

If my father had still been alive he would have had no sympathy for today's young British Muslims. How would he, someone who had chosen to leave his homeland to come to this country, have reacted to seeing the next generation so brazenly hostile to every principle he believed in? I can only imagine his response: 'These boys today,' I imagine him saying, 'these stupid young boys, they don't know how lucky they are! Islam! They say they're doing it for Islam?' And I can see the faces of other men, my father's old friends from the past, nodding their heads with sadness.

'They take it all for granted,' my father would have said, 'they don't know how hard it was for us – us men, we know because we lived it, didn't we? And if we had known when we worked those double shifts in the factories… trying to make something in this world… and for whom? For our children. And if we had known that they would spit in the face of our labour and our dreams, bring shame to the community, blacken the name of Pakistan… and all for what? And they say they're Muslims, and they say it's about politics.'

13 **to muddle through** to reach results without having a clear plan – 19 **brazenly** openly and without shame

'Politics is what you talk about before you have families, isn't that right Manzoor sahib?' one of the others might say. 'Before children and responsibilities, and making a life for your family.' And I can imagine the men drinking their steaming tea in silence, wondering to themselves where they had gone wrong.

When I was young I used to fantasise about renouncing my British passport and moving to the United States. I was fascinated by the idea of the American Dream, the suggestion that everyone had an equal chance to make something of their lives and to be considered equally American. Bruce Springsteen seemed to be the very embodiment of that dream: someone who had been born to a working-class immigrant family and who had, through his talent and tenacity, reached the very peak of his profession. Bruce Springsteen changed my life because in his music I saw the promise of hope and escape and self-improvement, but where once I longed to escape to the United States, these days I'm convinced my father did the right thing coming to Britain.

It has taken me three decades to realise that there is only one country which is truly mine. The life my father had built, the family he raised and the life I have fashioned are all due to living in Britain. Every opportunity, every job and every chance to pursue my dreams has been offered by this country, not by America, and not by Pakistan. My father used to tell me he regretted coming to Britain, but in truth it was the greatest gift he gave his children. I was born in Pakistan but made in England; it is Britain which is my land of hope and dreams.

- always surrounded by Pakistani
- spending time in Pakistan together
- racism
- no respect towards Pakistani

13 **tenacity** [te'næsətɪ] determination

Additional Material

The 'Rivers of Blood' speech

This is an excerpt of Enoch Powell's so-called 'Rivers of Blood' speech, which was delivered to a Conservative Association meeting in Birmingham on April 20 1968. Soon after the speech Powell lost his Cabinet job.

[…]

A week or two ago I fell into conversation with a constituent, a middle-aged, quite ordinary working man employed in one of our nationalised industries.

After a sentence or two about the weather, he suddenly said: "If I had the money to go, I wouldn't stay in this country." I made some deprecatory reply to the effect that even this government wouldn't last for ever; but he took no notice, and continued: "I have three children, all of them been through grammar school and two of them married now, with family. I shan't be satisfied till I have seen them all settled overseas. In this country in 15 or 20 years' time the black man will have the whip hand over the white man."

I can already hear the chorus of execration. How dare I say such a horrible thing? How dare I stir up trouble and inflame feelings by repeating such a conversation?

The answer is that I do not have the right not to do so. Here is a decent, ordinary fellow Englishman, who in broad daylight in my own town says to me, his Member of Parliament, that his country will not be worth living in for his children.

I simply do not have the right to shrug my shoulders and think about something else. What he is saying, thousands

8 **constituent** a voter who lives in Powell´s area – 13 **deprecatory** [deprəˈkeɪtərɪ] expressing disapproval – 18 **the whip hand** the control – 20 **execration** [eksɪˈkreɪʃn] expression of hatred *(Abscheu)*

and hundreds of thousands are saying and thinking – not throughout Great Britain, perhaps, but in the areas that are already undergoing the total transformation to which there is no parallel in a thousand years of English history.

In 15 or 20 years, on present trends, there will be in this country three and a half million Commonwealth immigrants and their descendants. That is not my figure. That is the official figure given to parliament by the spokesman of the Registrar General's Office.

There is no comparable official figure for the year 2000, but it must be in the region of five to seven million, approximately one-tenth of the whole population, and approaching that of Greater London. Of course, it will not be evenly distributed from Margate to Aberystwyth and from Penzance to Aberdeen. Whole areas, towns and parts of towns across England will be occupied by sections of the immigrant and immigrant-descended population.

As time goes on, the proportion of this total who are immigrant descendants, those born in England, who arrived here by exactly the same route as the rest of us, will rapidly increase. Already by 1985 the native-born would constitute the majority. It is this fact which creates the extreme urgency of action now, of just that kind of action which is hardest for politicians to take, action where the difficulties lie in the present but the evils to be prevented or minimised lie several parliaments ahead.

The natural and rational first question with a nation confronted by such a prospect is to ask: "How can its dimensions be reduced?" Granted it be not wholly preventable, can it be limited, bearing in mind that numbers are of the essence: the significance and consequences of an alien element introduced into a country or population are profoundly

8 **Registrar General's office** government department dealing with births, marriages and deaths

different according to whether that element is 1 per cent or 10 per cent.

The answers to the simple and rational question are equally simple and rational: by stopping, or virtually stopping, further inflow, and by promoting the maximum outflow. Both answers are part of the official policy of the Conservative Party.

[…]

We must be mad, literally mad, as a nation to be permitting the annual inflow of some 50,000 dependants, who are for the most part the material of the future growth of the immigrant-descended population. It is like watching a nation busily engaged in heaping up its own funeral pyre. So insane are we that we actually permit unmarried persons to immigrate for the purpose of founding a family with spouses and fiancés whom they have never seen.

Let no one suppose that the flow of dependants will automatically tail off. On the contrary, even at the present admission rate of only 5,000 a year by voucher, there is sufficient for a further 25,000 dependants per annum *ad infinitum*, without taking into account the huge reservoir of existing relations in this country – and I am making no allowance at all for fraudulent entry. In these circumstances nothing will suffice but that the total inflow for settlement should be reduced at once to negligible proportions, and that the necessary legislative and administrative measures be taken without delay.

[…]

As I look ahead, I am filled with foreboding; like the Roman, I seem to see "the River Tiber foaming with much blood."

[…]

9 **dependants** wife, children etc. – 12 **funeral pyre** fire for burning a dead body – 18 **voucher** ['vaʊtʃə] *here:* document that various groups of British nationals born outside Britain must obtain in order to settle in Britain – 22 **fraudulent** illegal – 23 **to suffice** [sə'faɪs] to be sufficient – 24 **negligible** ['neglɪdʒəbl] almost zero – 28 **foreboding** fear and worry about the future – 28 **the Roman** the Roman poet Virgil; the quote is from the Aeneid

The Observer *Sunday 24 February 2008*

Sarfraz Manzoor

Black Britain's darkest hour

In 1968, in one of the most controversial speeches of Britain's political history, Tory MP Enoch Powell warned the nation against opening the 'floodgates' to black immigrants. It caused a storm of protest. Sarfraz Manzoor recalls the impact on his family and, 40 years on, returns to Powell's constituency to meet those Powell wanted to 'send home'

[…]

Powell was 55 and shadow defence spokesman under Edward Heath. As Health Minister eight years earlier, he had been encouraging immigrants from the Commonwealth to work in the understaffed NHS. Now, he was about to make a speech warning in the most apocalyptic terms of the consequences of rising immigration. The speech remains the most controversial in British political history. In its most notorious passage, Powell, classicist as well as politician, quoted the Roman poet Virgil, warning: 'As I look ahead, I am filled with foreboding; like the Roman, I seem to see "the River Tiber foaming with much blood" '.

The speech radicalised those who opposed Powell. Blacks, whites and Asians met in church halls and planned protests against the damage being done to their town's reputation. (The Rock Against Racism movement also owed its creation to Powell after a drunken comment from Eric Clapton during a concert in Birmingham in 1976, when the musician told an

8 **constituency** [kən'stɪtjuənsɪ] area that elects a representative to a parliament – 11 **Edward Heath** Prime Minister of the UK from 1970 to 1974 – 14 **NHS** National Health Service

audience to vote for Powell to stop Britain becoming ‘a black colony’ inspired the founding of the anti-racism movement.)

The speech also implied that ethnic minorities would never be truly British. In 1968, my father had been in Britain for five years and Powell occupies a surprisingly significant place in my teenage psyche. My mental image of him was of a glacial man, always dressed in pinstripe suits, with unsmiling eyes, a face in a fixed scowl, shivering with racial fury. When I learnt that he was a poet and a brilliant scholar, double-starred first in Latin and Greek from Cambridge, it served as a reminder that bigotry was not the sole dominion of the ignorant. Powell’s name was regularly cited whenever my father wanted to remind me how easily Britain could turn against us. It sometimes seemed that he and my father were bound together in a conspiracy to force me to accept that I was not and never would be British.

More than Norman Tebbit, Powell frightened me. Tebbit wanted me to support England, but Powell wanted me to support England while living in Pakistan. Repatriation was a most terrifying word for a young boy who knew nothing but Britain and who feared what might happen should Powell and his supporters ever gain power. He taught my family the importance of always having a suitcase packed and a Pakistani passport.

For Powell, immigration was a threat to social cohesion. He believed the native population was in danger of being swamped by an alien culture.

[…]

The anxieties that Powell articulated 40 years ago of ‘homes and neighbourhoods changed beyond recognition’ are anxieties which have only escalated over time. The concern Powell

6 **glacial** [ˈgleɪʃəl] very cold – 7 **pinstripe suit** *Nadelstreifenanzug* – 8 **scowl** [skaʊl] threatening expression of the face – 10 **bigotry** [ˈbɪgətrɪ] the act of expressing unreasonable beliefs – 16 **Norman Tebitt** Conservative British politician who complained about a lack of loyalty because a lot of Asians didn´t cheer for the England cricket team – 18 **repatriation** act of sending someone back to their own country – 28 **anxiety** [æŋˈzaɪətɪ] state of being worried that sth bad might happen

expressed about Sikhs demanding special treatment is today a widespread apprehension that everyone is accorded special treatment – Muslims, Hindus, Sikhs, Afro-Caribbeans and asylum seekers – everyone except the native white population. It is that apprehension which has led to the onslaught against multiculturalism and this is why, after all these years, some continue to venerate Enoch Powell as a prophet. John Mellor calls him 'the best Prime Minister we never had': 'If he had been elected, he would have run this country like he was planning an attack in the desert.'

Enoch Powell was right, it seems to me, to highlight the danger of communities failing to integrate and right to say that the sheer number of immigrants coming into a country can have a serious impact on its culture. But having met those who suffered as a consequence of his Birmingham speech, and as someone whose childhood yearning to belong was haunted by his toxic legacy, it is hard to forgive him. This was a man who spoke fluent Urdu and would ask his Asian constituents if they preferred to talk to him in English or their mother tongue, a politician who did not speak out against immigration throughout the years that West Indians and Asians were arriving in this country and his constituency, who in October 1964 said: 'I have set and always will set my face like flint against making any difference between one citizen of this country and another on grounds of his origin.'

In trying to explain why he decided to raise the subject of immigration when he did, it's hard to escape the conclusion that it was politically motivated. The explicit purpose of the speech was to attack the Labour government's plans to pass a Race Relations Act which would have outlawed racial discrimination in employment and housing. But there was

1 **Sikh** follower of Sikhism originated in the 15th century in India – 2 **apprehension** anxiety about the future – 5 **onslaught** fierce attack – 7 **John Mellor** Conservative and MP from 1935 until 1955 – 17 **legacy** ['legəsɪ] sth that exists because of actions or events in the past *(Erbe, Hinterlassenschaft)* – 18 **Urdu** language spoken in Pakistan – 23 **flint** very hard grey stone

also, some suggest, an intention to destabilise the position of Conservative leader Edward Heath. In July 1965, Powell came a distant third in the Conservative party leadership contest. After the speech, Powell was transformed into a national public figure with a realistic prospect of leading the party. For that prize, Enoch Powell was prepared to pay in blood.

'I could not understand why people looked at me as if I should not be here,' Gulam Haider Ellam tells me, recalling the aftermath of the Birmingham speech. 'It made me angry because I was a British citizen, born in the British Raj.'

For an imperialist such as Powell, whose greatest ambition had been to be viceroy of India, being a British citizen was only useful so long as it served the empire. When those same citizens began to arrive in Britain, their claims to citizenship were less appealing. Powell concluded his speech at the Midland Hotel by declaring: 'To see, and not to speak, would be the great betrayal.'

But it was not his white constituents whom Powell was betraying. He was betraying men like Lance Bunkley, who tells me that the speech 'made me feel like I was a stranger in a strange land'. He was betraying Tanveer Khaja's father, who worked at the Goodyear tyre factory, and Parminder Gill's father, who toiled in a metal factory. He was betraying the Commonwealth doctors and nurses whom he had invited to come to Britain. He was betraying my father and every immigrant who suffered and saved doing work the whites thought was beneath them. And he was betraying everyone, of every colour, who believed that diversity could enrich as well as threaten a nation.

Powell's beloved empire and precious England had relied on the efforts of these immigrants, the very men and women he was happy to castigate for political gain.

10 **British Raj** [rɑːdʒ] British Indian empire before 1947 – 12 **viceroy** [ˈvaɪsrɔɪ] person sent by a king or queen to govern a colony – 17 **betrayal** the act of giving information to an enemy *(Verrat)* – 32 **to castigate** to punish

Leaving Wolverhampton, I felt humbled to have met some of those who lived through 20 April 1968. It is they, and all those who supported them, who are the true Great British heroes. The men and women who, unheard and unheralded, proved their devotion to this country through hard labour. Enoch Powell might have been predicting rivers of blood, but today's Britain was built because of their rivers of sweat.